Praise for Jerry

"Here is an extraordinary glimpse into a man who'll forever be remembered as among the very best of the elite Yellowstone rangers. Truly, Yellowstone is better for Jerry Mernin having called it home."
    —Gary Ferguson, author of *Hawks Rest: A Season in the Remote Heart of Yellowstone*

"I cannot imagine being a ranger and not having known Jerry Mernin. He was a genuine leader who routinely demonstrated the courage to speak up, take action, and challenge the status quo. Those of us who had the distinct honor of working with him proudly count ourselves 'Mernin Rangers.'"
    —Nick Herring, former deputy chief ranger, Yellowstone National Park

"Jerry Mernin was among the last of the Old School, a doughty professional with an eye for the ironies of protecting wild nature with humans teeming through it. His recollections show us a side of Yellowstone that few people are privileged to see."
    —David Quammen, author of *Yellowstone: A Journey Through America's Wild Heart*

"Few rangers have experienced as much adventure, danger, beauty, and satisfaction as Jerry Mernin. The many young men and women he mentored consider him a 'ranger's ranger.'"
—Carol Shively, former Lake District interpretive ranger, Yellowstone National Park

"No one exemplified better what it is to be a park ranger. As an NPS biologist I learned all I needed to know from three backcountry horse trips with Jerry. I treasure his lessons; words spoken only, as a rule and custom of Jerry's, deep in the wilds and never to be uttered anywhere else. This book comes as close as you can to riding with Jerry in Yellowstone."
—Douglas W. Smith, senior wildlife biologist, Yellowstone National Park

"Jerry Mernin was the model for my generation of park rangers, and his book conveys the essence of the park ranger position better than any other that I have read."
—Ron Mackie, former Yellowstone backcountry ranger and Yosemite wilderness manager

"Jerry Mernin was one of the best resource rangers—and the best bear management ranger—I knew in my 38 years in Yellowstone. I strongly recommend this account to rangers, new and experienced, and to the public that often sees only the surface of what makes a fine ranger."
—Mary Meagher, Yellowstone National Park research biologist, retired

"In my 22 years as a Yellowstone district ranger, I rode a lot of miles with Jerry Mernin. He was a remarkable person, an iconic ranger, and a dear friend. The rangers that protect our national parks are better now and will be better in the future because of Jerry Mernin, and that's a damn good legacy!"
—John Lounsbury, 37-year National Park Service ranger, retired

"Jerry's straightforward prose reflects his discipline and training while the humor and understatement of events reveal the renegade behind the ranger. Thanks in great part to men like Jerry Mernin, bears and men are still coexisting and getting better at it all the time. It was a distinct pleasure!"
—Lance Craighead, PhD, Executive Director, Craighead Institute

"If you are one of those people who wish you could have been a park ranger, then this is the book for you. You will get a firsthand account of the good, the bad, the exhilarating, the terrifying, the challenging, and the rewarding, all told by a man who could handle it with competence and humility—and then reward the rest of us with 'a good story well told.'"
—Mark Marschall, former Yellowstone and Yosemite backcountry ranger and co-author of *Yellowstone Trails*

"When I think back on my NPS career, I realize that almost everything I knew about being a ranger, I learned from Jerry. I bet there are many who would say the same thing."
—Rick Smith, National Park Service employee, retired

"Anyone who knew Jerry loves to tell Mernin stories, which have only grown bigger as the years go by. What a pleasure it is, finally, to have these wonderful tales written by the man himself. No Yellowstone shelf should be without it."
—Jeremy Schmidt, former Yellowstone ranger and winterkeeper

"A must read for any ranger, future ranger, or anyone interested in today's national parks. The park service and the world need more Jerry Mernins."
—Bob Barrett, former NPS backcountry packer and author of *Where Mules Wear Diamonds*

"Jerry Mernin was respected by everyone who knew him and had few enemies, an incredible accomplishment for someone who rocked the boat as many times as he did. One of the most cherished memories of my life was to spend time in Yellowstone's backcountry 'on patrol' with Jerry Mernin. I wish I could have been around him longer."
—Dan Sholly, chief ranger, Yellowstone National Park, 1985–1998

"Have you ever dreamed of being a national park ranger? This is the book for you. Jerry was a park ranger's ranger who loved his work in the parks and the wilderness."
—Smoke Elser, author of *Packin' In on Mules and Horses*

YELLOWSTONE RANGER

Stories from a life spent with bears,
backcountry, horses, and mules,
from Yosemite to Yellowstone

JERRY MERNIN

Compiled by Gary Brown

RIVERBEND
PUBLISHING

Yellowstone Ranger: Stories from a life spent with bears, backcountry, horses, and mules, from Yosemite to Yellowstone

Copyright © 2016 Jerry Mernin

Published by Riverbend Publishing, Helena, Montana

ISBN: 978-1-60639-090-0

Printed in the USA

5 6 7 8 9 10 MG 22 21 20

Cover and text design by Sarah Cauble, www.sarahcauble.com

Riverbend Publishing
P.O. Box 5833
Helena, MT 59604
1-866-787-2363
www.riverbendpublishing.com

FSC
www.fsc.org
MIX
Paper from
responsible sources
FSC® C011935

Dedicated to the many heroes of the National Park Service

"Do good, avoid evil; remember who you are and what you stand for; and watch out for the company you keep."

–Jerry Mernin

Acknowledgments

OVER HIS LIFETIME, JERRY MERNIN DEVELOPED DEEP FRIEND-ships in the national parks he lived and worked in. This circle expanded after retirement when he joined the Gypsy Rhythm Writers Group, which met regularly at the Bozeman (Montana) Public Library. Jerry's writing was enriched by the feedback he received there and in particular by that of Ingeborg Hays.

As Jerry wrote the chapters, he sent them to various friends to fact check and provide feedback. We don't know all of the people who helped him, but in the past year, recent versions of the manuscript were reviewed by Nick Herring, Alice Siebecker, AnnMarie Chytra, Mark Marschall, and Tess and Tom Moore.

The stories are based not only on his memories but also on interviews he conducted over the years with the participants and on incident reports, which he re-read while preparing this book. He would have, of course, taken responsibility for any differences between his versions and other accounts.

When Jerry died in 2011, he left a stack of individual chapters and an outline. Gary Brown, a long time personal friend and colleague, volunteered to tackle the formidable task of shaping those chapters into a book. Jerry and Gary met each other in 1958 at Yosemite and worked together often there and at Yellowstone where Gary was at one time the park's bear management specialist and eventually assistant chief ranger. Gary devoted two years of effort, 15 hours per week, to the manuscript, taking stacks of paper chapters and cross-referencing them with digital copies, deleting repetitious material, organizing them in coherent sections, and scrupulously keeping the voice intact.

At the end of that process, Marjane Ambler (a journalist and author by trade) added her expertise in copy editing and preparing the manuscript for submission to the publisher.

Several friends contributed to the photo research, including Gary Brown, Nick Herring, Alice Siebecker, and Tom Ovanin. Professional photos were contributed by James Fain, who first met Jerry at the North Rim of the Grand Canyon National Park in 1961. He and his family visited the Mernins at the South Entrance regularly beginning in 1974.

Cindy Mernin is especially grateful to all members of the National Park Service "family" who helped make this book possible.

Contents

Foreword   *by Cindy Mernin*   18

Introduction *by Marjane Ambler*   21

Prologue   *Listening to a grizzly bear breathe*   27

PART I EARLY YEARS IN YOSEMITE

Chapter 1   *Growing Up in Yosemite*   29

PART II LEARNING

Chapter 2   *My First Ranger Tales*   35

Chapter 3   *Stormy Lessons in Glacier National Park*   45

Chapter 4   *How I Became a Missionary about One-Match
            Fires*   54

PART III A YOSEMITE RANGER

Chapter 5   *Law Student Meets Bob Flame, Ranger*   61

Chapter 6   *Encounters with a Specter, a Fire, and a Bear* 68

Chapter 7   *Red v. the Mule-eating Stokes Litter*   78

Chapter 8   *Lessons in Humility*   96

Chapter 9   *Beauty Lies in the Eyes*   125

Chapter 10 *Remember Who You Are and What You
            Stand For*   127

PART IV TRANSITION AND GUNS

Chapter 11   *A Love Affair with Guns*   155

Chapter 12   *Never Look Back*   163

PART V YELLOWSTONE

Chapter 13   *On-the-Job Training for Canyon Rescues*   167

Chapter 14   *A Fateful Visit for Three German Women*   178

Chapter 15   *Barney Sanders's Tie (or, A Not-So-Good Day in Yellowstone)*   186

Chapter 16   *Changing Times Arrive in Yellowstone*   195

Chapter 17   *Bear in the Bathroom*   205

Chapter 18   *Patrol Cabin Etiquette*   211

Chapter 19   *God Bless Park Rangers' Wives*   218

Chapter 20   *The Day the President Rode My Horse*   228

Chapter 21   *Paying Tuition at the School of Hard Knocks*   237

PART VI BEARS, BEARS, ALMOST EVERYWHERE

Chapter 22   *My Introduction to Yellowstone Bears*   247

Chapter 23   *The Closing of the Dumps*   260

Chapter 24   *Park Visitors "Jumped" by Bears*   269

Chapter 25   *Hard Lessons Learned Capturing and Relocating Bears*   277

Chapter 26   *A Predatory Grizzly*   289

Chapter 27   *Some Bear Humor*   307

Chapter 28   *A Grizzly Bear Charge*   310

Chapter 29   *Country Without Grizzly Bears*   317

PART VII HORSES AND MULES

Chapter 30   *Dusty, my Thousand-pound Partner*   319

Chapter 31   *Irwin the Magnificent*   333

Chapter 32   *Bit Players and Supporting Roles*   340

PART VIII THE LAST RIDE

Chapter 33   *Outlasting Your Warranty*   349

Chapter 34   *Death, Loss, and Change*   352

Epilogue   *The Mernin Rendezvous*   359

About the Author   360

Index   362

YELLOWSTONE NATIONAL PARK

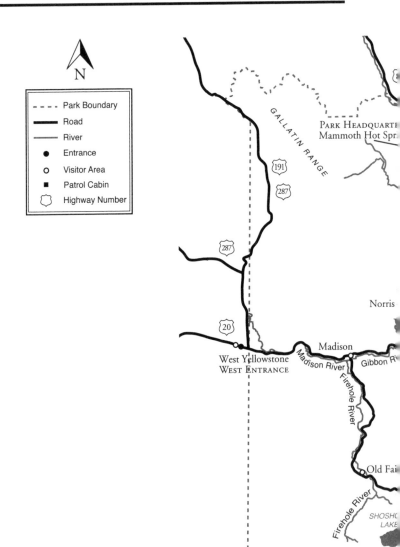

N

	Park Boundary
	Road
	River
●	Entrance
○	Visitor Area
■	Patrol Cabin
	Highway Number

GALLATIN RANGE

191

287

287

20

PARK HEADQUARTE
Mammoth Hot Spr.

Norris

Madison

West Yellowstone
WEST ENTRANCE

Madison River

Gibbon R

Firehole River

Old Fai

Firehole River

SHOSH(
LAKE

PITCHSTONE
PLATEAU

Bechler Ranger Station
Snake River Ranger Statio

SOUTH ENTRANC

YELLOWSTONE: CANYON VILLAGE

YELLOWSTONE: LAKE & FISHING BRIDGE AREA

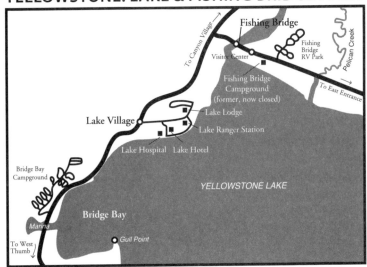

YOSEMITE NATIONAL PARK

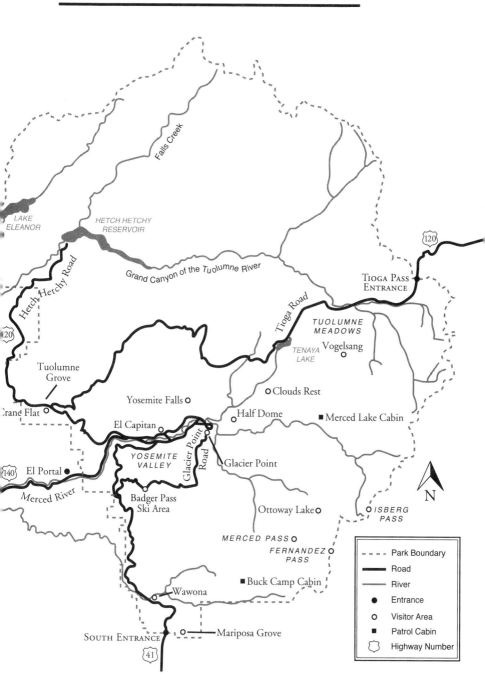

Foreword

By Cindy Mernin

IMAGINE A MAN WHO IS PERFECTLY SUITED TO AND COGNIzant of his life's passion. What an incredible gift! From his childhood in Yosemite National Park, to his education at Notre Dame, service in the Army, and near completion of law school at Hastings, Jerry Mernin never lost sight of the importance of the National Park Service mission or the value of rangers in promoting those ideals. As it turned out, he managed to find everything he ever wanted in his own backyard.

Jerry acquired basic ranger skills at the knee of his father, who himself had a long and illustrious career in the NPS. He never backed away from a challenge and always sought to broaden and improve his physical, emotional, and intellectual development for his entire life. He routinely would stay up to study new information when he should have been sleeping. During his final years, he faced off cancer (successfully) and even the degradations of Parkinson's disease with aplomb.

Much like himself, Jerry's writing is complex in its simplicity and can be easily underestimated. During his last decade, he joined a writers group that met weekly at the Bozeman (Montana) City Library. The diversity and intention of the regular participants encouraged him greatly, and the earnest, friendly exchanges helped him refocus and expand his writing ability beyond government documentation. Convinced that he should give an account of his singular experiences, he set about describing his endeavors, which occurred during an era of the Park Service that might be described as golden. He would spend hours typing and would eventually have to peck out his assignments letter by letter as his Parkinson's disease advanced.

Jerry was an advanced advocate of professionalism in law enforcement but not to the exclusion of other ranger responsibilities: wildlife management, firefighting, search and rescue, boating, E.M.T., winter and summer backcountry survival, care and use of stock, and, last but not least, being a good host to the public. What a diverse mix! Just knowing all the equipment used in each category, let alone how to function with it, and then to instruct other personnel in time for a rapacious summer season was quite a feat.

Jerry loved the diversity and challenge and the hard physical investment necessary for working in large natural resource parks. He was extremely safety conscious and planned out eventualities beforehand rather than being caught short while assisting someone a long distance from help and equipment. I never had to worry that he would fail to return home in one piece—he knew his limits under a variety of conditions and always carried a pack with enough supplies for bivouacking several days.

Jerry was ever the historian, and always had in mind the contrast of past and present. Realizing that one's recall can be inaccurate, he often visited the Yellowstone Center for Resources to check old reports of the incidents he needed to refresh. Accuracy in writing was as important to him as it was in handling firearms. I know that had he been able to travel, he would have done the same fact-checking in Yosemite.

It was often noted that Jerry's demeanor was very considered, formidable, and graceful. It reflected the very essence of his time and place and all that had passed before him. There is an almost monastic tradition of "rangering" that has been handed down as oral history, with limited written documentation beyond cabin logs and incident reports. The result is a wealth of stories and characterizations that emerge during gatherings and slack time to the amusement and edification of newcomers. This method of instruction drills a ton of information right into the heart and soul of the listener.

Jerry was good at telling stories, and it's difficult to convey the finer aspects of many stories without his gestures, theatrics, and voice inflections. Nonetheless, he tried his best to make his writing captivating and informative. Now, the onus of recording what happens in "a day in the life…" must pass to his remaining contemporaries and a whole new generation.

Introduction

By Marjane Ambler, author of *Yellowstone Has Teeth: A memoir of living year-round in the world's first national park*

A FEW YEARS AFTER RANGER JERRY MERNIN'S RETIREMENT from Yellowstone National Park, my husband and I met him and his wife Cindy at the park. During our visit, we went to the Canyon Visitor Center where they have a large, three-dimensional map of Yellowstone. As we explored the other exhibits, Jerry stayed in the lobby studying that map. We all knew not to interrupt him. He was having a spiritual experience, re-visiting the Yellowstone backcountry, tracing the trails he had traveled over his thirty-two years in the park and remembering the beloved mules and horses who had accompanied him. When he noticed us, he told us with deep regret that there were a couple of places he had not visited.

In 1952, Jerry (then an undergraduate at the University of Notre Dame) arrived at Yellowstone for his first National Park Service (NPS) job—fire guard at Pelican Cone. Little did he know how that summer would change his life and the lives of dozens of rangers whom he trained and mentored over the years. Having grown up in Yosemite where his father, also named Gerald Mernin, was then a district ranger, he could not imagine that another national park would capture his heart.

Gerald and Emma Mernin encouraged their son to choose another profession and not follow blindly in his father's footsteps. Consequently, Jerry attended Hastings College of Law while working seasonally at Yosemite for several years. When he turned his back on the practice of law and chose rangering as his profession, Jerry worked at Bryce and Grand Canyon national parks before returning to Yellowstone in 1964.

In May 1971, his life changed dramatically when Cindy Ferguson, a registered nurse from Baltimore, arrived at the Lake Hospital and caught his attention. They were married seven months later. Living with a ranger is never easy, especially at isolated locations. The long, dark winters tested their relationship and made having children too impractical. Trips to the outside to get a head of lettuce or a restaurant meal were rare during the winters before the park started grooming the roads, and on one remarkable night, a grizzly tried to break into their living quarters.

That was one of many close encounters between Jerry and bruins since grizzly and black bears roamed the park campgrounds regularly in that era before changes in park policies limited the food available from campers. Jerry put himself at the interface, spending night after night trapping bears and moving them. In 1966 alone he free darted and removed 13 different grizzlies and almost as many black bears from the Canyon Campground. Too often, bears had to be destroyed, but Jerry was notorious for waiting until the bear was within arm's reach before he shot. He wanted to make sure it was not a false charge.

When he became a supervisor, he repeatedly put his own life on the line rather than that of his subordinates in bear encounters and rappels down the walls of the Grand Canyon of the Yellowstone to rescue fallen visitors or recover their bodies.

Jerry and Cindy's home was also the ranger station for most of their years in the park meaning that she, like so many ranger spouses through the years, often stood on the front lines in times of crisis. Acquaintances knew she provided the delectable meals for visitors at home and in the backcountry when she went along. Readers will also discover the wisdom she imparted, such as when his soul ached for a lost equine companion.

One author described him as having the "sinewy build of a top skier, giving a hint of physical resources instantly available." (Early in his career, Jerry worked as a ski patrolman at Yosemite's Badger Pass Ski Area.) That innate strength, combined with his low, deliberate voice, could be intimidating, even to his peers. Always a stickler for proper attire, he wore his NPS Stetson low in front, a finger width above his eyebrows, according to the author, Bill Everhart (author of *Take Down Flag & Feed Horses*). His writing, however, is anything but intimidating. When Jerry talked, everyone listened, as much for his humor as for his wisdom, and his writing conveys those qualities as well.

Jerry was at his happiest when in the backcountry, astride one of his favorite horses, with the lead rope of a pack animal in hand. Nevertheless, he also participated actively in park management decisions when he felt that park resources, especially grizzly bears, were threatened. His supervisor for many years, former Chief Ranger Dan Sholly, said, "He was respected by everyone who knew him and had few enemies, an incredible accomplishment for someone who has rocked the boat as many times as he has." For example, in the 1980s, the park clamped down on outfitters with regulations that were extremely unpopular at first. Later, after a few years of outfitter certification training and other restrictions, most outfitters realized the value of the changes and began giving a Yellowstone Outfitter Award to a ranger each year; Jerry received one of the first.

Jerry's book is remarkable for his humility. He chronicles

many of his mistakes, as for example, when he risked the lives of himself and his horse George on the harrowing Clouds Rest mountainside in Yosemite. The stories also illustrate mistakes made by the National Park Service as it tried to balance the needs of visitors and wildlife over the years.

This book is no pedantic rant, however. It conveys the tales of a born story teller, whose stories were honed during decades around the campfire and the kitchen table. His skills were enhanced by his mother Emma's talent as a tutor and by his education at Notre Dame University and law school. Jerry often used the phrase "a gentleman and a scholar," and indeed he was both. His first book (unpublished) traced the timeline of the Nez Perce flight from the U.S. Army in 1877 through Yellowstone.

Despite the challenges of living and working in Yellowstone, you will not read any whining or complaining in these pages. Most people who have lived in Yellowstone love the park, but Jerry's passion may be unmatched. He turned down promotions that no doubt would have made life more materially comfortable for the Mernins but would have required more desk work or changing parks. A ranger who took a Yellowstone assignment should be willing to settle in, he said. "The park is so vast, it takes years before you are familiar with all of it." He hated the bureaucracy that would have come with promotions, often saying, "If you ever get in a shoot out, God forbid, save a bullet for yourself because the paperwork is worse than death."

After he was forced to retire by NPS regulations in 1996, his only regret was not having another thirty-two years to work in Yellowstone. For several summers after retirement, he volunteered in the backcountry. After he could no longer do that because of his Parkinson's disease, he mourned. Fortunately for all of us, his wife Cindy and his colleagues convinced him to chronicle his experiences in the national parks so young rangers could continue to learn from his mistakes at "the college of hard knocks."

While Jerry learned many lessons the hard way, he also was educated at the elbows of his elders and especially of his father. Throughout his career he was driven by his desire to protect the resources he loved and to live up to his father's standards.

Jerry's father always said, "There is nothing new under the sun." The Park Service introduces each generation of rangers to new techniques, new equipment, and new software. Nevertheless, Jerry's father was right: Rangers' work still relies upon timeless principles and techniques—such as how to tie a good-looking hitch, how to defuse a volatile situation, how to leave a backcountry cabin so it can save the life of a desperately cold traveler. Most of us can say we became wiser as we aged, but few have the gift of remembering exactly when we learned each life lesson. Jerry's stories of such moments may prevent embarrassment or tragedy for future rookie rangers.

Thankfully Jerry took Cindy's advice and painstakingly recorded his stories. He was a founding member of the Gypsy Rhythm Writers' Group at the Bozeman (Montana) Library, and they critiqued one another's work for several years. Despite his letter-by-letter, two-fingered typing, Jerry's stories emerged with all their humor, philosophy, and wisdom intact, and those who knew him can hear his deep voice as they read.

No doubt he omitted some stories that somebody will miss, but he left a collection that conveys how this ranger matured throughout his career, from his early days practicing gun-handling during empty evening hours in Bryce Canyon to his final reflections on aging and death.

His long-time friend and colleague Gary Brown compiled paper and digital copies of chapters and put them in order, devoting months to deleting repetitious material and scrupulously keeping the voice intact. Jerry and Gary met each other in 1958 at Yosemite and often worked together there and at Yellowstone where Gary was the park's bear management specialist and finally assistant chief ranger.

Brown's editing work was handicapped by the fact that Jerry was not available to answer questions. On December 13, 2011, Jerry died at the age of 79 of a massive brain hemorrhage. Several of the flags in Yellowstone were lowered to half-staff, a nearly unique sign of respect.

Prologue

Editor's note: Jerry Mernin had numerous encounters with bears, especially in Yellowstone, and especially with grizzly bears. Although he had to trap or remove bears from time to time, he loved bears and respected them. This story is quintessentially Jerry Mernin: honest, unembellished, and astonishing.

Listening to a grizzly bear breathe, and being given a second chance

AN EXPERIENCE IN YELLOWSTONE'S PELICAN CREEK CAMP-ground taught me that bears can be forgiving. I had been dropped off by one of the patrol rangers and was on foot, carrying the CO_2 capture rifle and following a 600-pound grizzly we had been trying to trap for some time. I was quite a distance behind the bear as he ambled into the lodgepole pine thicket separating two campground loops. I was paralleling his course, hoping to be ahead of him as he came into the light of the next loop.

It was dark, but I wasn't using my flashlight. My eyes had adjusted to the dark, and I moved carefully through the lodgepole. For quite some time I could hear the bear moving just ahead of me. Suddenly I realized I hadn't heard anything for a while, except for the distant campground sounds. Had the bear stopped? Or had he just moved out of range of my hearing?

I stopped to listen and to try to get my bearings. My heart sounded like a marching band's drum beating out a double-time cadence. As soon as I stopped I could hear breathing. My breathing or his? I glanced at the sky to get a better sense of where we were and then concentrated on holding my breath, bladder, and bowels. I still heard steady in-and-out, in-and-out breathing, and it wasn't mine.

My lungs were beginning to ache from holding my breath. I exhaled slowly, quietly, and then took a deep, quiet breath.

I could still hear the steady in-and-out breathing. How close? Five feet? Fifteen feet? Twenty? How far can you hear a grizzly bear breathe?

Although the night was quite cool, I was sweating. My heart thumped, my senses were on high alert, and my mind raced as different ideas sprinted through it. What to do? Yell? Run? Pull my .44? Flick on my flashlight?

The steady breathing continued. It was a long pause in a chess game: my opponent waited for me to make a wrong move.

I have no idea how long the whole scenario lasted, but it seemed to me an awfully long time. Finally I took a deep breath, turned away from the bear, and walked to the road as quietly, confidently, and carefully as I could.

I called the ranger on patrol, asked him to take me to my vehicle, and told him I was hanging it up for the evening. I went home without any further explanation. It took some time to wind down and even think of going to bed. Once in bed it took still more time to get to sleep. I finally dropped off, thankful for the tolerant, live-and-let-live attitude my erstwhile opponent had demonstrated. He showed a side quite contrary to the grizzly's usual (often well deserved) reputation for being tough, ferocious, and unforgiving.

Intellectually I know you shouldn't anthropomorphize, but I feel for some reason, this particular bear chose to give me space and respect even though I had crowded, and in effect, challenged him. He gave me a second chance. After more than 38 years, I still reflect on this encounter, and I can only say, "Thanks, bear."

Chapter 1

Growing Up in Yosemite

I SPENT MY INFANCY AND EARLY CHILDHOOD IN YOSEMITE
National Park because my father, Gerald Mernin, was a park
ranger. Dad was 6-feet, 4-inches tall, slender, and athletic.
He had the shoulders and arms of a light-heavyweight boxer
and a handsome, open, friendly face that could turn stern and
riveting at a moment's notice. Dressed in the ranger uniform
of the day, with sharply peaked Stetson, forest green riding
breeches and well-shined, knee-high cordovan riding boots,
he was an imposing figure who had the command presence of
a squad of Marines in full combat gear.

One incident illustrates this. Three timber workers from
Bootjack, a logging community in the foothills, visited Yosemite and became drunk and disorderly in short order. They
pushed their way into the crowded Degnan's restaurant in
the Old Village area, took uncollected tips from the tables,
uneaten food from people's plates, and were completely ob-
noxious. Two seasonal rangers tried to quiet the rowdy ones
but were threatened with bodily harm and to be used to wipe
up the floor. Having an innate instinct for survival, the two
rangers judiciously retreated and called Dad.

When Dad arrived he assessed the situation, asked the two

seasonal rangers to wait outside, and then stepped inside. The room went silent. The three men were sitting at the counter, each having a beer. Dad walked up behind them, tapped each one on the shoulder, and without saying a word, gestured them outside with his thumb. They got up promptly, quietly staggered out the door, and were taken to the lockup where they spent the night sobering up. The next day they appeared before the U.S. Magistrate, were fined and ordered to leave the park. Before they left, all three apologized to Dad for any trouble they may have caused him.

It is possible that becoming a ranger myself first came to me through osmosis from living at many different ranger stations at such an early age. By the time I was one year and ten days old I had lived at Crane Flat, Alder Creek, Glacier Point, and South Entrance ranger stations, as well as in Yosemite Valley. My favorite picture from this era shows my dad in uniform, mounted on a good-looking, thoroughbred-type horse, posing with me (at nine-months-old) in one arm. We were at Alder Creek Ranger Station at the time, and Dad was using the horse to patrol the Wawona road while it was under construction.

As I grew up in Yosemite I admired my dad and everything he did. I wanted to be just like him. But from my earliest memories, I recall Mom and Dad encouraging me to be anything I wanted but not a ranger. I could never figure this out because being a ranger seemed like a good idea to me.

When Dad was assigned to Wawona as district ranger, it was new country with new experiences for me. Dad was scheduled to attend the F.B.I. National Academy at Quantico, Virginia, in 1942, as the first national park ranger selected for this honor.

Dad, however, was not perfect. He had a temper and

sometimes had a hard time controlling it, and he had a dock-worker's colorful vocabulary that would make any journey-man mule packer envious. My mother never thought much of these characteristics and lived in frequent battle with them for more than 50 years.

Mom was from Sacramento, a business college graduate, and came to Yosemite partly as an adventure and partly to find a job. She found both and more. Mom had an amazing grasp of the English language and grammar and was a born teacher.

In our first years at Wawona she transformed me from a nearly failing student to an above-average student. When we transferred back to Yosemite Valley while Dad was in the ser-vice during World War II, I frequently finished my assign-ments early and was given free time to read recreationally. The first book I chose was *Wyatt Earp, Frontier Marshal* by Stuart Neal Lake. I liked the book so much that I stole it; I still have it and still need to make amends. I don't blame my mother for this.

Mom was a strong hiker but did not like being around horses because she suffered from serious hay fever. She was a good businesswoman, a frugal manager of finances. Dad was not, so Mom made ninety percent of the business deci-sions for the family. If Mom had been born fifty years later she could have been the CEO of a Fortune 500 company. She stood only five-feet four-inches tall. As a youth I resented this because with her as my mother I would never make it to Dad's six four. As an adult I forgave her simply because I realized it was easier for a horse to carry a six-foot man than one that is six four.

In her later years Mom was a world-class contract bridge competitor. She studied and worked hard to improve her knowledge and to play her best game, not just to beat the other person. I always worked to develop this attribute in myself.

Above all, I thank my mother because she presented such a strong image of an empowered woman who could succeed at anything to which she put her mind. When I was a supervisory ranger during the 1970s and the advent of EEO (Equal Employment Opportunity law), the memory of this image made it easy for me to accept and welcome women as park rangers, a previously all-male bastion. Thanks, Mom.

I came along considerably less than a year after Mom and Dad were married. About this time Dad was assigned to a different area of the park. Shortly after we got settled at the new location Dad made a courtesy call on a neighboring rancher, taking along Mom and me.

When the rancher's son saw me he got curious, trying to figure out the math involved, and asked Dad how long he and Mom had been married. The grandmother quickly intervened. "Tut, tut, my boy. The first one can come any time. After that they usually take nine months."

By all accounts, I was a handful: boisterous, active, strong-willed, and opinionated. Reportedly I was always tempting fate and pushing the envelope. One of my earliest memories is trying to run away from home on my tricycle, riding down the road from the government residence toward the Old Village with Dad chasing me on foot. My parents were strict disciplinarians and did not spare the rod to spoil the child. But at no time did I feel abused, unwanted, unloved, or neglected.

Mom and Dad did better the second time around. My sister Lynn was born in 1937. Lynn was my complete antithesis. She was quiet, sweet, loving, and adorable. She could wrap Dad around her little finger. Lynn and I were not particularly close as youngsters. The four and a half years difference in our ages meant a lot of baby-sitting for me and cut into my roaming and exploring. As she grew up she enjoyed the excitement and diversity of the city. I found it harder to sleep in the noise of the city and was always happy to get back to the mountains.

Things changed when I got out of the Army and was living at home while going to law school. Lynn was attending Dominican College in San Rafael, studying to be a teacher. Classmates who visited her were often very attractive young ladies. I found it much more enjoyable to visit with them rather than to study law.

I think fondly of my childhood and young manhood in Yosemite. I am grateful for the time I was able to spend there. But when I reflect on the past I am most grateful for my parents and all I received from them. And though I didn't make it to six four and was never a world-class competitor in any activity, I wish I hadn't managed to pick up Dad's temper and colorful vocabulary.

After December 7, 1941, and the bombing of Pearl Harbor, the United States entered World War II. Park management asked Dad to agree to stay in Yosemite through 1943 if they sent him to the F.B.I. Academy. Dad agreed, went to the Academy, came back to Yosemite, finished 1943 there, and then volunteered for the armed forces. Even though he was married with a family and did not have to serve, he was determined to be part of it.

When Dad went into the service in early 1944, Mom, Lynn and I moved from Wawona into Yosemite Valley. It was here, probably in the fall of 1944, that I inadvertently stumbled into one of my first life-altering moments.

Walking back from The Old Village Pavilion where I had

been to a movie I noticed a sign that had been vandalized by someone scratching their initials on the face of it. I thought, that's too bad, that's morally wrong, it's also illegal, that it was a misdemeanor, that misdemeanors were punishable by fines and/or jail for up to a year, that it was not a felony. I stopped midstream in my profound musings, amazed that I knew so much about law. Maybe I should study law, I thought. And that started me down the slippery slide that led me to law school some years later.

Chapter 2

My First Ranger Tales

I WAS RAISED ON A HEALTHY DIET OF RANGER TALES. SOME critics accuse ranger tales of relying too much on the fantasy of fairy tales, which usually begin with, "Once upon a time…" and end with "…and they lived happily ever after." Actually, ranger tales are somewhat more grounded in fact or at least the teller's perception of fact. They often start with "There I stood…" and end with "…and that's no shit."

Ranger tales run the gamut of all aspects of a ranger's work. They can be exciting, terrifying, humorous, boring, or mundane. Usually they are told to entertain, sometimes to enlighten, sometimes simply as a response to another person's story.

After years of listening attentively to and in awe of my dad and his peers exchanging stories, I can remember the first time I realized I had a ranger tale of my own, though I was yet to become a ranger.

In 1952 I was a sophomore at University of Notre Dame and got a summer job as a fireguard for the National Park Service in Yellowstone. I rode out to Yellowstone with fellow UND student Fred Ionata. We entered Yellowstone through the East Entrance. Going up over Sylvan Pass and past Sylvan Lake impressed on me that we were entering a different world.

When I reached park headquarters at Mammoth, I found Scotty Chapman, the assistant chief ranger in charge of fire operations, who hired me for the fireguard position at Pelican Cone. Scotty got me a bunk on the third floor of the former cavalry barracks (later to become the park's administration building). Here I was, nineteen-years-old, and I was firmly launched on my first Yellowstone adventure and my second life-turning experience.

Our week of fireguard training included weather taking, smoke chaser operations, compass work, lookout responsibilities, horse packing, and just about everything a fireguard needed to know.

I had helped repair the ground phone line to Pelican Cone and was hanging around the Lake Ranger Station area where I had bunk space, awaiting word on when I should man the lookout for the season. It was a weekend. I didn't have a car and had no plans for my days off. Lake District Ranger DeLyle Stevens saw I had time on my hands and asked me if I wanted to pack a load of metal fence posts into Pelican Springs Patrol Cabin.

"Sure, you bet," I said. At that time I was happy to do anything with horses. I was especially pleased to be able to do something that involved both horses and backcountry. Stevens showed me a bunch of metal fence posts and told me which pickup truck to use.

I gathered a few things and drove out to Pelican Corral where the two horses assigned to Jack Knowles, the fireguard/packer for Pelican Cone, were kept. I had met Jack, his wife Ella, and their son Bobby (about four years old). Jack had been the Pelican Cone lookout the previous year.

At the corral I gave the horses a feed of oats while I "man-tied up" the fence posts (that is, I wrapped them in canvas tarps) and tied them into two separate packs. Each pack was about seven feet long, two feet in circumference, and weighed about 60 to 70 pounds.

I put the riding saddle on a trim, dark, good looking, fif-teen-hands-tall mare. The single rigged Decker packsaddle went on a big-footed, big-bellied, roan paint horse that stood over sixteen hands high. He was as gentle as an elderly saint.

The fence posts were placed on the packsaddle tepee-style and secured with a basket hitch. In retrospect, it would have been better to pack them parallel to the horse and secure them with a barrel hitch. But at that stage of my packing career, I used the only hitch I knew.

We were off by the crack of noon, youth and enthusiasm heading north to adventure under increasingly cloudy skies. The dark mare stepped out eagerly, the packhorse trotted to keep up. The loads swung erratically in response to the packhorse's increased stride. While the packhorse shied at the swinging load, the mare danced daintily to keep ahead of the disconcerting fence posts. My right hand maintained a death grip on the pack horse's lead rope as my arm was stretched to its limit trying to preserve the link between the perky mare and the reluctant packhorse.

It started to rain. I had anticipated this and had put on my Levi jacket before we started. My efforts to button the jacket were continually frustrated by the packhorse that kept my right arm stretched back as he tried to keep up with the mare. Then the first lightning bolt shot from the sky and hit directly in front of us. It was immediately followed by a deaf-ening crash of thunder. Both horses shied and pivoted back the way they had come. Aided by good luck and the agility of youth, I stayed in the saddle. I finally got the horses turned around and headed north just as the second bolt of lightning struck, with another crash of thunder.

This brought a jolting repeat of the first go-around. It was repeated six more times. At last the horses settled down and just jumped at each bolt of lightning and clap of thunder. It rained harder and harder. I got wetter and colder. The lightning and thunder kept up for an hour. Youth's energy and enthusiasm kept me going. That and the awareness I finally had a tale. There I rode…and that's no shit!

The transformation I experienced when it dawned on me that my misery was the beginning of a ranger story was amazing! Even though I was cold and dripping wet, I began to watch the horses closely. I found I could gather in the mare and take the slack out of the packhorse's lead rope to minimize the effect of their response to the lightning and thunder. After this, the trip went smoothly. We made better time. Finally, the weather began to clear.

As the storm abated, my mood improved. When we arrived at the cabin, I tied the horses and unpacked the fence posts. I had trouble folding the stiff, rain-soaked manties into compact bundles to pack out. That was my first experience with this challenge. Little did I realize that I would face it often in years to come.

The return trip was routine. The horses and I both enjoyed it. At the corral I unsaddled and checked the horses carefully for sores and rubbed marks. I found none. My first solo packing venture was a modest success. After I gave my companions a feed of oats I drove back to Lake Ranger Station, took a long hot shower and ate a candy bar and a bag of peanuts to make up for the dinner I had missed at the government mess hall. I went to bed early and happy. As I relaxed and faded into sleep, I mentally rehearsed the sentences of my first ranger tale.

While somewhat disappointed that I did not get a post where I would be working with horses, I resolved to make the best of it. Jack and I worked around Lake a few days, then with Ella and Bobby, moved to Pelican Springs Patrol Cabin, which would be Jack's base of operations for the summer.

The trip and the next few days were particularly interesting for me. It was my first stay in a Yellowstone patrol cabin. I saw my first winter-kill bison carcasses and my first grizzly bear. Jack and I worked on the phone line to the cone, using climbing spurs to climb the trees that the single strand of phone wire hung from. It was hard work, but I relished it. I was doing real ranger work. I didn't mind the mosquitoes or the wet, muddy trails or my blisters or the raw places on my legs from the climbing spurs. When we got back to the cabin, Ella included me in the meals she prepared, and I ate well. Life was good.

The day came for me to man the cone for the season. Jack packed me to the lookout, went over all the procedures, and then he and his horses headed down the mountain. Jack's departure reminded me that in my relatively tender nineteen years, this was the first time I was responsible for what I purchased, prepared, and ate for my meals. I was the only one responsible for seeing that I had clean underwear and that the dishes were done, and a whole list of other things. I was starting a new life. I was left on top of the mountain in silence and warm sunshine with a host of new responsibilities, a beautiful view, and no one around.

Before this, being alone had never bothered me. There was always someone down the road, next door, or coming over in a few minutes or hours. But this was different, on a mountain top, all alone, no one to talk to, and no one to ask questions, no one expected to come up until Jack would resupply me in a week. I was alone and lonely. I felt somber, moody, and apprehensive. Then I happened to pick up a cookbook and noticed a recipe for baking powder biscuits. It looked easy and interesting. I had the ingredients, so I made a batch of baking powder biscuits. The biscuits turned out well, and while I was eating hot biscuits with butter and honey, I noticed the shelves of paperback books left by previous lookouts. I picked one up and began to read it. The day ended nicely with hot biscuits and an interesting book.

I spent the rest of the summer enjoying the solitude, the beautiful scenery, and my own company. I relished lookout life and have never again minded being alone. I read, enjoyed the fabulous views, and watched the sun set behind a mountain range to the west just as a full moon rose from behind a different range in the east. I was alone, except for the elk and bison grazing on the open hillsides below the cone.

I took weather readings morning and evening and called them in on the ground telephone line. I watched lightning storms, recorded lightning strikes that hit the ground, checked each strike later to make sure there was no fire, and learned to distinguish thermal steam from wood smoke. I reported fires. I did all the things a lookout was supposed to do.

About the first week of August, I got word that my grocery bill at the Lake Hamilton Store was due. I thought I had arranged for credit for the whole season. This was before credit cards, and I didn't have a checking account. While I didn't have the cash to cover the bill, I did have two un-cashed paychecks. This set the stage for a new adventure. It started to rain. We received quite a bit of moisture with very little lightning. I was given permission to come down from the lookout after calling in the five p.m. weather readings, as long as I was back up to record the next morning's weather at eight a.m.!

Youth and crass ignorance combined to create an episode that should never have happened. I left promptly after I called in the five p.m. weather. I carried a fire rucksack with a jacket, a couple of candy bars, and a four-cell fire headlamp that had fresh batteries. Dan Yuhr, a seasonal boat ranger and friend from my weeks at Lake, would meet me at Pelican Bridge with a pickup. He would take me back after I had paid my bill and done some shopping.

With wild abandon and more energy and enthusiasm than good sense, I began running down the phone line to Pelican Springs Cabin (about three miles away). Going down the phone line was shorter than taking the trail. It also gave me a chance to see if any trees had fallen across the line or if any limbs were touching it. The line was clear. I made good time to the cabin. Other than splitting wood this was my first exercise in a month.

Still overflowing with energy, I ran, walked, and jogged the next four miles to Pelican Bridge. As planned, Dan was waiting for me. I was feeling good as we exchanged greetings and drove to the Hamilton Store at Lake. I cashed a paycheck, paid my bills, bought a few items, and arranged for credit. Then we stopped at the Lake Lodge soda fountain. I ordered an extra-thick strawberry malt. It was so good I had a second one.

Soon it was time to begin the second part of my epic journey—get back to the cone in time to call in the morning weather. Dan took me back to Pelican Bridge, and we parted company. He headed back to Lake Ranger Station and bed. I headed to Pelican Cone, about twelve miles away. The moon showed intermittently through breaks in the clouds. Mist rose from the valley floor. It was quiet and moody. The only human-caused sound was Dan's pickup enroute to Pelican Corral and beyond. When my eyes adjusted I found I didn't need a headlamp to see. I kept it handy on my belt. As I started hiking I was definitely less enthusiastic than when I had bounded off the cone a few hours earlier.

As I walked, I savored the feeling of Pelican Valley in the mist, with an almost full moon breaking in and out of the clouds. The damp, cool quiet made walking comfortable, even as I stumbled periodically on the ruts in the trail. I tried to keep a reasonable pace. I was looking forward to bed. As time passed, I became aware of the strain in my hips and knees and the muscles in my legs tightening up, but I tried to ignore it by focusing on the trail and keeping up a steady pace. Pushing along on auto pilot, concentrating on keeping moving and not stumbling, I heard just in front of me, almost in touching distance, two simultaneous sounds that bolted me to full alert and pumped shots of adrenalin into my heart, and caused me to stop breathing and freeze mid-stride.

A bunch of elk, apparently bedded down near the trail, sprang into motion and ran by me with hooves pounding and rattling. In the same instant, just in front and only a few feet away on my right, what sounded like a huge bear exhaled forcefully, a loud *whoof*. The bear immediately began clicking and masticating its teeth! I held my breath and stood still. My heart pounded. I wondered what to do as I listened to the elk run away. Finally, I couldn't wait any longer and clicked on my light. I got an instant response of clicking and gnashing of teeth, huffing nostrils, and smacking lips. The sound was to my left and a little farther away than the first time I had heard it.

In the shadows at the edge of the light I saw the large bear.

He appeared to be heading away, but his head was pointed back towards me. I quickly turned the light off. I wasn't sure if the bear was still moving away. I waited, hardly breathing, my heart racing. I could no longer hear the fleeing elk. Once more I clicked on my headlamp. The bear immediately responded with more gnashing and clicking of teeth, but farther away. I shut off the light and waited. My mind was in turmoil as I debated my options. Finally I started to walk slowly up the trail, all senses alert. It was apparently the right thing to do as nothing followed me, as far as I could tell. Pumped with adrenaline, I picked up the pace for a time. Then, as fatigue took over, I slowed down and shuffled along.

By the time I crossed Pelican Creek and started climbing the final 1,600 vertical feet (in four miles of trail) to the cone, I was walking on empty. The sun finally came up, and I made it to the top in plenty of time to call in the weather. My epic ended, but my suffering did not. My legs were so stiff and sore I could hardly bend them. I couldn't raise them high enough to use the rungs of a ladder. I hobbled around for two weeks. Fortunately no one came up to witness my misery. More fortunately I didn't have to go anyplace. I just had to look for fires (there weren't any), take the weather, and bake my daily batch of biscuits. When Jack came to pack me down in September, I left Pelican Cone as a more confidant person, much more comfortable with myself than when I went up. In retrospect, I was unbelievably lucky. Making that trip alone for no better reason than I had ranks among the most foolhardy things I've ever done. My supervisors should have known better even though I didn't. But those were different, simpler times and shouldn't be judged in the context of today's awareness and standards. It was my decision to make the trip. I am the person ultimately responsible for my actions and my physical well-being.

I learned later that a bear's rapid exhaling of breath (*whoofing*) indicates surprise, and the gnashing of teeth and smacking of lips indicates agitation, anger, or aggression. By standing in place, I did the correct thing. At that time I was doing it for other reasons. A life turning point! I had my second ranger tale—and that's no shit.

Chapter 3

Stormy Lessons in Glacier National Park

WHEN I GRADUATED FROM NOTRE DAME IN 1954, I HAD A job as a fireguard waiting for me in Glacier National Park, Montana. I took the Northern Pacific Railroad from Chicago and arrived in Belton, Montana, with my duffel bag and a daypack, ready for the summer.

I caught a ride to Glacier's park headquarters, reported to the fire cache, was assigned a bunk in the bunkhouse, went through fireguard training, and eventually wound up at Goat Haunt Ranger Station along the Canadian border, at the south end of Waterton Lake. To get there I had to cross into Canada, go through Waterton

National Park to Waterton Park town site, and then take an NPS patrol boat down the lake and back into the United States to Goat Haunt Ranger Station. It was quite an adventure for my young, newly graduated mind and my longest venture outside the USA.

Bob Morris was the ranger in charge; he was also my supervisor and the one who brought me down the lake to my new home. He was a quiet, easy-going individual, probably in his late thirties who wore dark horn rim glasses that periodically slipped down his nose making him look professorial and scholarly. He characteristically wore a well-worn uniform that was clean but was never spit and polish. It wasn't his style, nor was he in that kind of job. From the very beginning I liked him both as a person and as a supervisor. He was fair, looked out for his subordinates, gave them considerable latitude, and was appreciative when they did good work and showed initiative. I couldn't ask for more than that.

My summer went by in a blur. I dutifully went over the fire equipment; we had no fires. I rode a lot, and I hiked a lot. Hiking was mostly on my days off, usually alone. I paid attention to bears but worried more about being chased by a moose than by a grizzly. I saw my first wolf (on the International Boundary while hiking to Cameron Lake). On foot or horseback, on government time or my own, I traveled almost all the trails east of Boulder Pass and north of the Going-To-The-Sun Road, many of them several times. The farthest I hiked in a day was 35 miles; my knee was sore for the next week. It was my first introduction to aging and to the subsequent frailty of body parts.

By chance it was a visit by the Sierra Club that led to the two most interesting days of the summer. One hundred Sierra Clubbers started a ten-day "wilderness" hike at Many Glacier, went through Ptarmigan Tunnel, over Stoney Indian Pass, up to Goat Haunt, and over Boulder Pass to the North Fork Road. This was when it was the vogue to enjoy wilderness in the company of many kindred spirits. Though the goal was to live simply and to enjoy nature, their efforts were supported by a pack string of 100 horses.

I visited one of their camps. It was a beehive of activity amid a metropolis of tents. All participants had Sierra Club cups hanging from their belts. They appeared happy, healthy, and satisfied with their lot so why should I complain? I benefited by their presence because it gave me the opportunity to make three horse rides to deliver messages. Even then I subscribed to the concept that any day spent on a horse in good country was not subtracted from the totality of your days of life but was a bonus to be added to them.

When the Sierra Club group dropped into the North Fork Road to pick up their cars and the 100-horse support group was returning to Many Glacier, the latter camped a few miles west of Goat Haunt. The following morning, the head outfitter rode in with two of his packers to catch the morning Waterton tour boat to get them out of the backcountry in time to return to school. The outfitter lamented to Bob that now he was really going to be short-handed for the rest of his trip.

Gesturing at me with his thumb, Bob said, "I've got a solution for you. My fireguard is a pretty fair hand with stock. He's off the next two days. Hire him." The leathery, salt-soaked outfitter looked me over as if he were deciding to bid on an unknown horse. "Can you be ready in an hour?" he asked. "I can be ready in a half hour," was my reply, as I stood there blushing at Bob's compliment and at being the center of attention.

"I'll be by in an hour," the outfitter said, apparently deciding to buy the pig-in-a-poke without further investigation. "We have an extra sleeping bag. That'll be one less thing for you to pack."

I THANKED BOB FOR GETTING ME THE OPPORTUNITY TO SEE new country that was high on my priority list. He said I could take an extra day to get back if I needed it. A little over an hour passed. The outfitter and one of the packers came back with a bunch of horses. My new boss handed me a saddled, blaze-faced sorrel with four white stockings and said it would be my saddle horse for our trip. I checked the cinch for tightness, tied a Levi jacket, a rain jacket, flashlight, toothbrush, and some candy bars behind the cantle, and adjusted the stirrup length. I was barely settled on my horse when my new boss handed me the lead rope for a string of five packhorses that were saddled but not carrying loads. They were mine for the trip.

The rest of the outfit showed up. There were around ten horse handlers, packers, and myself leading about 100 packhorses. The whole entourage was soon lined out by an abundance of whoops, yells, shouts, and whistles. My string and I were near the end of the line. An experienced packer and his string rode drag, meaning they brought up the rear and kept everyone moving.

My saddle horse was a comfortable mover and had no problem keeping up with the pace. Not so with the lead horse in my string that continually dragged. My right arm was soon tired and stretched out, and at the rate we were going, I was worried I would finish the trip with my right arm six inches longer than the left. A temporary solution led to the first big lesson. I noticed a loop had been braided in the end of rope going to the lead horse. Apparently I wasn't the first person to experience this problem. I dropped the loop over my saddle horn; it was a relief to let the horse drag against the horn and give my arm a rest. We jingled along quite some time before "I saw the elephant."

We dropped down, crossed a creek, and were plunging up the other side when the lead packhorse pulled back hard on the secured rope. My sorrel, caught mid-stride, was yanked back onto its hind legs and came within a dime's width of being pulled over on me. My horse teetered there, seemingly forever, until the packhorse moved forward and released tension on the lead rope, allowing my horse to get his feet under him. I immediately unhooked the lead rope from the saddle horn and carried it in my hand for the rest of our journey. Since that experience I've never towed another animal tied hard and fast to the saddle horn. As the saying goes, "Once burned, twice cautious." The bonus insight from the near catastrophe was that I started to go slower and more cautiously over and around obstacles and to make sure each animal in my string had enough time to maneuver. These were invaluable lessons that have served me well.

As soon as we had started the trip I busied myself with memorizing the description of each horse in my string and remembering his place in the lineup. Since we would be camping along the way, I knew this would be important information in the morning when it came time to catch my six out of the hundred that would be loose in some meadow.

I was enjoying the scenery when I became aware that clouds were gathering and the sky was darkening. By the time we made the top of Stoney Indian Pass, the sky left no doubt that we were in for a storm. When it started seriously raining, our leader stopped and put on his long rain slicker, as did the others, but I was limited to a Levi jacket and a rain jacket that reached only to my hips. We hunkered down in our saddles and continued amidst an increasing rain. The farther we went the harder it rained. The lightning intensified and came closer.

For two or three hours it was a strident symphony of rain and lightning followed by drums of thunder, then more rain. Lightning close, lightning far away, lightning to our front and, at the same time, lightning to the rear followed immediately by rolling kettle drums of thunder amid torrents of rain. I counted five separate trees struck by lightning that flared into roaring blazes only to be doused back to darkness by the wash of water. We continued our march marked only by a decrease in the volume of rain and a welcome increase in the interval between flashes of lightning.

We stopped in a large meadow, and our leader rode out of the darkness and told me to unsaddle and to turn my horses loose. He added, "Then come up to the fire and dry out." I didn't need to be told twice. My horses were happy to stand in place and grab what grass was available without moving. I unsaddled my last horse, bundled up his packsaddle, placed it on the ground, blankets next to it. I turned him loose and dropped his halter by the saddle, then, one-by-one, unsaddled the others. I had a pile of saddles, a pile of blankets, and five manties.

I laid out a manty as smooth as I could in the dark, then placed the saddle blankets on the manty to form a mattress, and covered my "mattress" with the other half of the manty. I covered the saddles, fished out my flashlight, and walked through the continuing drizzle to where the ten packers were warming their hands and drying out around a now substantial fire. I was wet and beginning to shiver as I walked up to the fire and began to warm up. Steam began showing as my Levis heated up. Someone gave me a cup of coffee, and I began to feel almost decent again. I got something to eat and felt even better.

My new boss gave me a sleeping bag. I returned to my bivouac site, unrolled the bag on my impromptu mattress, and prepared for bed. I wrapped my boots in my jacket to use as a pillow and put my damp pants in the sleeping bag next to me hoping my body heat would dry them out overnight. I covered my nest with a manty and crawled in. In short order I was sound asleep. The last sound I heard beside horse bells was more rain falling on my manty.

I awoke sometime in the early morning hours with the realization that my rear end was wet. Somehow I was sleeping in a pool of warm water, and when I moved out of that position my butt was cold. As nearly as I was able to decide, my choices were warm, wet butt or cold, drier butt. I spent the rest of the night sleeping fitfully, debating which butt was preferable. When I heard people yelling I figured it was time to get up. I put on my damp jeans and boots and was glad to see it was not raining. Then I found out why my rear was wet: the manty I was sleeping on stuck farther out than the manty covering me, so when the top one shed water, the water drained onto the bottom manty to the lowest point available—where my butt was. Another lesson.

After something to eat I joined the others in catching our respective strings. The time I had spent memorizing my horses paid off. I finally had them all caught and saddled with the same blankets and saddles they carried yesterday. I was proud of myself. I had no sooner gotten them tied in their places in the string when the boss rode up. He looked things over in an instant. "Good," he exclaimed, "You got them saddled with the right saddles, and you got them in the right order. Good for you!" I was happy that my efforts had paid off, and I got a compliment to boot.

After a delightful day, we arrived at the Many Glacier corrals in the late afternoon. After taking care of the horses and eating supper, it was getting close to full dusk. The boss told me there was space in the bunkhouse if I wanted to stay over and head back tomorrow. I told him I was hoping to be at Goat Haunt at work by eight in the morning, and Bob had said he would leave the station's work boat at the Waterton Park marina for me to use whenever I got there.

Well-fed and dry I walked out to the Many Glacier road

and stuck out my thumb. The third car to go by picked me up and gave me a ride to Babb, Montana, on Highway 89. My luck held as I had waited only about fifteen minutes until a businessman from Waterton came out of the Babb Bar and gave me a ride all the way to the marina. It was a cool breezy evening with clouds drifting around an otherwise full moon when I got out of my beneficiary's car. My pocket watch showed it was midnight as I walked the rolling docks to where the U.S. government's boats were kept when in town.

The work boat was basically a heavy duty row boat powered by a temperamental, 20-horsepower outboard motor. I opened the storage bin under the seat, took out a life jacket and put it on the seat by me, and stashed my extra gear. Preoccupied as I was with starting the outboard I paid little attention to the lake, which was choppy with significant white caps. The wind seemed to be coming from the south. With the full moon there was enough light to navigate, and I headed south. The lake was much rougher than I had seen it, but not being any kind of sailor or waterman I did what I thought I should do—I powered into the waves. Just as I was thinking it would be wise to modify my approach, the motor died. Shit! What now? I tried to restart the motor. No luck.

My boat and I were being tossed about like a four-year-old boy's rubber ducky in a bathtub. Belatedly, I saw the life jacket on the seat next to me. I should have put that damn thing on, I thought, but I didn't dare stop trying to get my boat under power. We were being tossed closer and closer towards a rocky cliff. At least I knew how to swim! I mentally thanked Mom for insisting I take swim lessons years ago.

Surprisingly the engine fired! At half speed I nursed my boat away from the impending doom at the rocky cliff. I found that at half speed, we could negotiate the waves better, and by quartering into the waves my boat did much better. Good lessons learned the hard way. As we continued south the wind and waves diminished, and by the time we reached the international boundary there was only a slight chop to the lake. I finally was able to put on my life jacket. When I tied up at the government dock at Goat Haunt the lake was calm and the full moon was cloud-free. When I showed up to take the 8 a.m. weather, Bob was surprised to see me. "How was your trip?" he asked. "Oh, fine," I replied. "Nothing un-usual." I figured a white lie was better than trying to describe the abject terror I still carried with me.

Years later when I reflected on the summer of 1954 and its lessons, I marveled that I ever made it to age twenty-five.

Chapter 4

How I Became a Missionary about One-Match Fires

WHEN I WAS NINE MY FATHER TAUGHT ME HOW TO USE WAX paper to set a "one-match fire" and explained why it was important to leave such a fire ready to go in backcountry cabin stoves. My nine-year-old mind was able to understand the superiority of wax paper in setting any fire, but it took a few experiences over the years to fully appreciate the rest of the lesson. Years later, a personal experience made me a missionary on the subject.

In 1941, Dad was Wawona District Ranger in Yosemite National Park, and Ostrander Lake was in his district. It was accessed by a nine-mile trail off Badger Pass to Glacier Point Road. A few years previously the Yosemite Park and Curry Company (the park's primary concessionaire) had built a handsome stone and log ski lodge there to encourage folks to get into the backcountry on skis in the winter.

I was with him when he found the last occupants had not left fires set and ready to go. Dad was mildly pissed. While he split kindling and crumpled up wax paper to set a fire, he explained, "When you leave a cabin, always leave a good fire set in the stoves…in case the next users are cold, wet, and so exhausted they don't have the energy to start a fire…use wax paper if you have it…wax paper doesn't absorb moisture like newspaper…and wax paper burns hotter than newspaper or paper bags."

"Use pitch wood if you have it for kindling," Dad continued, "It burns hotter than regular wood…keep your kindling small…using fuzz sticks is even better." "What are fuzz sticks?" I interrupted. Dad stopped what he was doing and selected a straight-grained piece of kindling from the pile. He opened his pocket knife to its utility blade and, placing one end of the kindling on the chopping block, used his knife to slice several thin curling feathers of wood from top to bottom of the stick but did not cut them off. He wound up with a kindling stick with a half dozen thin wood curls on one end. That was my first introduction to fuzz sticks.

In January 1964 I arrived in Yellowstone National Park. Less than a month later I celebrated Washington's Birthday at Thorofare Ranger Station deep in Yellowstone's backcountry while on an 18-day ski patrol with South District Ranger Bob Morey and Law Enforcement Specialist Ed Widmer.

THIS WAS ONE OF THE FIRST LONG SKI PATROLS IN YELLOWstone after a double fatality occurred in Grand Teton National Park, which had led to a virtual hiatus in winter ski travel in the two parks. One method bureaucracies have for dealing with tragedies is to initiate more paper work. As if a memo would make a task safer, Morey had to write the chief ranger outlining the purpose of the patrol, what was to be accomplished, who was participating, and what each participant would gain from the trip. With the chief ranger's written approval, the rangers involved were free to do what rangers had traditionally done—range, cover the country, learn the area, and perform tasks to benefit the resource.

The tragedy that led to this exercise happened four years

earlier in 1960 and involved three experienced Grand Teton rangers: Stan Spurgeon (assistant chief ranger), Gale Wilcox (district ranger), and John Fonda (assistant district ranger). Spurgeon and Wilcox had crossed the frozen northern end of Jackson Lake heading toward the Lower Berry Creek Patrol Cabin when disaster struck. Fonda fell through the ice. Wilcox immediately skied to his assistance and broke through the ice as well. While dragging Wilcox to shore, Spurgeon got completely soaked and exhausted but to no avail. Wilcox and Fonda both perished.

The temperature was 20 degrees below zero and the snow pack deeper than average. Floundering through the deep snow to the cabin sapped almost all the strength Spurgeon had left. Before he collapsed he managed to get into the cabin and light the fire that had been set in the stove. The next day Spurgeon attracted the attention of a snow plane party and was rescued.

Fonda Point on the east shore and Wilcox Point on the west side of Jackson Lake remind us that life can be fleeting when an individual, no matter how competent or experienced, missteps in the backcountry.

My own misadventure that made me missionary about leaving one-match fires happened in November 1972. At that time I was the Lake sub-district ranger. Along with shorter days, this particular November brought much colder temperatures, including several minus thirty-degree nights. I still had one backcountry cabin to supply with rations for winter ski patrols. I always kept horses as late in the season as possible since life without horses and mules is just not as full. Besides I was hoping for warmer weather to supply Pelican Springs Patrol Cabin, my last non-rationed cabin.

At the urging of those in charge of the corral operations,

my supervisor gave an ultimatum to get the horses in—soon! So the next day I loaded up Dusty, my horse for the past eight years, and Max, a packhorse, and headed to Pelican Cabin with a heavy load of winter rations. I got a late start waiting for it to warm up a bit, and it was almost what in later years I called a "Snake River Start"—off by the crack of noon.

Initially we made good time. Dusty was a fast-moving Thoroughbred and Max a strong, durable horse that listened to his own drummer and sometimes was a challenge to handle. Everything went well for the first eight miles. When we got to the south fork of Pelican Creek, with only two miles to the cabin, I got a clue that this might not be my day. The trail drops steeply into the creek bottom and rises abruptly to climb out of the ford, which is a wide place in an ambling, slow-moving creek. The ford crosses the creek at an angle and is about two horse-lengths across and about knee deep on the average horse. On either side of the ford are deeper pools, from belly deep to the top of an average horse's withers. Although we had crossed this same place from six to twelve times in past years without hesitation, Max decided this time he was not going to cross. I tried repeatedly but to no avail.

Exasperated but holding my temper, I took a couple wraps of the lead rope around the saddle horn, nudged Dusty at the appropriate moment, and dragged Max across and made it to the top of the hill. So far, so good. I had won the battle but the war remained to be decided. We made it to the cabin. I tied up, unpacked Max, loosened cinches and carried the rations into the cabin. Although I had done a lot of preliminary work, more remained to be done than I had anticipated. I decided that if I could be back across Pelican Creek by dark, I could get it all done. The trail beyond Pelican Creek was routine, and we could do it easily in the dark.

My plan made, I got to work and started one fire for warmth. I put rations away, selected out-dated rations to take out, made an extra supply of fuzz sticks, swept, made up the packs to take out, and took out the hot ashes from the bed of the stove I had fired up. Then I tightened cinches on my horses' saddles, packed Max with a light pack to take out, and I was done, right on schedule.

My last chore was to set a fire in the stove I had used. Using plenty of wax paper and fuzz sticks I prepared a one-match fire Dad would have been proud of. The temperature was zero as I swung up on Dusty and headed for home, dragging Max with us. A low of twenty below was predicted for the night.

I was enjoying the crisp ride through the increasing dusk as Dusty stepped out at his comfortable, sure-footed, mile-eating stride. We made it to the Pelican crossing with daylight to spare. All we had to do was cross the creek, but fate—and Max—had something else in mind. In his bone-headed manner, Max would have nothing to do with crossing. Try as patiently as I could, he wouldn't cross, no matter what I did. As the last daylight was running out I tried dragging him. On my first effort, with one wrap around the saddle horn, Max pulled back and pulled the lead rope out of my hand. I retrieved the rope, waited until we all calmed down, then tried again.

In my most relaxed manner I urged Dusty forward. Max resisted, and I took three wraps around the saddle horn. At the last instant Max gave in, jumped forward, and rammed into Dusty's right hip with such force that he knocked Dusty off his feet and into a deep pool of water next to the ford. In a split instant I was wet from the waist down! Dusty churned the water, made it to his feet, and lunged back onto the bank he had just come from. As wet as I was, I managed to stay in the saddle and hang onto Max's lead rope. I was gasping from the cold so much I couldn't even swear. As Dusty and Max shook themselves I contemplated my situation. It was dark, below zero, I was wet from the waist down, I had two wet horses, and I could feel myself getting colder by the minute.

So we trotted back to Pelican Cabin and I got inside. With one match I started both fires, warmed up, dried out, took care of the horses, and spent the night. And that is why I became a missionary about one-match fires.

I spent 32 years as a permanent ranger in Yellowstone, and while I wasn't perfect, no one could ever accuse me of not leaving a wax-paper, fuzz-stick, one-match fire ready to go.

Chapter 5

Law Student Meets Bob Flame, Ranger

FOLLOWING MY SUMMER IN GLACIER NATIONAL PARK, I volunteered for the draft, having had two years of deferment to finish college. I went into the U. S. Army in December of 1954, took eight weeks of basic training at Fort Ord, California, and then remained at Fort Ord for clerk-typist school. How I graduated I don't know since I was a lousy typist, but I was assigned to Fort Barry in Marin County, California. Barry was a two-company post and the regimental headquarters of the 30th Anti Aircraft Artillery charged with the missile defense of the Bay Area and bases in California's Central Valley.

Being a failure as a typist but consistently having the shiniest shoes in the company, Sergeant-Major Tuttle made me the colonel's driver. I spent the rest of my tour driving Colonel Dallas Haines around the Bay Area and Central Valley. I received an early out from the Army after 21 months and three days in order to attend law school.

In the fall of 1956 I entered Hastings College of Law in San Francisco. Hastings is a part of the University of California and the oldest law school in California. I lived with my folks in San Francisco and rode the city bus to and from downtown San Francisco and Hastings. Sometimes I rode with my dad who was working in the National Park Service regional office at the time.

Law school was a grind. And big city living and commuting downtown was more of a challenge than I had ever anticipated. Hastings held classes from 8 a.m. to 12 noon. The rest of the day was yours to study or to make a living, whichever was needed. I tried to study since, courtesy of the G.I. Bill and my parents, my basic needs were taken care of, but studying was a drag. Sitting in the law library with dozens of other nose-to-the-grindstone, would-be legal scholars, reading case law, taking notes on the most boring, hair-splitting minutia, trying to follow a judge's line of reasoning, almost made the Army look good! It certainly made me wonder what I was doing there. I often lamented my logic in enrolling in law school, but I resolved to give it a go.

I soon developed a routine. After my last class I took an hour for lunch and ate a sandwich I brought from home (and, as my mother instructed, trying to remember to chew each bite 20 times). With lunch over, I would walk rapidly up and down nearby Market Street and then head to the library for the rest of the afternoon. Before long I looked forward to my Market Street trips. One day I walked farther than usual, and around Second and Market I noticed a used bookstore. For some reason I went inside. In the California section, I noticed a series of books by Dorr Yeager, a National Park Service naturalist. There was *Bob Flame: Ranger, Bob Flame in Rocky Mountain*, and several other Bob Flame books. While I recognized Dorr Yeager's name, I had not heard of Bob Flame.

Curious, I picked up *Bob Flame in Yosemite*, opened it to the first page, and read "Bob Flame, ranger, rode to the top of the pass. He pulled in his palomino mare. He felt a cool breeze at the back of his neck…." What bullshit, I thought.

No self-respecting ranger would ever be caught riding a palomino mare. I returned the book to the shelf and left the store without wasting more of my time on fantasy.

At that time I held many definite opinions, not all of them founded on observation. I had yet to discover there is no such thing as a bad color in a good horse. I thought palominos and paints were more for show than for serious use. It was fine for a Hollywood cowboy like Roy Rogers to ride a palomino, but I didn't think a ranger would. I returned to the library and forced myself to read more case law. I found little joy in law school. The best part of the week was the weekend, which usually included long walks with Dad, often along the beach.

In the early winter, I applied for a seasonal ranger position in Yosemite for the following summer. Sometime during the winter I visited Yosemite and made an appointment to meet with Chief Ranger Oscar Sedergren. I told him I had applied for a seasonal ranger position and hoped to be considered for more than an entrance station position (which was the typical entry level assignment). He looked me up and down and made no commitment, but he did ask me how much horse experience I had. I replied I was a fairly experienced rider but was only a beginning packer. He said he would keep my request in mind.

Somewhat to my surprise, I made it through my first year of law school, and since I had been hired as a seasonal ranger, immediately headed to Yosemite. I got there in early June 1957, went through seasonal ranger training, and found out that I was assigned to Buck Camp, a relatively remote, one-man ranger station in the south end of the park. Located about 15 miles by trail from Wawona, the district headquarters, Buck Camp had many square miles of High Sierra scenery, miles and miles of trails, and no roads. For me it was a boyhood dream come true—a backcountry ranger.

Before heading to Buck Camp I would have to work at the South Entrance until more seasonal rangers arrived for duty. I spent three weeks at this very busy station selling park entrance permits. If we came up short of money at the end of a shift, we made up the difference from our own pockets. This experience changed me for life, or at least it changed the way I counted money and sorted bills. To this day all bills in my wallet must be face up, right side up, and sorted by denomination.

One day District Ranger Walt Gammill told me the horses and tack had arrived at Wawona, and he wanted me to look them over to pick the saddle horse and pack mule I wanted for Buck Camp. I was also to select a saddle for me and a packsaddles for the mule. There were four horses and four mules. Walt described them, told me which he recommended, but left the choice to me. Walt was a relaxed, laid-back, easy-going gentleman. He was definitely not a micro manager. His only question about my ability was asking if Dad had taught me how to get along in the backcountry. I said yes. Things were simpler then.

I spent the day sorting gear, picking a saddle, trading parts from three bridles to make up a presentable one, and taking a short ride on each horse to make my decision. I selected the palomino mare that Walt had recommended (without realizing the irony of that choice). I also chose a nice looking brown mule called Coyote. Walt said I might as well go to Buck Camp the following day with a second mule and the fireguard, Jim Burleigh, to help me get set up. Jim could bring the extra mule back after spending a layover day with me at Buck Camp. Also, he said the phone company would be working on the phone line to Buck Camp, and I should call into the district office once in awhile to let them know everything was all right.

Jim and I were up early the next morning and fed, brushed, and saddled the stock. I made up the packs, then, very tediously and laboriously, tied two needle-and-thread-diamond hitches. They didn't look bad: The diamonds were even, the hitches were tight, and I heaved an immense sigh of relief that my first solo packing operation was ready to go. Jim had no idea of my apprehension; he thought I knew what I was doing.

We headed up the road through Chilnualna (a square mile of private property and mostly summer houses surrounded by the park). Just beyond Chilnualna was the trailhead to Buck Camp. The packs rode amazingly well. An old packer's adage says if the packs make it the first half-mile, they'll probably make it the rest of the way. The closer we got to Lou Stockton's home, the straighter and taller I sat in the saddle. I had traveled all through the Buck Camp country with Lou while I was in high school and again while in the Army.

When we rode up to the house, Lou and Myrtle (his wife, who was almost a second mother to me) came out. I was sweating profusely; this was my first test. Lou looked things over critically, plucked at the ropes, rocked the packs, and when the packs came to rest dead center, he said he thought we'd make it. I exhaled the breath I was holding and felt pressure growing on my hatband as my head expanded. I was such a proud puppy I almost peed my pants for joy.

The rest of the trip was hot, dusty, and uneventful, but I felt increasing excitement: We were going to *my* station! When we arrived, youth, energy, and the pride of possession took over. We unpacked, fed the stock, checked the pasture fence, activated the water system, cleaned the winter's supply of mouse "do," cooked a Spartan supper, left the dishes for morning, and went to bed happy, tired campers.

Not bothered by mice scurrying through the woodpile all

night, we awoke in the morning refreshed and re-energized. More cleaning, repairing, organizing, and exploring, and then it was time for Jim to head back to Wawona with the extra mule. I went with him a few miles and then turned off to check Buena Vista Lake, a popular campsite. I rode home cross-country and was taking a shower on the front porch when the phone line repairmen showed up. With the phone working, I called in, talked to Walt, who seemed pleased with the progress I reported.

When the linemen left, life at Buck Camp fell into a pleasant routine. Up early, care for and saddle the stock, patrol, patrol, and patrol. I tried to cover it all. I rode cross-country, followed informal, marked trails; I regularly visited the more heavily used campsites, contacted everyone I could; tied the stock, explored on foot, found new travel routes, returned to the stock, made it home late, slept soundly, and repeated the process. Life was good.

I felt very possessive of the area, almost as if it were mine. I was responsible for its care and well-being. I loved what I was doing and had no complaints. When I stepped into the saddle in the cool of the morning my horse's stride eased yesterday's aches and pains, and I looked forward to the day's work. My life's dreams and my job were one.

I really liked my mule Coyote who had an interesting personality, led well, kept up well, and was no problem. The mare was a different matter. When she was good, she was very, very good. When she was bad, she was a pain in the ass. Her way of protesting when she didn't want to do what I asked was to rear straight up, stopping just short of going over backward. It was very disconcerting, and I demonstrated my disapproval with voice, spur, and the side of my boot. We went through three episodes before I could anticipate her impending insurrections and redirect her focus. I called her Lady when she was good, Babe when she wasn't so good, and a variety of expletives when she threw her tantrums. We both learned a lot from our association.

Coyote went everywhere with us. Every day he carried the same light load of tools, radio packset, sleeping bag, first aid kit, and rations. I got more proficient and adept every time I secured the load with a box hitch. By the end of the season I could tie it with my eyes closed and in less than one fourth of the early season time.

One warm day early on, while I checked out all the trails and regular campsites, I rode up to Fernandez Pass. The trail was steep, narrow, rugged, and in places the exposure was significant and impressive. When we surged up the last pitch to the top of the pass I pulled in the mare to let her breathe as I took in the view. I stretched in the saddle, took a deep breath, and enjoyed the scenery. As I sat there, a breeze blew across my neck, and cooled the sweat that had accumulated on the way up. A thought flashed through my mind—Bob Flame, ranger! Well, I'll be damned!

My face flushed with embarrassment as I compared myself to Bob Flame. I looked around to see if anyone was watching. There was no one. Fernandez Pass was as remote from crowds as any place in California. I smiled, recalling the opening line of Dorr Yeager's book. "Bob Flame, ranger, rode to the top of the pass. He pulled in his palomino mare. He felt a cool breeze at the back of his neck." I resolved to find and read "Bob Flame in Yosemite" to see what other experiences Bob and I might have shared.

Chapter 6

Encounters with a Specter, a Fire, and a Bear

THE DAY I ENCOUNTERED THE SPECTER OF BOB FLAME ON Fernandez Pass turned out to be an especially interesting day because I also ran into John Muir—more or less. Coming down from the pass I decided to check the campsite at Horse Thief Canyon. Even beyond the romance of its name, Horse Thief Canyon had been a special place for me from the time I had first followed Lou Stockton there some ten years earlier.

Not on an established trail, Horse Thief Canyon was not easy to find. The route to it was shrouded, and its entrance was obscured by heavy pine forest. If you left the Moraine Meadows Trail at the correct place and traveled approximately east and uphill a mile or so, you would quite likely be rendered both speechless and breathless when you broke out of the timber. In front of you was a half-mile wide, one-mile long, lush, boulder-strewn mountain meadow, guarded on three sides by impressive granite peaks. The meadow had a glacier-fed creek running the length of it that was as clear, cold, and colorless as if poured from a bottle of gin long kept in the freezer. Triple Divide Peak stood as a lofty sentinel at the very head of the canyon.

Its isolated location, stunning beauty, and labyrinth of rock, water, and meadow gave it a special aura even in a country where outstanding settings were commonplace. Each time I had camped there had been memorable, even enchanted. On this sunny and warm summer day, it was as lovely as ever and had yet to be camped in this season. Most of my mind was devoted to appreciating the stillness and beauty as I rode around the area. Pleasant memories added to my mood. But it was getting late, and we had miles to go to get home. Then Babe, seeming to recall how far we were from oats and rest, went into her "stepping out, going home" pace.

As we rounded a large boulder, my mare and mule suddenly shied violently and jumped to their left. I somehow managed to stay in the saddle as I was abruptly startled back to reality. The snorting attention of my mare and mule was focused on a slender, frail individual with a long, white beard and shaggy white hair. He was trying to steady himself after suddenly sitting upright from a prone position. I felt I had seen this person before; it was John Muir—or at least a facsimile of that icon of the Sierras.

"I didn't mean to scare your horses," the white-haired apparition said in a high-pitched, unsteady voice.

"Are you okay?" I asked, still sitting on my mare. "Where are you headed?"

"I'm going to Red's Meadow," John Muir said. "I left Glacier Point three days ago. I've made this trip before. This time is harder though. I'm 83, you know."

By now I was off my mare, listening to the slight figure in front of me. He was William Kat, a retired carpenter from Yosemite Valley. Then it dawned on me why he looked so familiar: I had attended the first three grades of Yosemite Elementary School with his granddaughter, Marion.

With his lean build, long gray hair and beard, Kat looked just like Muir. He was crossing the Sierra, and this would be his last trip since it was harder this time than it used to be.

The more we talked, the more awe I felt. Kat had a small pack, a blanket but no sleeping bag. For food he had 12 walnuts, a half-pound of cheese, and half a loaf of dark bread. He expected to be out for several more days. Did he have enough food? "Oh, yes, it doesn't take very much to keep me going," he said. Do you have matches? "Yes," he said, explaining that the matches were only for emergencies; he never started fires. Fires left too much of a scar on the land. (Interesting! Remember, this was 1957, not 1987.)

Did he have a map? He dug into his pack and pulled out a very nice map of the John Muir Trail. I was envious. The only map I had was a topographic map of Yosemite, and it showed very little beyond the park boundary. I complimented him on the map. I asked where he had gotten it and said that I would like to get one for myself.

Kat said the map came with the book, *Starr's Guide To The John Muir Trail.* He said he would send me the book and the map when he got out. Since this was his last trip, he was sure I would get more use out of it than he would. Despite my initial refusal, Kat persisted. I finally tore a page out of my three-inch by five-inch park service notebook, wrote my name and address on it and handed it to Mr. Kat. Then, he continued on his way, and I headed for Buck Camp.

I couldn't get the old gentleman off my mind. The next morning I collected a few cans of food suited for backpacking and returned to Fernandez Pass. I got there late morning after following Kat's footprints all the way to the top. I could see down the trail on the other side for several miles, but Kat was long gone. I wished him well and returned to Buck Camp and my routine.

One day's activity blended into the next, and the season

progressed rapidly. The last week of July arrived with a lightning storm. I found myself on a small (one acre, plus) but relatively hot lightning-caused fire just north of Merced Pass in a fairly open stand of mature lodgepole pine and fir trees.

I got there in the early afternoon just as the wind was kicking up. I jumped off my mare, tied her and the mule, grabbed a shovel, and, aided by a shot or two of adrenalin, started building fireline. During a lull I moved the animals to a safer location and unpacked the mule, but I left him and the mare saddled in case I had to move them out in a hurry. I substituted a hardhat for my Stetson, got my gloves, and went back to the fire.

I worked frantically, knowing that no help was on its way; I was the only one in a position to do anything on this fire. I literally worked until I dropped, then got up again when a breeze pushed the fire across my scratch line and repeated the process two or three times until things slowed down in the early evening. I found a small stream close by that was barely a trickle but had useable pools of water. I watered the stock, gave them a bite of grain, grabbed a fire ration for myself, and went back to the fire.

I FOUND A PLACE WHERE I COULD CALL THE FIRE CACHE WITH my packset radio. They wanted to know how big the fire was and if I could handle it by myself since they were shorthanded, etc. I said the fire was around three acres, and I could use help but would do what I could without it, and I was short of rations. They said they would do what they could. I ate a fire ration and saved the packets of sugar and Pream for snacks later on.

When the fire quieted down I unsaddled my stock and let them graze for a while. Between working on the fire, taking care of the horse and mule, trying not to over eat my supply of fire rations, and calling in periodically, I didn't have time to fret or brood. I can say definitively that three fire rations a day was not near enough calories to sustain the physical activity needed on a fire. I was hungry long before I had scheduled my next meal.

I was by myself for three or four days and worked frantically during daylight hours to keep up with my obligations. I slept the well-deserved sleep of the exhausted when I got the chance to do so. Finally two fireguards out of the fire cache in Yosemite Valley, Ray Warren and Wally Ebersold, arrived on foot carrying big packs. Now there were three of us to work our buns off and to enjoy camping out in Yosemite's backcountry splendor. One challenge was cutting down a five-foot-diameter red fir with just a double-bit axe and a Pulaski. We were glad we got it down. There was still fire smoldering in the top of the tree.

I was on the fire approximately ten days and was elated when I was able to leave and head back to Buck Camp. How good it felt to be "back in the saddle again" (my apologies to Gene Autry). When I got home it was well after dark. In short order I got several doses of good news and bad news. Good news: The cabin was still standing. Bad news: A bear had broken into the cabin and trashed things thoroughly, eating most of my food, including a whole carrot cake Myrtle Stockton had sent up with me when I came up from Wawona the day before the fire. The SOB deserved to be shot for that dastardly deed. Fortunately, the bear had missed a half-bag of pancake mix and a bottle of maple syrup. The lanterns worked. The stove was intact, and there was plenty of stove wood. I started a fire to heat water for a shower.

I unsaddled, rubbed down Lady/Babe and Coyote, gave

them a good feed of oats, watered them, and turned them out in the pasture which still had lots of grass left. I returned to the cabin and mixed up a double batch of pancakes. I ate them all, covered with copious amounts of maple syrup, and enjoyed them immensely after ten days of fire rations. I found an intact can of fruit cocktail and consumed it. Then I took a shower. Happiness was, indeed, a midnight shower on the porch of Buck Camp Patrol Cabin after days on a fire. When I finally got to bed I slept so soundly that I didn't hear a single mouse scurrying in the woodpile.

I spent the next day cleaning up the mess the bear made. A partially consumed bottle of cooking oil was mixed in with the broken glass, dishes, and Bisquick; pots and pans were scattered all over; all the canned goods were pulled from the shelves, and many had been bitten into and torn apart enough to consume the contents. Most of the cans chewed into and consumed were meat and fruit. Most of the canned vegetables were intact. Bears are omnivores and will eat just about anything, but this particular bear didn't seem to like vegetables. How he (she?) could tell meat and fruit from vegetables was beyond me. I doubted if the bear could read. Could the bear somehow smell through the tin cans? Or was there some odor left on the cans and label from the canning process? It was a mystery to me then and remains a mystery now. I do know I would not wish cleaning a cabin trashed by a bear on anyone, even my worst enemy.

The next day I went to Wawona to resupply. I stayed with Lou and Myrtle Stockton, and Myrtle outdid herself pampering me. When I returned to Buck Camp, I had another of Myrtle's carrot cakes packed carefully in one of Coyote's panniers. Lou Stockton helped me pack up and in the process showed me a couple of packing wraps and twists that were new to me.

A few days after my return to Buck Camp, I had some great company. Cary and Marguerite Jackson spent three days camped nearby. Cary was a former Buck Camp ranger, and he and Marguerite were longtime family friends. They had taught me a tremendous amount about horse use the summer I spent with them at their place in Fish Camp, near the south entrance of the park. Their visit provided me with great company, lots of information about horse protocols, past local history, travel routes, and some good food.

I WAS SORRY WHEN THEY LEFT FOR THE REST OF THEIR TRIP. My knowledge of my job had increased and my packing skills had been enhanced tenfold just by watching them around stock and by trying to help them. Both Cary and Marguerite were good, patient teachers, and I am indebted to them for nurturing my special love of horses and horse use.

Over the Labor Day weekend Dad came up to help me pack out and to revisit the country he had once been responsible for as Wawona District Ranger. Walt Gammill insisted Dad take a horse. Dad was looking forward to the walk but thanked Walt for his hospitality and took the horse. He traded off riding and walking and had a good trip in.

We had one long day ride together during which he complimented me on my improved horse-handling skills and on being aggressive in covering the country. The next day we cleaned the cabin and repaired much of the corral I had neglected all summer. Dad complimented me on the amount of stove wood I had split and stacked, but he basically gave me the devil for not dealing with the mouse situation and for not fixing the corral sooner. He said the unkempt appearance reflected poorly on the NPS and on me. I had to admit he was correct.

Had this weekend occurred today instead of over 50 years ago, observers would say a father had spent quality time with his son. I saw it more as an opportunity to be educated by a master. From either point of view, it was a good way to end my summer at Buck Camp and my first season as a park ranger.

The final vignette of the season unfolded at Badger Pass, Yosemite's ski area, the following winter. I was up skiing for a few days and ran into Oscar Sedergren, the chief ranger. He said he had been reading all the patrol logs from the previous season, and he was very impressed with how thoroughly I had covered the country and how many visitor contacts I made. Sedergren said that outfitter Johnny Jones had told him I had contacted all but one of his many drop camp parties. Jones said that all his guests had enjoyed my visits and I was welcome any time in his camps. I was both pleased and a little flustered at the recognition. Compliments are like money: They are nice but are not the real reason you work hard. I did it because it is the proper way to do a job I feel is important, because it is the way my dad would have done it, and then, finally because I wanted my dad to be proud of his son.

My first season as a ranger in the summer of 1957 turned out to be a watershed event in my life. I developed, contributed, and, most of all, immensely enjoyed what I was doing. Summer was over, however, and with reluctance I returned to San Francisco and my second year as a student of law at Hastings.

I found it difficult to adapt to the city, to Hastings, to the routine of class, study, and hurried coffee breaks. Most of my mind still lingered somewhere between Royal Arch Lake and Fernandez Pass or wandered around Triple Divide Peak and Buck Camp.

Reminders of Yosemite continually distracted me. I got home one day to find a package in the mail with no return address. In the package was *Starr's Guide To The John Muir Trail And The High Sierra Region* by Walter A. Starr, Jr., including the map I had admired. Inside the book's front cover, written in pencil, was "Wm Kat"; below that, written in ink, was "to Jerry Mernin." There was no note, just the book and the map. A promise made, a promise fulfilled. Or as Robert Service says in his classic poem, *The Cremation of Sam Mc-Gee*: "Now a promise made is a debt unpaid, and the trail has its own stern code."

Without a return address I had no way to thank Mr. Kat for his gift. I never saw William Kat again, nor did I ever hear about him. But every time I look at the book or unfold the map, I fondly remember the man and his indomitable spirit. So I guess he was correct when he said that I would get more use out of the book and map than he ever would.

The following day after class, I inhaled my sandwich and walked down Market Street to the used bookstore to buy *Bob Flame in Yosemite*, but it was not there. Only *Bob Flame, Ranger* was available.

In the 50-plus years since that milestone event on Fernandez Pass, I've been unable to find the book. Friends have looked on the internet and checked with the Library of Congress with no luck. In fact, experts tell me there are only four Bob Flame books—Yellowstone, Rocky Mountain, Death Valley, and Among the Navajo. None takes place in Yosemite, and in none of the four does Bob ride a palomino mare. I'm still looking. Everyone needs at least one Holy Grail in his life. If I can't find it, or at least find a book where someone riding a palomino mare feels a cool breeze at the back of his neck when he reaches the top of a pass, I'll have to admit I was beginning to lose my marbles at the tender age of twenty-four.

I continued the drudgery of Hastings and the study of law. I worked hard at it, but my enthusiasm just wasn't there. During the late winter I was sidetracked from my studies by newspaper accounts of a trans-Sierra expedition bogged down near the crest of the Sierras because one of the team broke his leg. Three of his party had skied out to Yosemite Valley to get help. I thought it had nothing to do with me, but it was an interesting diversion. A winter storm settled in and prevented a helicopter rescue. Fixed wing aircraft flew over and dropped a radio, food, supplies, and a Stokes litter mounted on a toboggan in case they had to drag the injured member out over the snow.

Finally a helicopter was able to slip in to the bivouac site, pluck the disabled skier out during a break in the weather, and fly him to the hospital in Yosemite Valley. The rest of the party skied out to the valley, leaving the toboggan-mounted Stokes litter behind.

I knew that the Stokes litter was a wire basket into which an injured person could be strapped and that it was named after its inventor, a naval medical officer. I didn't know was how well I would get to know (and despise) that particular litter. But that's another story.

Chapter 7

Red v. the Mule-eating Stokes Litter

As the 1957-1958 school year inched toward summer recess, things began to look up for me. I was going back to Yosemite for another summer in the backcountry on horseback. Even though I had to continue my routine of morning classes and afternoons grinding through case law, I could see the light at the end of the tunnel. Not only could I look forward to Yosemite, but I was shopping for a car of my own.

I decided on a 1958 Volkswagen, two-door sedan, with the new, larger rear window. I paid $1,800 and was happy because of the freedom and mobility it gave me. I also got a pair of Hyer crepe-soled riding boots (crepe soles were better for walking, especially on granite). At the same store, I purchased a pair of traditional spur straps to put on the spurs Lou Stockton had loaned me last season. I was ready for summer.

I arrived at South Entrance in early June, ready for a week or two of selling entrance permits. Clyde Lockwood was my new supervisor; Bob Peterson had transferred to Yosemite Valley. I had been assigned to Merced Lake for the summer. While I was disappointed not to be going back to Buck Camp, this assignment would give me a lot of new country to explore. Merced Lake brought more responsibility because of the close proximity (one mile) of Merced Lake High Sierra Camp (MLHSC).

At that time Merced Lake was one of five High Sierra Camps on the High Sierra Loop, along with Vogelsang, Tuolumne Meadows, Glen Aulin, and May Lake. Each camp was located a short day's hike from the next one. The camps were basically tent cities operated by the Yosemite Park and Curry Company; the camps offered hikers and horse backers comfortable beds with clean sheets, hot showers, and good, home-cooked meals. Clientele included people on guided horseback and hiking trips, drop-ins lucky enough to find a vacancy, as well as regular guests who came back year after year for a week, ten days, or even a month. There was also a primitive, multi-site, NPS campground on the shore of Merced Lake, about a quarter mile from the High Sierra Camp. This made quite a backcountry metropolis to keep track of.

After a week at South Entrance, I was sent into the valley to work until it was time to go into Merced Lake. I was assigned to the information desk in the lobby of the park headquarters building. Here I answered the phone, the park radio, and visitor questions; took lost and found reports, issued fire permits, directed people to offices, and kept busy.

One day the chief ranger called me into his office and told me the park had to bring out the toboggan-mounted Stokes litter that had been air dropped to the trans-Sierra skiers last winter. He had suggested that the skiers help get it out. Two of them had just returned from dragging it down to the snow line, and it was at a campsite on the upper reaches of the Lyell Fork of the Merced River.

The chief ranger said that once I got situated at Merced Lake he would have the two skiers hike up to Merced Lake, take me to the campsite, and help me pack it to the valley. Me!? Pack it!? I stood there in surprised silence and tried to maintain a poker face. I kept myself from blurting out the honest response: Packing a seven-foot long toboggan with a Stokes litter on a mule and getting it to the valley was *waaaay* beyond my level of ability and experience. However, I answered the only way a seasonal ranger who might want to become a permanent ranger could answer the chief ranger who had just presented him with a seemingly preposterous, insurmountable task. I said, "Yes, sir." At my first opportunity, I went to see Bob McGregor.

McGregor was in charge of the NPS horse operation. He was a childhood hero of mine and on my "wannabe" list (men I "wanted to be like" when I grew up). He was calm, quiet, knowledgeable, highly regarded by his peers, and the consummate horseman, mule man, and packer. I thought he walked on water. I listened carefully to everything he said, watched attentively everything he did. He was a study in understated elegance around horses and mules.

When I asked him about it, Bob said packing the Stokes and toboggan wasn't as hard as I thought it would be. He said to have boxes in the panniers, put just enough weight in them so they rode properly, and adjust the panniers to hang high on the pack mule's back, close to the sawbucks of the pack-saddle. Then put rolled-up cot mattresses or sleeping bags on top of the panniers to build a platform above the sawbucks and pack the toboggan on this platform. He gave me a second lash rope and cinch, one to secure the base load and the other to tie on the Stokes and toboggan. Easy, he said. While I wasn't totally convinced it was easy or that I could do it, I had faith in Bob and felt much better about my prospects.

Bob found a pair of pack boxes, put them in a pile of equipment with my name on it, and then took me into the main tack-room to pick out my saddle. He then showed me that the front window to the tack room had no latch on it. If I needed something after hours and the door was locked, I could climb in, get what I needed, then tell him about it the next time I saw him. I felt flattered that he trusted me with that secret.

That summer I worked for Herb Ewing, the Tuolumne Meadows district ranger. Herb had been born and raised in Yosemite and was the third generation of his family to work for the NPS in Yosemite. Beyond that, Herb had risen from seasonal ranger to district ranger, all in the same district. He had his own way of doing things, and while I didn't always agree with him, Herb knew his district and all aspects of its operation very well. He told me what I needed to do to open up the Merced Lake Ranger Station but left the details of my daily activities up to me. Overall, he was good to me, gave me a lot of freedom and flexibility, and taught me a lot .

After meeting with Herb, I went to McGregor to find which stock I would be using. Bob gave me Lady/Babe for the second year and also a good-looking, well-built sorrel mule, about 15 hands high. The mule was similar in looks and size to many of the mules used in Yosemite at that time and had alert, intelligent eyes that didn't miss much. He was calm, gentle, easy to handle, led well, but, as later events demonstrated, had his own perspectives of what he should be doing. I called him Red Mule, or less formally, Red.

I went into Merced Lake the third week in June. The night before I left, Bob had let me keep Lady and Red in the barn so they wouldn't have to play ring-around-the-rosy and compete with the rest of the stock to establish the feeding and pecking order for the night.

I made the mistake of going to the barn in uniform, which encouraged passers-by to stop and see if the ranger could pack or not. (It was also hard to keep your shirt clean while packing.) I had loaded and balanced the panniers the previous night, so the packing went fairly quickly. I thanked Bob for his help and numerous courtesies and departed in good time for the Happy Isles Trailhead. I was pleased to have a good-looking pack for the first one I had tied that season.

I don't want to dwell too much on looks, appearance, and image. Expertise, experience, dedication, drive, and a whole bunch of other qualities will count for more in the long run. But when it comes to young rangers on horseback, image can be an important factor in their success. I have run into outfitters in the backcountry who remembered meeting me three years previously and could still describe the horse I rode and even recall I had a good looking pack.

To get to the Happy Isles Trailhead in Yosemite Valley I took the trail behind the corrals, followed a trail along the edge of several campgrounds, crossed several roads, paralleled the Merced River a ways, and finally got to the trailhead where I started for Merced Lake, fifteen miles away. The trail was asphalt for the first few miles. Vernal Falls was about a mile, Nevada Falls a few miles more. Lots of people. Hundreds. By the time I reached Little Yosemite Valley, there were fewer people. From there on to Merced Lake I found only a dozen or so. As we traveled, we moved from the hustle and bustle of civilization, to crowded trails, to virtually empty trails, to remoteness, and finally to solitude.

I rode through the skeleton of the soon-to-be-reconstructed High Sierra Camp, noting numerous hand-lettered signs warning horsemen to use the trail around the camp and not to ride through the heart of the camp as I was doing. While I didn't feel particularly wicked over my transgression, I could see that it could be a big problem if the camp was set up and a pack string came through on a windy day.

The bare tent frames would soon be canvas-covered tent

cabins. There were about 20 or so frames arranged in a square about the size of half a city block. In the center of the square was an ample-sized fire ring. At the south end was a large tent frame with a flagpole in front of it. I assumed this frame would be the dining room and would house the cook tent as well. To the east, alongside the by-pass trail, were several corrals and a barn. I didn't spend much time looking about the yet-to-be-opened camp but pushed on the final mile to my new home.

It was a warm, pleasant, summer afternoon as I rode out of the timber into a comfortable opening and first laid eyes on Merced Lake Ranger Station. The cabin stood 50 or so yards south of the junction of the Vogelsang/Tuolumne Meadows trail with the Merced Lake trail. A creek, which flowed down from the mountains to the east, rolled past the trail junction to join the Merced River to the west and out of sight of my cabin. It was a serene, spiritual, even sublime setting to me. No one was around. I was glad to be able to enjoy the peace and quiet of the moment by myself. Then, prompted by thoughts of what still needed to done, I rode into the open area around the cabin and tied Lady and Red at the hitch rack in front. There was a small holding corral behind the hitch rack, and an outhouse stood about 30 yards south of the cabin. And that's all there was to the Merced Lake Ranger Station complex.

The log cabin had three rooms—a kitchen with a wood stove, a sink set up for running water, and a good supply of cooking and eating utensils; a living room with a handsome rock fireplace, a dining table, several comfortable chairs, and a comfortable bed rigged up to serve as a couch. The bedroom had four beds, several extra mattresses, and three sleeping bags. It was opulent by Buck Camp standards. The phone in the living room worked, the lanterns all worked, there was plenty of split wood, and the place was clean. What more could a person ask for?

I unpacked and unsaddled Red and Lady, then turned them out to roll, stretch, and cool down in the holding corral. I went upstream on the nearby creek, found the intake box for the water system, and activated it. By the time I got back to the cabin, I had water running out of the sink and shower spigots.

I unpacked, threw my sleeping bag on the bed by the front door, put my personally purchased supply of beer in the creek to cool, shut the gate on the drift fence just north of the cabin, started supper (warmed a can of something), brushed and grained the stock, and put a bell on Lady. It was time to relax after a 10-hour day. I had a beer to celebrate my safe arrival and my good fortune at being where I was. After supper I turned Lady and Red out for the night and then sat on the back porch, enjoying the quiet. I couldn't believe how lucky I was, sitting there in the deepening dusk, listening to the horse bell in the distance and wondering what all the poor folks in San Francisco and the rest of the world were doing. Taking into account psychic income, I considered myself amongst the wealthiest people in the world.

After a good night's sleep, I fed Lady and Red and left them in the holding corral while I checked out the area. Looking over the station tools and equipment I selected and sharpened an axe and shovel to carry on patrol, then checked the grazing area and drift fence. I let Lady and Red out to graze for an hour mid-day. When I brought them back for an afternoon in the holding corral, I gave them each a handful of grain (on the advice of the Jacksons and Lou Stockton) to teach them that the corral and the cabin were the source of good food and luxuries.

The next day began one of the more enjoyable weeks of the summer. I rode all the trails, checked all the campsites, and visited with all the backcountry users I encountered. My routine became the same as the previous season—ride three or four days, then rest the stock a day while I did cabin and area chores.

At Isberg Pass I read the register log (placed by the Sierra Club at each pass, which recorded those entering the park). I was dismayed at the number of times I saw the sentiment, "Keep horses out of the Sierra!" When I first saw that sentiment at the register at Fernandez Pass, I was with Lou Stockton and asked him about it. Lou said a very vocal group of backcountry users felt that horses and mules made too much impact on trails and at campsites; a lot of people just objected to horse manure. Since that time I have paid close attention to what horses and mules do and don't do and tried to lessen the impacts of their use. It has become a continuing, lifelong endeavor.

Everywhere I went I enjoyed the country. When I headed back to the valley the first time, I re-shuttered the cabin and got an early start, left the drift fence gates open wide, and rode around the High Sierra camp on the by-pass to imprint the proper route on my mind and Lady's. Somewhere between Echo Valley and Little Yosemite, I met several pack strings from the Merced Lake High Sierra Camp. I pulled off the trail to let them pass. A middle-aged woman with reddish hair (the manager) told me she hoped I wouldn't let the packers ride through camp, unlike last year's ranger who ignored the problem.

In a rare stroke of diplomacy I said I would stop by and discuss it with her as soon as I returned from the valley. "Fine," she said, "stop by anytime." Dad had given me an important bit of advice when he found out I was going to Merced Lake—always get along with the cook. It turned out to be very good advice that year and for the rest of my career in the NPS, and now that I'm retired, this advice is still worth following.

When I got to the valley, McGregor said to let my stock out in the corral to roll, and he would put them in the barn for the night. This trip established the pattern I would more or less follow on the rest of my resupply trips. I stopped by the ranger's office, signed up for bunk space in the government dorm, and not necessarily in this order, showered, got a cold beer, then a chocolate malt. (Sometimes I would repeat the malt and beer process.) Later in the day I shopped for groceries, did my laundry, and washed the horse and mule blankets. While clean blankets did not guarantee healthy backs for your stock, it was an important step in the right direction.

I found out from the chief ranger that members of last winter's troubled trans-Sierra ski party were available to help pack out the toboggan-mounted Stokes litter anytime. I was as ready as I was going to get without two or three more years of packing experience. The chief said he would tell them to contact me at Merced Lake. "Yes, sir!" And so I progressed toward one of my young life's more challenging ventures. Two days later I returned to my station. Needless to say, I rode around the camp on the by-pass trail and not through the center of the camp.

The following day I went back to the camp to introduce myself to the managers and staff. I tied my horse and mule at the far end of the hitch rack used by the packers, walked to the side door of the kitchen, and, remembering Dad's advice to get along with the cooks, dutifully knocked on the door. On being acknowledged, I went in with hat in hand.

A slender, balding, mostly grey-haired man in his sixties was sitting at a table replacing the mantle on a Coleman lantern. At the stove, a husky, slightly overweight, red-haired woman, probably in her mid-to late fifties, was stirring a large pan of pudding as well as tending two other pans on back burners. The man and woman were the camp managers, Elmer and Ila Lennox, also known as Pa and Ma. They were from Castroville, California, where they owned a restaurant that was managed by relatives in their absence. This was the Lennoxes' third season managing Merced Lake High Sierra Camp.

Just as the fairy tale Jack Spratt and his wife differed from each other, so did Elmer and Ila Lennox. Pa Lennox was quiet, thoughtful, slow moving, and could keep everything around the camp operating. Ma Lennox exuded energy and was a fine cook and baker of goodies (her pies were great). She was always in a hurry, a gracious hostess, and never seemed to tire.

Between them, they did a fine job of managing the camp. Guests were well fed and well cared for; employees worked hard, got along, and enjoyed the country; packers supplied the camp needs. On that visit, I had a cup of coffee and listened as Ma Lennox described her pet peeve—packers who rode through the center of the camp stirring up dust that blew into all the cabins. I said I would be happy to talk to any of the packers who violated the important protocol. That satisfied Mrs. Lennox, and she invited me down that evening for a piece of pie after the guests finished their evening meal.

When I got up to leave, I complimented them on the coffee. Pa Lennox was proud to take credit for the "perfect" cup of coffee. He said that making the coffee was his responsibility wherever they went. As I rode back to the ranger station I smiled to myself at Pa Lennox's pride and intensity.

But, as the summer rolled on, I smiled less and respected him more because it was that pride and intensity that distinguished Merced Lake High Sierra Camp from other high Sierra camps. To this day I take my hat off to Elmer and Ila Lennox for the way they managed the camp.

After supper I turned Lady and Red loose for the night and walked back down to the camp. I went by the NPS campsites on the lakeshore, visited with the parties there, and then went over to the cook tent for my pie. After enjoying my pie and two cups of Pa Lennox's good coffee, I went out to the campfire circle, answered a few questions, and listened to their tales. I slipped away, hiked home under the stars, and was glad to hear Lady's bell in the distance when I got back. My last thought before falling asleep was that it had been a good day, and I got paid for it to boot. Little did I realize that I would soon be earning my pay.

A few days later I got a phone call from Bart Hooley, a member of last winter's trans-Sierra ski party, ready to set a date. On the date we had agreed upon, I returned home from a patrol and found two athletic, competent-looking men about my age: Bart Hooley and his partner, whose name I no longer recall. We had a pleasant evening to get acquainted, exchange insights on our mutual project, and come up with a plan.

Hooley and his partner were accomplished skiers, climbers, hikers, but in no way were they horsemen or horse packers. Through a combination of hiking and skiing, they had reached the ski party's bivouac site and had brought the toboggan-mounted Stokes down to the snowline at that time. Now, they intended to take me to the site, help me pack up, and then they would be finished with their chore. Somehow I didn't think it would be that easy, but I kept my misgivings to myself. The next morning we got a relatively good start.

Using McGregor's directions I had a good-looking pack with the top making a good platform well above the sawbucks of the saddle.

For the first time, I felt slightly optimistic about the retrieval project as Lady, Red Mule, and I followed Bart and his partner up the trail that went around the backside of Vogelsang Peak to Vogelsang High Sierra Camp. We reached the Lyell Fork of the Merced River about mid-day and found a well-established campsite with abundant rushing water, lots of wood, good grass, a level place to pitch a tent, and spectacular views.

It also had the toboggan and the Stokes litter. Shit! The litter was mounted on the toboggan and the whole outfit weighed around fifty pounds and was about seven feet tall. What a big, awkward, heavy, miserable, ungainly son-of-a-bitch that would be to pack! When Hooley saw my dismay, he looked at me and said, "Don't blame me. I wasn't the one with the broken leg." I could imagine Dad telling me, "You hired out to be rugged. Get with it." I unpacked the red mule, loosened his and Lady's cinches, and let them graze while the rest of us had lunch. Then it was time. I tied Lady close by, repacked Red, and snugged the cinches up tight. While one person held Red, two of us lifted the toboggan-mounted Stokes and quietly approached the mule.

Red stood calmly, head down and relaxed, seemingly half asleep, watching us out of the corner of his eye. He didn't move as we placed the toboggan and Stokes on his back; he didn't move as we moved the load forward so it was balanced fore and aft. But when Red casually raised his head, his ears bumped into the toboggan. He promptly let us know he didn't like that by arching his back and bucking off the toboggan and Stokes. We calmed him down, petted him, led him around, talked soothingly to him, and tried again. Same result, only this time, he more explicitly demonstrated his displeasure. We collectively breathed deeply, gave Red the opportunity to gain his composure, and tried once more. Same result, third attempt.

By the fourth go-around, our technique had improved, and we actually got the load tied down. Wow! Fat city! It had taken us an hour just to get it tied down. I caught my breath, gingerly took the lead rope from Bart, gave Red a few moments to adapt to the change of circumstances, and then carefully tried to lead him around to get used to the pack. It worked well—for one step. Then his ears touched the toboggan and he bucked circles around me until the pack and saddle slipped off to the side. Red, smart mule that he was, must have decided that expressing his opinion was not worth hurting himself over. He let me unbuckle and uncinch everything and let it drop to his feet. Once he was free of the pack, packsaddle and blankets, he snorted and jumped away from the mess. He immediately turned and faced the GD, mule-eating Stokes litter as if he didn't want to let it sneak up and attack him again.

Again we re-saddled and repacked Red. Again he bucked, whirled, fussed, farted, and kicked enough to make us either redo or refine the pack. Each session took 30 to 45 minutes of stress and sweat. We were getting better, faster, and more effective each time we repacked him, but our patience was running out as well. I was wringing wet with sweat and was contemplating cutting the Stokes into little pieces and hiding them, but there were witnesses. Besides, I had been told to bring the damn thing down to the valley.

On the next attempt, the pack stayed. I checked the cinch on Lady's saddle, mounted, got Red's lead rope from his holder, and started down the trail. Within a short distance, Red shied at something, bucked around Lady and me, pulled the lead rope out of my hand and ran, bucking and kicking, down the trail. When we caught up to him, he was waiting, head down, in the middle of the trail, pack intact and only slightly askew.

He did this two more times. On his fourth attempted run, I held him, courtesy of less slack in the lead rope and multiple wraps around the saddle horn. I don't know what changed Red's mind, but after the fourth attempted run-away he just decided to put up with the pack, even though he still bumped his ears when he raised his head. Whatever it was, I was glad he changed as even the enthusiasm of youth has its limits. We made it to my cabin right at dark after a fourteen-hour day, all five of us pooped and happy to be done. Amazingly, Red survived the whole episode utterly intact with no bruises, blemishes, or marks that he didn't have before.

After breakfast the next morning, Bart and his friend asked if I wanted them to help me pack the toboggan for the final 15-mile leg of its trip to the valley. I said no thanks; I wasn't sufficiently recovered to face packing that abominable Stokes again so soon, and besides, I didn't have plans or need to go into the valley for at least another week. So Bart and his friend hiked into the valley. Several weeks passed, during which time I had to look at the Stokes and toboggan every time I went in or out of the cabin. I had a trip to the valley planned and, by chance Will Neely and another interpreter from the Tuolumne Meadows staff had spent the night with me while on an orientation tour. I asked them to help me pack up.

Things went so much better I almost thought I was packing a different load on a different mule. By and large we had a routine trip until we dropped down from Nevada Falls. Going onto the heavily traveled section of trail we had our first genuine pucker-factor experience.

Along a section of ledge trail built into the mountainside we passed an upward bound couple who stepped off the trail and stood on the inside next to the cliff. As we came abreast of them, the woman said, "Oh, what a sweet looking mule," and reached out to pet Red on the nose. As Red abruptly pulled his head back, his ears slammed into the toboggan. Red did a brief, double-step dance in place, and his back humped up as I gasped and sucked in air. My sphincter tried to cut grommets out of the saddle. With one hand, I tried to pull in Lady, and with the other hand, took wraps around the saddle horn with Red's lead rope.

Miraculously, we made it by that couple. I stopped, let my breathing settle down, and contemplated our situation knowing we would probably meet a couple hundred more hikers before we got to Happy Isles. The image of Red bucking the toboggan and packsaddle off and running through a crowd of people flashed into my mind. Whatever we did could have dire consequences. This close, I decided to go for it.

I pulled Red up close and wrapped several dallies around the saddle horn. With Red's nose snugged up to the pommel of the saddle and his jaw resting on my thigh, we were as effectively joined as Siamese twins. I don't know whether it was the sight of my entourage or the grim look on my face, but the rest of the people we met stopped, stared, did a double take, and then got out of our way. It was a routine trip. I am not sure what happened to the Stokes and toboggan after I left it with McGregor.

A week to ten days after hauling the toboggan and Stokes into the valley, I returned so I could get the horse and the mule shod. We came in late the afternoon before the shoeing. Lady and Red were kept in the barn for the night. The next morning Waine Westphal, the horseshoer, said he would leave them in the corral when he was finished. I spent the rest of the day running errands, and it was almost quitting time when I returned to put my partners in the barn for the night. When I got to the barn, Bob McGregor was just tying Lady in her stall. He said Red was outside in the corral.

In a hurry, I grabbed Red's halter and went to get him, irritated at myself for being late and causing McGregor to work overtime to take care of my stock. I stepped out of the barn and across the corral from me were 12 to 15 red mules, standing half asleep in a group, heads down, swishing their tails to keep flies off themselves and their neighbors. They were all pretty well matched in size and color. I stood, my eyes squinting in the bright sunlight, trying to pick out which one belonged to me. On the far side of the group, one red mule raised his head, glanced at me, and then walked slowly and nonchalantly toward me.

It was my red mule. Red was a little nonplussed but took it in stride when I hugged him first and then put his halter on. I felt so complimented when he came up to me without any urging, that I gave him an extra double-handful of grain. And I stopped being in such a hurry. Taking care of your four-legged friends and spending time with them was every bit as important as being prompt for your two-legged friends (even when they were the ones buying the beer).

With my horse and mule freshly shod I returned to Merced Lake and promptly started the process of wearing out their shoes again. While on patrol, I regularly checked campsites, and at some of the most heavily used campsites I started burning the garbage pits. I would take the burned debris and odor-free cans way out in the woods and cover them in the hole left by the root ball of a tree that had blown over. That way the garbage pit could be used again, and we wouldn't have to sacrifice another pit site. This was a time before the "pack in, pack out" policy was developed. It was as close to minimum impact camping as that period had to offer.

About mid-summer an interesting incident occurred that wouldn't see its conclusion until the following season. I decided to go to Tuolumne Meadows for a resupply of food and grain, rather than down to the valley. I arrived at Tuolumne in the late afternoon, and Herb Ewing, my supervisor, met me at the barn and showed me where to unpack and store my gear. There were a half dozen horses and mules in the corral, including two palominos, one of them a mare. Herb's horse, Buster, a palomino gelding, was the top horse in the community pecking order. He was not a gentle ruler and made sure everyone knew he was boss.

I was apprehensive as I turned my two out into the corral. With ears laid back, Buster promptly approached Lady, who dutifully turned away to avoid him. "Don't you think we should separate them?" I asked Herb, as Red dodged away to join the group watching the activity from the far side of the corral. "No, they'll be all right as soon as Buster lets 'em know who's boss," Herb assured me. As Buster chased Lady around the corral nipping at her rear, I repeated my question, and Herb assured me again that things would be all right.

The next morning Lady had three bite marks courtesy of that meat-eating SOB Buster. "Guess Buster had to show her who's boss," observed Herb. I said nothing and chalked it up to tuition in the college of hard knocks.

By the time the season ended, Lady's bites were pretty much healed. Two days after the camp staff left we had an

18-inch snowfall. The country was beautiful and so deserted it was ghost-like. I took advantage of the weather to give the garbage dump behind the station a good burning. On Sunday, the day before law school started, I was up early, rode to the valley, turned Lady and Red over to Bob McGregor at the barn, said some goodbyes, and headed for San Francisco. At ten that evening I was in bumper-to-bumper traffic on the Oakland Bay Bridge with all the people heading back to the city after a weekend in the Sierras. I asked myself, "What the hell am I doing here when I could be up there?"

Chapter 8

Lessons in Humility

MY THIRD YEAR AT HASTINGS COULD BE SUMMED UP AS
SSDD, Same Stuff Different Day. Ride the bus downtown,
go to class, bolt my sandwich, walk Market Street, study, take
a hurried coffee break, study, then ride the bus back home.
Then repeat the process. By spring, I was so glad to be done
at Hastings that I completed my four-hour final exam in one
hour. I almost ran to my VW loaded for the summer and
parked nearby. I promptly headed to Yosemite and my second summer at Merced Lake. I didn't look back.

In the back seat of my VW I had my own recently purchased riding saddle: a three quarter, double-rigged, rough-
out leather, barely broken in, medium weight, stock saddle
built by D. E. Walker for the Visalia Stock Saddle Company.
I paid the previous owner, who had lost interest in horses,
$100 for the saddle, two blankets, two bridles, and a halter.

I got a big surprise when Bob McGregor gave me two
horses and a mule. That way I would have a horse to aid
a sore-footed or slightly injured hiker without having to let
the person use my horse. Or at times when I didn't need the
mule I could leave him with one of the horses while I rode
the other. By spreading out the workload, shoes would last
longer, and there would be less chance to throw a shoe as we

got closer to the scheduled shoeing date. Made sense to me. Beside, whatever Bob McGregor suggested was fine by me.

The first horse was George, a ten-year-old, big-bodied, big-headed, well-built three-colored paint horse with solid legs and good-sized hooves to support it all. George had a black and white mane and tail; a reddish brown, roan body, mixed with white markings Tobiano fashion, and a white blaze across his forehead and down the length of his nose. George stood around 15 and a half hands high and possessed the biggest head of any horse I've ever known before or since. That big head contained a remarkable brain and a mind that was always alert, learning, and thinking.

At first impression, I felt George would definitely be strong and durable, but I worried how fast he could move and how comfortable he would be to ride. I stopped worrying after my first ride—he could move out well and was as graceful, comfortable, and agile as any horse I had ridden to date. As the season progressed, I grew very fond of and attached to big-headed George. The second horse was a 20-year-old slender sorrel, a thoroughbred type that Bob said was a good traveler but would not stand up to heavy use. Sorrel, as I called him, was a good relief ride. He was competent, experienced, had no bad habits, and was pleasant to be around.

My mule was a good looking black mule, 16 hands tall, with two white socks on his hind legs and a white star in the middle of his forehead. Socks stood quietly when someone was around him. He was easy to work with but definitely followed his own drummer. He was not inclined to be caught easily.

The first trip of the season to Merced Lake was routine. I enjoyed being on horseback again. On arrival, I quickly got the station open, water running, and started checking campsites and trails. On these forays, I took both Socks and Sorrel with me. George proved to be giving and bold. Fairly early in the season I went to Tuolumne Meadows for a resupply of groceries and grain. I arrived late afternoon, unpacked, unsaddled, let the boys cool down, and then gave them a bait of grain. Herb Ewing showed up and started putting out hay for his eight horses and mules and for my three. Herb's palomino, Buster, again ruled the roost, making sure everyone knew who was boss. Followed by his palomino lady friend Bar Heart, Buster chased everyone away from each feed bin as we filled it until he had sampled the hay in each one and finally settled on one for his and Bar Heart's exclusive use.

I felt more than a little bit of apprehension when I turned my boys into this mix. Buster hustled across the corral, ears laid back, head and neck down and stretched out, eyes focused on the newcomers. Herb chuckled. "Buster's got to show them who's boss," he said. Socks and Sorrel promptly scattered as Buster came across the corral. George, unconcerned, continued straight ahead, seemingly only interested in finding the best spot for a dust bath. Ears back, teeth bared, Buster charged George. Without telegraphing intent, George suddenly whirled around and twice kicked both of his hind feet full force into Buster's ribs. WHOMP! WHOMP! The sound of the impacts was loud enough to be heard a hundred yards away.

The blows staggered Buster, almost knocking him off his feet. With the air knocked out of him, Buster stood wheezing and gasping, back arched in pain, trying to catch his breath. George showed Buster no more interest but continued on to the watering trough and took a long satisfying drink before finding a good place to roll. Herb said, "We better separate them." It was my turn to say, "No. They'll be all right once they decide who's boss." I did my best to keep a straight face and not to show even a hint of a smile. When we left, Buster was standing by himself, head down, back humped uncomfortably, as far away from George as the corral would allow. George had finished his roll in the dust and was munching hay with Socks and Sorrel at one of the feed bins.

I took my duffle bag and headed for the shower tent, not a bit unhappy with the day or the way it had ended. When I came out the next morning to catch and grain my boys, Buster was still as far away from George as possible. Twice more that season I came out to Tuolumne to resupply. Both times Buster hustled up to check out the newcomers, and both times he lost interest in asserting his authority when he saw George. The mantle of authority rested lightly on George; he simply ignored Buster.

Another incident showcased George's alertness and responsiveness, as well as his athletic ability. It was both exciting (at the time) and amusing (in retrospect). We were making a grain resupply trip into the valley and were striding along at a good clip through a campground just south of Ahwahnee Meadows. As we exited through the trees toward the road we were going to cross, I stopped George on the road's shoulder to check for traffic. Glancing to the left, I saw a white convertible make a fast, unsafe pass around a slow-moving string of eastbound vehicles. In the process, the driver of the white convertible forced a westbound vehicle onto the shoulder. All this unfolded right under my eyes as George and I waited to cross the road.

Being young, idealistic, and not wanting crime to continue unabated in my presence, I tapped George with my spurs so I could get closer to try to remedy the situation. In a single leap, George went from the edge of the trees, across the shoulder of the road and into the middle of the eastbound lane of traffic, directly in front of the speeding white convertible. (In reality, in my zeal to contain crime, I may actually have "jabbed" George with the spurs instead of "tapped" him.)

Who was more surprised, the driver of the white convertible or me, was unclear. At any rate, he stopped and I pulled George back to get him out of the way. In my concern for George's safety, I may have pulled harder than I thought, because he dramatically reared straight up and stood poised on his hind legs better than Trigger ever did for Roy Rogers or Champion for Gene Autry. While this was not what I had in mind, I decided to take advantage of the situation since I had the driver's attention.

With George still balanced on his hind legs, his front feet pawing the air, I fixed my most authoritative stare on the driver. He was dumbfounded, staring back at me, mouth and eyes wide open. I pointed my right index finger at the driver and gestured for him to pull over on the side of the road. He nodded assent. George came down to all fours and, with neck arched, majestically backed off the road.

As I tied George and approached the white convertible, it was difficult to maintain my composure and keep from smiling while I talked to the driver. He was very contrite and apologetic as I checked his driver's license and dutifully copied down the information. I gave him a written warning and finished my trip, smiling all the way to the barn. That this incident didn't wind up as a colossal catastrophe dumbfounds me to this day. A great number of things could have gone wrong, possibly even injuries to me, to George, or to bystanders. I'm still amazed at George's poise and athletic ability—and at my unbelievable luck.

Two weeks later, on one more resupply trip into the valley, I had a more personal mini-adventure. We were stepping along, heading for the barn on a section of trail by the Merced River. People were sunbathing, wading, and swimming in the deeper holes. Some distance ahead I saw someone leave the beach and take the trail toward us. As we got closer I saw that it was an attractive young lady in her late teens. She was graciously endowed with physical attributes that her swimsuit accentuated. Now this was an era before political correctness reminded us that women should be appreciated for their total person and not just for their physical assets, regardless of how attractive those might be.

I tried to mask my hyper-ventilation by sitting up straight in the saddle and focusing a thousand-yard stare on the trail ahead rather than the young woman passing just to my left. I was succeeding modestly well until WHAM! I was jerked viciously backwards. My back slammed into George's rump; my NPS Stetson flew off my head; and the lead rope ripped through my grasp leaving a rope burn that I nursed all summer. I barely managed to stay in the saddle. Thankfully, the young lady had continued walking and didn't look back.

Apparently George had passed a tree on the left while Socks tried to pass it on the right, with the lead rope between them. As I dismounted to pick up my hat and Sock's lead rope, I swear he had an evil gleam in his eyes and smiled at me. It almost seemed he was biting his lips to keep from laughing (or braying) out loud. I could imagine him thinking, "Gotcha that time, Dad."

The more I rode George, the more I came to admire him. Not only was he durable, dependable, and surefooted, he would willingly, even eagerly, go wherever you pointed him. This last attribute was a two-edged sword that almost bit us on the butt. One day I decided to ride to Clouds Rest to patrol and check out an area I had not yet visited. I rode in from the northeast via the trail from Tenaya Lake that was little used at that time. I had not been over it before. I had left Socks and Sorrel at home and was enjoying another good day on George. The country was new and interesting, and with a good horse, life just doesn't get any better.

Clouds Rest rises to almost 10,000 feet and is the high point in a dramatic granite range that runs northeast to southwest. Viewed from the north, Half Dome and Clouds Rest present an awe-inspiring picture. Our final approach was at a right angle to the range. The faint, little-used trail passed through an increasingly thinning forest as it gained elevation and basically disappeared in the final open slope just below the prominent granite hump that was Clouds Rest. To my left were a couple hundred yards of pine needle-strewn open slope. Straight ahead was a deer trail with recent tracks of perhaps a half dozen deer leading to a pass in the range about 100 yards away.

George and I went up to the pass and stopped for a breather and to enjoy the view. Wow! What a view it was. Depth, distance, majesty. Granite peaks, domes, and outcrops everywhere, mile after mile. Tenaya Creek flowing way, way below. I looked right and left for the trail; to the right the deer tracks scattered on a forested slope. To the left, it appeared that a trail had been built into the granite face of Clouds Rest a little below us. Impressive.

From my own experiences and comments from competent horsemen, I knew that good horses are more sure-footed and careful than most people ever give them credit for. As a result, I often stayed mounted while others led their horses over rough and/or sheer-sided sections of trail. Though the beginning of this trail was not inviting due to the exposure, I stayed in the saddle. George didn't hesitate; he did not seem bothered by the fact that the trail was built in solid granite with relatively narrow, increasingly steep, and then sheer drop-offs. It bothered me.

I studied the trail more closely. As we approached the face of Clouds Rest, the trail got narrower, and the distance from the trail to the creek below increased from hundreds of feet to thousands of feet. I worked to keep my breathing calm and steady when I finally, fully realized we were riding along a massive granite cliff created by Mother Nature thousands of years ago and not a scenic trail designed by the NPS and built by Civilian Conservation Corps (CCC) crews thirty years ago.

By reason of George's steady, measured, and careful pace, we were somewhere midway across the north face of Clouds Rest. Tenaya Creek was a slender ribbon of white water several thousand feet below my right stirrup, which at times hung in empty air beyond the cliff's face. Holy shit! What now, Lone Ranger?

My breathing was coming faster and shallower as I focused entirely on our route, no longer trying to soak in the scenery. When we came to an abrupt break in the cliff, George stepped across a foot-wide gap without hesitation. I decided no more of this. Very slowly and very carefully I pulled George to a stop. Even more carefully I dismounted, leaned against the cliff to steady myself, and waited for circulation and feeling to return to my knees. I petted George and scratched the underside of his jaw, more to calm myself than to reassure my horse. George expressed his appreciation for the break by depositing a large pile of manure.

After considering options for a while, I decided this was as good a place as any to try to turn around. Standing on

George's left, I took the lead rope in my left hand, reached around in front of George with the rope, and, hugging George, reached around with my right hand, took the rope and laid it across the saddle seat. So far, so good.

Then, very carefully and slowly, I slid between George and the cliff wall to George's backside, taking the lead rope off the saddle as I went by. Standing in back of George, I gently pulled his head around, talking to him gently, indicating I wanted him to turn around. He tried but his butt bumped the wall, forcing his front feet dangerously close to the edge of the cliff. Damn! After more deep breathing on my part and a couple more gentle requests, George hunched his back, tucked his butt in, and made it all the way around. I was so relieved, all I could do was hug George's big head, scratch his ears, pet his neck, and let my breathing and heart rate calm down to a near normal level.

George and I made it back the way we had come. This time I walked and led my friend. When we got back to where we had started, I was very happy to be traveling on dirt trails once again.

I was able to pick out the real route across the open slope and into the forest on the opposite side. We followed it to Half Dome, contacted a number of hikers, and made it back to Merced Lake by mid-evening. When we arrived, Socks and Sorrel were there to greet us and get their evening ration of grain. George received an extra helping for once again saving me from myself and from a potential tragedy.

This story has a postscript. A week after the Clouds Rest episode a Curry Company guide came up to me while I was at the High Sierra Camp and asked if I had been to Clouds Rest lately. I said, yes, about a week ago. He said he thought so; he also had been there about a week ago guiding an all-day horseback ride out of the valley. I was the only one he knew who would take a horse out on a place like that. I looked him in the eyes and said nothing. I was so mortified at what I had done that it took years before I could tell anyone the story. To take a needless, foolish risk yourself is one thing, but to also involve a loyal trusting friend is unforgivable.

There was more to 1959 than just horses and mules. About a week after I first arrived at Merced Lake that June, the High Sierra Camp opened. It was good renewing acquaintance with Ma and Pa Lennox and Erwin (Tom) Thompson and getting to know the three new camp helpers. A number of the regular guests showed up to savor the early season freshness.

One of my interesting guests was Dr. Carl Sharsmith, a botanist, professor, and longtime seasonal naturalist from Tuolumne Meadows. He was doing a backcountry grazing survey. His finding of significant overgrazing at certain locations would have far-reaching impacts on concession and government stock use. It got my attention as well and was a matter I always heeded in the years that followed.

Another overnight visitor was a government packer who three years previously had a confrontation with then Merced Lake Ranger John Townsley. At that time, the packer had worked for the Curry Company and had persisted in bringing his pack string through the center of the High Sierra Camp even after being warned by Townsley.

Ila Lennox delighted in telling me how John had met the packer with his pack string in the center of the camp. When the packer refused to turn around and tried to ride past John, John had grabbed the horse's reins just behind the bit with his left hand and with his right hand pulled the packer off his horse and kicked him in the seat of his pants, sprawling him onto the ground. Ila said that John then took the packer by his shirt collar and led the whole entourage outside the camp. When I later asked the packer for his version of the story, he agreed with Ila. And when I asked him what he thought of the incident, he simply said, "The big son-of-a-bitch meant what he said."

Years later Townsley was superintendent of Yellowstone National Park. During his tenure (August 1975 until September 1982), he tried to keep Yellowstone's law enforcement profile low key. I never got the opportunity to ask him how he would characterize the definitive, hands-on approach the 1956 Merced Lake ranger utilized in dealing with the packer. (Townsley died of cancer in September 1982 before I could ask that question).

Early in the summer, Tom Thompson went with me on an overnight horse patrol to Ottoway Lakes. We rode up the Merced River checking and cleaning campsites and climbed up and over spectacular, granite-strewn Red Peak Pass, dropping into the remote, rock-surrounded Ottoway Lakes. As we dropped into the stunning basin I could see we would be sharing solitude with another stock party already camped there. This didn't appear to be a problem as the area was large enough and the campsites were separated from each other by sight and by all but the most egregious sound. The site available to us was the smaller, higher up, more secluded site. It was the one I would have chosen anyway.

We rode into our site and unpacked. Stiff and sore as he might have been from his first ride of the season, Tom was grinning ear to ear, as happy as a teething puppy with a new chew toy. We got our camp laid out, grained the boys, and turned them loose to graze until our bed time. While Tom explored the area in back of our campsite and took pictures, I walked down to show the colors and visit our neighbors. As

I walked, I looked the camp over. It was well organized and neatly set up. A half dozen or so people were gathered around a camp fire, some seated on chairs, some on logs, some standing. Below camp about a dozen horses and mules were quietly grazing. A Curry Company guide/packer whom I knew quite well came out to greet me.

My guide friend said this was "Mrs. T's" camp and invited me to join them for cocktail hour. "Mrs. T" was Mary Curry Tressider, daughter of David and Jennie Curry who came to Yosemite in 1899 and established Camp Curry. It had morphed into The Yosemite Park and Curry Co. and now was the main provider of visitor services in Yosemite. Mrs. T was a charming, middle-aged lady (60ish) who had been raised in Yosemite and who was deeply devoted to it, her company, and to park employees and their families. Many people in Yosemite thought she walked on water.

I was not at that time (and still am not) a comfortable, cocktail party conversationalist. Friends that know me well have long suggested that when most of the social graces were handed out, I must have been someplace else having a short beer. I've never challenged that assessment. Shortcomings and inclinations aside, I went in with my guide friend who introduced me around. Mrs. T asked how my parents were, how the summer was going, if I could stay awhile, and if I would have a drink with them. On inquiry I found out they didn't have any cokes or soft drinks other than soda or tonic water for their mixed drinks.

I had been worrying about this since my guide friend had said it was cocktail hour. My mind was whirling with conflicting protocols, real and imagined. While it was after five, I was in uniform and on duty. In the backcountry you were always on duty so long as anyone knew you were a ranger or if anyone needed a ranger. In my mind, it was anathema to drink on duty or in uniform. But I did recall hearing that when park superintendents were in uniform representing the park at dinner parties it was appropriate for them to drink moderately. I grasped this straw as my way out of my conundrum. Jesuitical reasoning aside, I was more of a superintendent of Ottoway Lakes than anyone else present, so I would assume that responsibility.

I said yes thank you, I'd take a scotch and water if they had enough. I was poured a stiff jolt of Scotch and offered a bottle of water and a container of ice cubes to add to my taste. Ice cubes! in the backcountry, and this was their fifth day out. I was impressed. Being a "superintendent" wasn't so bad after all. At first sip I half expected to be struck by a bolt of lightning for my blatant sophistry. When it didn't come, I relaxed and enjoyed the scotch and the ice cubes. The conversation focused on the country they had seen and whether they would stay there another night; it was such a beautiful camping spot. They asked me about my job, if I liked it, and wished they could have had a similar job when they were younger.

I finished my drink and ice cubes, savoring the ice cubes more than the drink. I thanked them and returned to my less opulent campsite. Tom had had a good photography session in my absence and was as impressed as I about them still having ice cubes after five days. Tom and I had supper, and then sat visiting until the sun set and the basin drifted into full darkness. The horses were grazing, their location indicated by the bell on George. When the bell grew silent, I figured the boys had enough to eat, and it was time for us all to hit the sack. We caught our critters and tied them up for the night as I felt it was better to count ribs come morning than to count horse tracks going away from camp.

Tom and I were up early the next morning. We had a long way to go to get back to Merced Lake and get Tom rested for work early the following day. Remembering the "Keep horses out of the Sierra" sentiment in the Fernandez Pass register box, I looked around before leaving our campsite. In just a couple minutes, I re-naturalized the scuff marks where we had tied the horses over night, scattered manure that had been dropped while we were packing up, and made sure the site looked better than it had when we arrived—and it looked quite good then.

We waved at the group drinking coffee around Mrs. T's campfire and headed down the trail to Merced Pass, down Il-lilouette Creek, up to Nevada Fall, past Little Yosemite, and on to Merced Lake. When we got back to the High Sierra Camp the staff greeted Tom as if he were a long lost brother, rather than one who had been away for only two days and one night. Tom was tired from the long, unaccustomed ride (25 to 30 miles) but couldn't stop grinning as he headed for his tent and a shower. I was feeling pretty happy myself as I headed for my station and a shower.

Less than a month later, Mrs. Tressider and several of her lady friends were visiting Merced Lake High Sierra Camp when I ran into them at the evening campfire. The group, accompanied by its own guide/wrangler, had ridden from Tuolumne Meadows to Vogelsang High Sierra Camp, spent the night and had just come down to Merced Lake for a few days. One of the ladies with Mrs. T was Betty Preston, wife of Yosemite Superintendent John Preston. Preston had been superintendent of Great Smoky Mountains National Park ten years before while Dad was chief ranger there. I recognized Mrs. Preston from that time, recalling she was a pleasant, gracious lady, as are many NPS superintendent's wives—they either start or wind up that way after years of practice.

The ladies were discussing whether Mrs. Preston should ride out alone. Evidently Mrs. Preston had to leave the group earlier than planned and that presented a conundrum—if the wrangler went with her, Mrs. T and her party would be without his services on their planned day ride. Mrs. Preston was insisting she could ride out by herself. When I came up, Mrs. T seemed glad to see me and promptly introduced me to her circle of friends. Now I was a late bloomer in the chivalry realm and a slow learner to boot (still am as a matter of fact), but as I became aware of their challenge, I offered to ride out to Tuolumne Meadows with Mrs. Preston. It was a patrol day for me, and I would do as much good patrolling to Tuolumne as I would riding in any other direction. When I saw the relief in Betty Preston's face and the broad, spontaneous smile lighten up Mrs. T's features, I knew I had made the right offer. What I didn't know was that it would lead to another embarrassing experience for me. So here's to chivalry, long may it prosper, even (especially) in today's climate.

The ladies arrived at a game plan. Mrs. Preston would have only a small toilet kit, and the rest of her clothes and duffle could go out with Mrs. T's party. Good plan said I, since it meant I wouldn't have to bring a pack animal and that would make a round trip easily doable. It was past my bedtime, and I headed home followed by a chorus of appreciation and thanks from the ladies.

I was back at the camp the next morning riding Sorrel, who was well-rested and eager to go, and George got the day off. When we departed, the horses were stepping out very well. Mrs. Preston made polite small talk for a while, and then we lapsed into silence, enjoying the scenery and the ride, with periodic rest stops to give the horses a breather as we climbed to the Vogelsang camp. I saw a discarded candy bar wrapper lying blatantly in the middle of the trail ahead of us. Trying to keep the heavily traveled trails free of trash and litter was one of the mundane, tedious duties of being a back-country ranger.

Stopping and getting off my horse to pick up litter that someone else had dropped (sometimes deliberately) was definitely a drag. So over the years I had experimented with just stopping and leaning out of the saddle to pick up litter. That worked better. When that got routine, I experimented with reaching down while at a slow walk. It was a combination of focus, balance, and timing that led to success: staying close to the horse, bending down briefly, grasping the piece of litter, and getting back astride promptly. Once back astride, a brief shift in weight made sure the saddle was balanced and centered, and all that remained was to reach back and put the trash in the saddlebag. It had gotten so routine that I could do it at a fast walk. I usually kept the front strap on the right-side saddlebag unfastened to simplify the storage of litter.

We were moving along at a good pace as we approached the errant candy wrapper, and I reined Sorrel to pass closer to it. As we went by the wrapper, I leaned out of the saddle and swooped up the piece of litter. I had barely gotten upright in the saddle when Mrs. Preston exclaimed, "Oh! That was magnificent. What an athletic move!" Nothing can compete with the effusive praise of a gracious, attractive woman when it comes to inflating the youthful male ego—even if the woman is old enough to be his mother. I sat straighter in the saddle as my head immediately swelled two sizes. My shirt grew tight across my chest, and I almost had to grab the saddle horn to keep from floating out of the saddle. You can be assured the performance with the next piece of trash had a bit more finesse worked into it. That effort merited similar praise from Mrs. Preston, who added, "You made that look so easy!"

Our trip was progressing well. We were going down a long grassy stretch of trail leading into the Lyell Fork of the Tuolumne River when I met my nemesis. Ahead was a routine piece of paper on the trail. I bent down to pick it up, and I missed! Damn. I pulled Sorrel around and tried once more. Missed again! Somewhat annoyed and quite a bit irritated with myself, I reined Sorrel around until we were just about over the offending piece of paper. I focused, concentrated, and swept down in a concerted effort to get the piece of paper. With a thud I wound up sitting on my ass in the middle of the trail! Sorrel stood calmly next to me, casting a look of disdain in my direction, as if to say, "What's for an encore?"

"Are you all right?" asked a startled Mrs. Preston. "Did you hurt yourself?" "I'm fine," I answered. It's just my ego that's shattered, I thought, as I got to my feet with the latest piece of paper. Chagrin turned my face beet. Here I was, sitting in the middle of the trail with my horse giving me a funny look and the woman for whom I was showing off—and being my boss's wife to boot—worried about my well-being. It just doesn't get much more embarrassing than that for an eager, unsophisticated young ranger trying to make his way in the world. In the first few stunned seconds that I sat on my rear I discovered what had contributed to my mishap (beside male ego). The piece of paper had been resting in an abandoned rut and was six to eight inches lower than the meadow surface. Bending down to ground level from a tall horse was challenging enough, but leaning down another six inches was beyond my level of expertise.

Superintendent Preston had not been waiting very long before we arrived so at least that portion of the escort went well. I took care of the stock while the Prestons and Herb Ewing visited. When Sorrel cooled down I gave him a feed of grain, water, and we were ready to head back to Merced Lake. We had a routine trip back, and I even successfully picked up a couple pieces of litter from horseback. However, I looked around first to make sure no one was watching. I had enough come-up-ances for one day.

I had just finished feeding and brushing Sorrel when I heard a bell approaching from the south: George and Socks came to check for their overdue feeding of grain. I gave them a taste of grain to keep them interested in coming by the station and then turned the three of them loose for the night.

After I retrieved a beer from my stash in the creek, I sat on the station steps sipping my beer and reflecting on the day. As dusk settled on Merced Lake Ranger Station, I finally concluded that I had had a good day. I had a good ride in good country and had done family friends a good favor. My fall had taught me that compliments graciously given should be graciously received, but you shouldn't let them go to your head.

Despite all the positive events of the summer, I periodically thought about the dark cloud on my horizon. Hastings College of Law had notified me I would not receive my law degree. My cumulative grade point average had dropped to 69.7 percent. I would need to retake some courses to get my GPA up to 70 percent or higher. It was probably the result of too many four-hour law exams finished in one hour in order to get to Yosemite faster. I reluctantly made arrangements to return to Hastings in the fall.

In July 1959 as the fire season was entering full swing, my sister Lynn visited for two or three weeks. Lynn was so different from me that an outsider would think we came from different families and had grown up in different generations. Lynn and I were both raised in an era before computers, television, I-Pods, Blackberries, and such (we didn't even have a radio). Despite our Yosemite upbringing, Lynn adapted well to city life and was very urban oriented. I preferred open country and remote areas. She was quietly sociable and relatively at ease meeting new people. While I was not exactly anti-social, it took me a lot longer to make friends, and I never felt totally relaxed and comfortable in large groups or in meeting strangers.

Lynn was very content in the present, met the future gracefully as it arrived, and accepted new technology as soon as it developed. I focused on the skills of the past, wanted very much to be a good horseman and packer, and even resented the use of helicopters in the mountains. If I could have been assured of the availability of hot showers and cold beer, I would have been happy to have been born 100 years earlier.

We had become much closer when we both were living in San Francisco. One day my sister's attractive friend asked permission to smoke. This was when people still smoked indoors and didn't know or care about second-hand smoke. While the young lady pulled out her cigarette and fumbled for a light, I waited for the conversation to resume. My sister got her friend a light.

After her friend left, Lynn turned to me with an icy stare and a command presence that would have done Dad proud. She told me in clipped tones that men were expected to light ladies' cigarettes. Period. For the first time in my life I gave a dutiful "Yes, dear" response. After that I went out of my way to make amends. I carried matches everywhere, lit ladies' cigarettes right and left, and would dash across a room and light a cigarette before the escort even realized his date had a cigarette out. I got a lot of smiles and compliments from the ladies and also gained a reputation as the fastest match in the West! Guess you could say Lynn had an impact upon me.

I was looking forward to my sister's visit. As with any missionary, I had my own hopes for her beyond just an enjoyable visit. For some reason it was important to me that she be able to enjoy the backcountry as I did and to be as comfortable there as I was. While Lynn had ridden a number of times as a child and was no stranger to horses and mules, she had not ridden for several years before she joined me for the 15-mile trip to Merced Lake Ranger Station on Sorrel with a McClellan saddle. It was no surprise that she arrived both tired and saddle sore.

Consequently, Lynn didn't ride with me on my next few days of patrol. She made the place much cleaner than it had ever been in my tenure. Tea towels hung from oven handles, and dish racks lost their grunge. Floors were swept, windows were washed inside and out, and the whole place was dusted. I was in awe of the station's and my unbelievable good fortune. She had to learn to cook on a wood stove and to operate the best and brightest Coleman lantern, which usually flamed up unmercifully when it was first lit.

I ate better than I ever had, not just one can heated up at a time as I did for myself. Dr. Sharsmith passed by one day while checking his grazing analysis plots and was the beneficiary of fresh-out-of-the-oven blueberry muffins. And Lynn learned empathy for the women of previous generations—cooking on a woodstove on a warm summer day.

As I was returning from a patrol, I stopped to talk with a party heading to Vogelsang. About the first words from them were, "Are you the ranger with that neat outhouse?" They gushed on about how interesting they thought the outhouse was. When the next two parties heading uphill said almost the same thing, I urged George along faster. When George and I arrived at the ranger station, the mystery was solved as soon as I opened the outhouse door (cautiously) and looked inside. Straight ahead, plain and undecorated, was the first hole, labeled "men." To the right was a seat decorated profusely with doilies cut out of paper towels and napkins. It was accentuated by colored surveyor's tape tied as ribbons. A lotta work, a lotta doilies, a lotta fun. And it was carefully labeled, "WOMEN ONLY!" The message came across clearly and definitively—if you peed standing up, go no farther. If you were raised to be seated while relieving your bladder, you could step to the right; but wipe your feet first, mind your p's and q's, and above all, watch your aim!

The next day I let George have a rest and took Sorrel on a patrol to Half Dome. I tied Sorrel at the bottom and was about a third of a way to the top when I became aware of lightning activity on the north side of Mt. Clark. It was a relatively brief storm, but there were several ground strikes before the storm blew over. I was debating whether to wait and not chance being on top of Half Dome in a lightning storm when I saw smoke rising. That made up my mind, so I hurried down to Sorrel and back to Merced Lake.

When I arrived, I called the fire cache on the phone. As I expected, they wanted me to take on the fire and to let them know if I needed help. I started gathering equipment—radio pack-set, shovel, axe, Pulaski, canteen, fire rations, sleeping bag, file, compass, snacks, and more. I changed my riding boots for my hiking boots, my Stetson for a hard hat. Lynn, who had been helping collect gear, made me a couple sandwiches and filled my canteen. I told her I had no idea when

I'd be back. She should answer the phone and keep a log of calls she made and received. I thanked her for all her help, told her to take good care of herself, not to worry, and to follow Dad's advice—breathe deeply. Then I climbed on George and headed down the trail at a fast walk.

It took me awhile to find the fire. The burned area turned out to be about a half-acre of moderate fuel on a moderately steep hillside. The lightning-struck tree of origin was still burning vigorously, part of it blasted to the ground. Three or four mature sugar pines with bases scorched and smoldering had not yet started burning farther up the tree. A couple of old, dry, dead-and-down pine trees were about to be ignited by the ground fire marching aggressively toward them through the pine needle and duff floor.

I dug some fireline to slow the uphill progress, threw some dirt to knock down the fire on the lightning struck tree, and then radioed the fire cache. I described the fire, said I didn't need help, asked them to call Merced Lake High Sierra Camp to see if one of the guides would get my horses and take them back to the station, and got busy digging line. I worked non-stop until midnight, interrupted only by a call from the fire cache saying that one of the guides was on his way to get the boys and take them to the ranger station.

By midnight, I had the fire mostly out. When I stretched out to try to get some rest, I was cold! I had not brought a sleeping bag because it had been too big and bulky to carry in my already overloaded canvas bag. My solution was to heap some dry wood on the butt end of a downed log that was still smoldering. I rested warmly, even slept some until daylight when I began my final mop-up. My warming fire was the hardest thing to put out. It had kept me warm, but it was noon before I was finally certain it was out. So much for comfort and warmth on a fire. Having seen the last smoke around noon, I left the fire about 5 p.m. and headed for Merced Lake Ranger Station (with the okay from the fire cache). I left most of the equipment on the fire to pick it up the next day when I came back to check for smoke.

When I got home, I was happy to see smoke rising from the cabin chimney. Lynn was fixing supper, and there was hot water. I indulged in a tank-draining shower and felt much better. My quality of life improved even more significantly after I was sipping a beer from the creek. After supper Lynn pointed to a paper towel on the floor behind the stove. Under the paper towel was a mousetrap with a dead mouse in it. So my urban-oriented sister had finally displayed a limit to semi-primitive living. That was understandable, as everyone I knew had some limits. She could light a recalcitrant Coleman lantern, cook on a wood stove, and slept multiple nights as the sole occupant of an isolated backcountry cabin despite the fact that many of her acquaintances thought she was afraid of the dark. But she had drawn the line at removing a dead mouse from a trap.

My sister surprised me once again when it came time for her to get back home for early registration for her senior year at college. That she chose to walk to the valley rather than ride Sorrel was not surprising. However, the speed with which she made the trip greatly impressed me. I walked to camp with her and drank a cup of Pa Lennox's good coffee while she said her good-byes to the staff. Then I asked her to call me on the phone as soon as she arrived. She headed for the valley at a good pace. I returned to the ranger station and had barely worked up a sweat splitting wood when the phone rang. It was Lynn. She had made the 15-mile trip at a rate of between five and six miles an hour.

As the 1959 season progressed it got so dry that park management prohibited campfires in the lower elevations of the backcountry. The trails were well posted with no-campfire signs, and everyone was watchful and worried. I was picking up a supply of grain at Tuolumne Meadows when a fire was reported a couple miles from Half Dome. They immediately dropped a crew of smokejumpers on it. I was told to join them as soon as I could and to patrol and mop-up the fire after the smokejumpers had controlled it.

When I got back to Merced Lake, I dropped off my grain, repacked with several days' rations for me and my boys, and hurried to Half Dome. When I got to the fire it was late afternoon and the fire was mostly out; all that remained was some mop-up. I checked in with the fire cache and was told to stay with the fire until it was out.

Two jumpers showed me around the fire, indicated an intermittent stream that provided a limited supply of water, wished me luck, and started down the trail to catch up with the rest of their crew. I unpacked and unsaddled the boys, belled George and turned him loose to graze, and tied Socks and Sorrel. Changing my Stetson and uniform shirt for a hardhat and a work shirt, I began mopping up.

I worked aggressively, taking breaks only to rotate grazing opportunities among the horses, and when it got too dark to work, I ate a cold fire ration and went to bed. Having slept better than expected, I got up early and boiled water. I watched the sun come up while sipping a cup of instant coffee and wishing it was a cup of Pa Lennox's real coffee. I reminded myself that I had hired out to be rugged—when I had to be.

Then it was more mopping up. About mid-morning I was working on a stubborn smoking stump when I heard voices behind me. "Excuse me. Excuse me," a voice said, "I'm a seasonal park naturalist. I usually don't get involved in law enforcement matters, and it's my day off, but I have to tell you it's against the law to have fires up here because of the very high fire danger."

I must have presented a disconcerting appearance as I turned around with a blank look on my soot-smeared face. My clothes were grimy and my hands and arms were black up to my elbows with charcoal and ash. The slender, bespectacled seasonal park naturalist , looked at me, then beyond me at the burned twenty acres, recovered from his shock to say, "Oh, oh. OH," then concluded with, "Oh, my goodness."

With a slight, nervous chuckle, the seasonal naturalist stepped back, his gaze shifting from the fire to me and back to the fire. As he stood there looking sheepish, I stepped toward him and introduced myself as the Merced Lake ranger. The naturalist's three companions, who had stayed back while their friend handled the unaccustomed law enforcement situation, came up. They smiled and started laughing. I began to enjoy the circumstances as well. The naturalist soon put his embarrassment aside and joined the circle of laughter.

In time, I remembered Dad's frequent saying: "Part of every person's mission in life, especially in the NPS, is to give other people something to talk about." The young naturalist had started to fulfill this mission. As I continued patrolling the fire, I smiled at the seasonal naturalist's skewed perception of what he had seen and how he had embarrassed himself by acting on a false premise. Then I realized I knew a seasonal ranger who couldn't distinguish between a CCC-constructed trail and a narrow rock ledge Mother Nature had left on the face of a cliff. And I bet the naturalist would have been smart enough not to try to ride a horse across the face of Clouds Rest.

There were more similarities than differences between the two incidents. To their credit, both seasonal employees were trying to do a good job when they over-extended their comfort levels. The naturalist had shown good judgment in leaving his friends behind while he contacted a potential violator. Score one for the naturalist. The ranger had risked his horse unnecessarily. Not so good.

As the end of the 1959 summer season grew closer, a friend suggested I check with the Curry Company personnel office about openings as ski instructors and ski patrolmen in the Badger Pass winter operation. Since I was not enthusiastic about returning to Hastings, I impulsively went to see the assistant personnel officer. He put my name on a list and said he would contact me later in the fall.

I continued to brood about whether I should return to get my law degree. On one hand, I didn't want to disappoint Mom and Dad, nor did I want to quit a project I had put a lot of time, effort, money, and agony into, especially so near the finish line. But what was I doing in law school in the first place when the only thing I ever wanted to be was a ranger?

Then one day I realized I already had the answer in a letter Dad had written to me five years earlier. At that time I had told Mom and Dad I was thinking of laying out of school a semester so I could work that fall as a packer for a hunting outfitter. Dad's response was simple and succinct: "Son, somewhere along the line you've developed a taste for horse shit. It is for you to decide whether you will eat beans or caviar for the rest of your life. Whatever you decide, your Mother and I will support you. Remember, when you're around horses, always talk to them before you walk behind them. Love, Dad."

"Plop, plop, fizz, fizz, oh what a relief it is!" were some of the words to an advertising jingle for a heartburn medication at the time. That's basically the way I felt after I made up my mind. A life-turning moment!!!

I called Mom and Dad, told them that I would not be returning to Hastings, that I intended to work in Yosemite as late as I could, and that I had decided on a career with the National Park Service.

Their response both surprised and impressed me. They would support whatever I wanted: they had opposed my becoming a ranger only because they wanted me to know something different and to be able to make a real choice. They did not want me to become a ranger just because Dad was. They knew of several young people who had stayed in Yosemite because they didn't know anything else and, as a result, felt trapped, unhappy, and limited in later life. Maybe for them. I didn't expect it would be that way for me.

At first opportunity, I told Herb Ewing my plans had changed, and I would be available for as long as there was money to pay me. Herb didn't seem particularly surprised about my decision. After Merced Lake closed, I would be at Tioga Pass Entrance Station. It had turned out to be a great summer, and in retrospect I can't believe it all fit into one season. Miles and miles of patrol, exploring new travel routes and long abandoned trails, multiple fires, lots of company, interesting acquaintances, new adventures, and a changed career path. My growing confidence and competence made me feel I was equal to any challenge I might face. If I could choose a period of my life to experience again, it would be the summer of 1959, just to see if it all happened the way I remembered it.

I would miss Pa Lennox's coffee, but more significantly, George, who had a major impact on me. I regret only that our association was so short. He was the boldest, most self-assured horse I ever had the privilege to use. He taught me you have to look beyond the exterior to see the real depth of a horse; good looks, classic build, and conformation are less important than heart, soul, courage, and giving; and if you pay attention, you can learn from any horse.

A good friend once told me he was not sure there was a heaven, but if we made it there, he thought we would be re-united with all our four-legged friends At the time, it was just a random philosophical musing. I simply agreed with him and, not being prone to spending much time on semi-esoteric subjects, I let the conversation drift to a different topic. As years passed and I experienced a number of really memorable critters, that evening's brief conversation periodically came back to me. If heaven were as my friend speculated, it would definitely be a place to aspire to, if only to better understand our departed four-legged partners.

If I were ever able to communicate with him, I would defi-nitely thank George for all that he did for me, for the times he saved me from myself, and for the times he made me look good when all I really deserved was to be dumped on my silly butt. I would thank him for the impressive loyalty he showed, for his consistency, and for always being there when I needed him. I would apologize to George for the miscues I gave when I acted before thinking. I would apologize for my overconfi-dence in directing him onto the north face of Clouds Rest and not being smart enough to turn around sooner. I would thank him for his calm poise, his steadfast confidence, and his concentration and focus that in essence gave me a second chance.

George changed forever the way I looked at horses. They were no longer merely fine beasts of burden that you treated with respect and used. They became entities that you built a partnership with and accomplished jobs together. He set a very high standard for those that followed him. If I were to compose an epitaph for George, I would simply say, "George, you were a hell of a fine horse. It was a privilege for me to know you. I wish I could have been around you longer."

I recall the lump in my throat when I turned in the horses that fall of 1959. It was a bittersweet occasion: bitter because I wasn't ready to part with the boys who had taught me so much that season and sweet because I no longer had the specter of law school hanging over me. I would be staying in Yosemite and I had a clear goal for the future.

Chapter 9

Beauty Lies in the Eyes

AFTER I TURNED IN THE BOYS, I DROVE UP TO TUOLUMNE Meadows and found that I would be sharing the quarters adjacent to the Tioga Pass Entrance Station with Ferdinand Castillo, who had been in charge of Tioga Pass for many years. Ferdinand, a World War II Marine, was very patriotic. He insisted on respect for the flag and proper flag protocols, asking visitors to shut off their vehicles' engines, exit their vehicles, and stand quietly during the ceremony.

Meticulous in uniform, Ferdinand was the ultimate ranger host welcoming people to their national park. He was both memorable and popular, and repeat visitors invariably asked for him. Often regular visitors would wait in the parking lot until he came on duty so they could say hello to him and renew their acquaintance. I believe he was in his forties though he looked about half that age and had the irrepressible spirit of a teenager. Gracious host that he was, Ferdinand welcomed me into his residence so enthusiastically that I felt he had been waiting all season for me to arrive.

Located on the crest of the Sierra Nevada Range, Tioga Pass is framed by Gaylor Peak on the north and by Mount Dana towering more than 13,000 feet above a wide sweeping meadow. Tioga Pass was a magnificent gateway to Yosemite.

But beauty is in the eye of the beholder. One evening an over-weight, middle-aged motorist chewing on a cigar roared up from Highway 395, slammed on his car's brakes, and asked me, "Hey, buddy, how far is it to the scenery?"

North of the kiosk was the handsome, three-room cabin I shared with Ferdinand. Typical early NPS and Yosemite design, the granite and wood building was aesthetically pleasing and built to last forever. The living room had a good-looking stone fireplace, and on special occasions Ferdinand would fire it up and cook steaks on the dying embers. Good food, good memories, and a fine way to spend an evening in the days before television.

Things settled down to a peaceful routine. Open the station at seven, greet visitors, check the weapons of hunters from outside the park, seal the weapon with a cord and lead seal to make the weapon inoperable, and check any harvested game being transported through the park. Also, check the outgoing lane to make sure they had their permits. Smile and have your picture taken with park visitors several times a day, issue backcountry permits, and enjoy the scenery. The days were pleasant and comfortably busy. You didn't have to hurry folks through, and you had time to visit if you and the visitor were in the mood to do so. For an entrance operation, Tioga in the fall is as good as it gets. But it wasn't Merced Lake, it wasn't Buck Camp, and it wasn't backcountry.

My quiet routine of Tioga Pass Entrance was short-lived. I had signed up to take the Federal Service Entrance Exam, which was the test the NPS used to select permanent rangers. I had chosen to take the exam in San Francisco, and the date was quickly approaching. So ended the summer and fall that I didn't ever want to end.

Chapter 10

Remember Who You Are and What You Stand For

Nineteen-sixty turned out to be my last year in Yosemite. The year actually began on December 15, 1959, when I reported for work as a ski patrolman at Yosemite's Badger Pass Ski Area. I was happy to have been chosen for the ski patrol rather than as an instructor. I didn't feel I skied "pretty" enough to be an instructor, and a ski patrolman's work was more in line with ranger responsibilities.

Beyond just skiing and first aid, a ski patrolman was expected to be a host, assist skiers, pack slopes, smooth out rough spots, fill sitzmarks, etc. Limited by its modest terrain, Badger Pass was basically a beginner to intermediate ski area. However, numerous devotees came up regularly from Fresno, Madera, Merced, and other local communities. It was busy, especially on weekends.

Stan Albright was in charge of the ski patrol. Of the six paid patrolmen, four were seasonal rangers, and one was a seasonal NPS maintenance worker. On weekends, volunteer National Ski Patrolmen from Fresno came up to ski and assist. Some of these folks had been patrolling for a number of years and were very experienced and competent. Park rangers manned the first-aid room and reviewed the packaging of any patient who was being transported to Lewis Memorial Hospital in Yosemite Valley. The hospital was run by Dr. Avery Sturm, who had been in Yosemite at least since 1939 (when he set and cast my broken left arm).

Unlike most ski areas, the Badger Pass Ski Patrol used traction splints and applied traction to broken legs (tibias/fibulas) right on the ski hill. This was due to the influence of Dr. Sturm, who had observed that broken legs healed faster and better the sooner the broken edges of bone were aligned (set) and the less they grated against each other. Every ski patrolman went through evening sessions at the hospital to learn this procedure.

If this sounds out of the norm for a first aider to set a broken leg out on the ski hill, I guess it was. I didn't know of any other ski areas at that time that practiced this procedure. If you've ever seen the intense relief that comes to a person writhing in agony from a broken leg the instant traction is applied and the leg is set, you tend to become a believer. Things were probably simpler then. I mentally toast Doc Sturm whenever I reflect on his forward thinking, his faith in rangers and ski patrolmen, and the effort and energy it took to establish and oversee such a pioneering program. Here's to you, Doc, long may your legacy continue to shine.

DURING THAT WINTER I LEARNED A LOT ABOUT TRAUMA, pain, people, perspectives, and politics. Cappy Cook, still a seasonal, was the Badger Pass ranger. Rick Anderson and Bob Hartung were ski instructors with the Yosemite Ski School. Bob had come to Yosemite as a student minister with the Christian Ministry in National Parks, worked on the trail crew for two seasons, and had been a seasonal ranger for one summer. This was his second winter at Badger Pass. He and I roomed together, sharing a Yosemite Lodge employee cabin.

The ski season started inauspiciously—no snow. When I reported for work on December 15, I spent the better part of a week "manicuring" the slopes of vegetation that might stick up above a minimal snow pack and trip a skier. Then we spent a day setting up the Akja rescue sleds, basically a re-inforced aluminum sled/canoe designed to go in either direc-tion. It had long, detachable handles on each end that could be used to guide the Akja on the snow or to lift and carry it like a stretcher. Each Akja had a pad, sleeping bag, blankets, first aid kit, and canvas cover. The first aid kits contained several kinds of splints, including a traction splint, a variety of bandages, wraps, and tapes. They were well thought out and stocked for Badger Pass needs and injuries.

I was working the "bunny" (beginner's) hill when I had my first experience applying traction. I was near the bottom of the hill with skis off shoveling snow when I heard a clatter of skis followed by a thud and then a scream. Looking up, I saw a female skier who had fallen in a tangle right next to the rope tow about half way down from the top. She was writhing in pain, alternately screaming and sobbing as another skier tried to get the injured person's skis off.

I hurriedly put my skis on and was skiing to the bottom of the rope tow when I saw Stan Albright grabbing the rope to get to the woman who was still screaming and crying. As I grabbed the rope to start up the hill, I saw Stan bail off the rope tow, kick off his skis, and kneel next to the sobbing woman. I could hear Stan talking to the woman in a calm and reassuring tone as the rope tow took me by him on my way to retrieve an Akja. The woman had stopped screaming in response to Stan's assurances but was still breathing rapidly and whimpering quietly.

When I got there with the Akja, Stan had the woman actually smiling and breathing almost normally. I positioned the Akja, undid the cover, and gave Stan a blanket for the woman. He indicated to me that traction was called for and helped me set up the splint while all the while explaining what we were doing and comforting the woman. When we were set up, I started applying traction while Stan talked steadily, reassuring the patient every step of the way. When the broken bones popped into alignment, the woman gave a start and then said, "Oh, that feels good!" I became a true believer in traction from that moment on.

By the time we got the woman to the first aid room, her breathing was normal, and she was actually resting comfortably. Two things about this incident impressed me. The first was how important it was to reassure the patient. In this instance, simply talking to her kept the patient from going into shock. The second was how much relief traction provides.

Another early season incident taught me multiple lessons. It was a late Sunday morning of a busy, busy weekend. I was taking my first run after my lunch break and stopped at the Akja at the top of one of Badger's main runs. Several hundred yards away, near the bottom of the hill, a National Volunteer Ski Patrolman was working on a fallen, apparently injured skier. The patrolman finally looked up and waved frantically, indicating he wanted the Akja right away. I outdid myself, going straight down the fall line at high speed. With no weight to stabilize it, the Akja began fishtailing and almost dumped me. Not a good time to lose it, I thought, especially when people are depending on me. Concentrate. CONCENTRATE!

I managed to stay upright, arriving barely under control after this pell-mell trip down the hill. Although disquieted by my critical near miss, I found that adrenalin helped me as

I stabilized the Akja. I kicked off my skis, stuck them criss-crossed in the snow to alert oncoming skiers, and did the same with the injured person's skis. Unpacking the first aid packet, I covered the victim with a blanket and set up the traction equipment. I was comforted to see that the patrolman on scene was the Fresno Volunteer Ski Patrol leader. After 16 seasons of volunteer ski patrol he was one of the most knowledgeable and capable first aiders around. The injured party appeared to be a fourteen-to sixteen-year-old boy rapidly going into shock from pain. The patrolman was lying across the young man's chest to limit his movement and hugging him to keep him warm. The boy's breathing was rapid but shallow, and he was sobbing in pain.

When the traction splint was in place, I suggested to the patrolman that I hold the boy while he applied the traction. "No, you do it," he said. "But you have so much more experience than I do," I answered. The patrolman looked at me, tears running down his cheeks, and said, "I can't! This is my son!" I understood.

We got into position, and I applied traction. When the broken bones clicked into alignment, the boy gasped, said "Ohhh!," took a deep breath, stopped crying, and began breathing more normally. The father looked at me and mouthed the words "Thank you, Thank you," as tears of relief flowed unabated. Once more the miracle of traction properly applied to a broken leg on a ski hill worked its magic. By the time I finished tying off the traction, color had started returning to the boy's face, and he was breathing normally. Thanks again, Doctor Sturm.

As the season progressed my experience increased, and I became more comfortable applying traction. I never ceased being amazed by the relief a person experienced as soon as the traction took hold. One day I was involved with five cases: two as applier, three as assistant. Badger Pass sometimes had a busy first aid room; I remember one day when thirteen patients were hauled there by toboggan.

About a third of the way through the season I got word the chief ranger would like to talk to me. Both flattered and curious, I showed up at the ranger office the next day at 7:30 a.m. and met with Chief Ranger Elmer Fladmark. It turned out Cappy Cook was rapidly running out of time on his seasonal ranger appointment (somehow they had miscalculated the time he had already used on his seasonal appointment). Would I think about trading jobs with him? Cappy would continue living in the ranger residence at Badger but would work for the company as a ski patrolman in the job I had. I, in turn, would leave that job and become a seasonal ranger once again as I still had plenty of time remaining on my NPS seasonal appointment.

My mind was in a quandary. This was my winter to ski and things were working out well, but my ultimate goal was to be a permanent ranger. I asked the chief what I would be doing. A variety of assignments with some at Badger Pass, but he wanted to rotate that assignment so everyone had a bit of relief from the valley routine. I would be assigned some patrol shifts, and I would probably get some midnight to eight shifts. I saw a light at the end of the tunnel. I said candidly that I would look forward to the Badger assignments, but the midnight to eight shifts would work as well for me since I would have the days free to ski. I diplomatically added that I would be glad to work just about any assignment.

So I started the next week as a ranger. Over the weekend I moved from the Yosemite Lodge employee cabin I shared to the Ranger's Club, where I was assigned a private room because I worked the night shift. Wow, fat city, my own room. I was following a family tradition since Dad had resided in the Ranger's Club during his earliest years in Yosemite.

The midnight to eight shift was referred as MOP, for midnight, office, and patrol. The MOP person was supposed to spend every other hour in the office, so people could find a ranger if they needed one. The hour that followed an office hour was to be spent on patrol, which was intended more as a fire patrol then as a law enforcement patrol. If there was snowfall of four inches or more, you were to contact the on-call permanent ranger to check the road and decide whether to notify maintenance to plow.

Some things were spelled out, but most matters were very flexible. There was no 24-hour Communication Center so the MOP person was basically on his own. The hospital had a nurse on duty, and there were night clean-up crews at the Ahwahnee Hotel and the Yosemite Lodge. Most of the the valley was asleep. Settling into a routine, I would have breakfast and then drive to Badger Pass where I would check in at the first aid room to let them know that I would be skiing and would be available as needed. Since I was skiing in uniform, I had the privilege of cutting in front of the lift line, but I tried to be casual about it as if I were patrolling the slopes and not just free skiing.

Not being assigned to any slope, I could roam as I pleased to wherever the skiing was better or to wherever there was an accident. Extra hands were usually welcome, and since I had worked with everyone involved, things usually worked out quite well. I got in a lot of skiing, a lot of first aid experience, and a lot of practice bringing toboggans off the ski hill. Life was good for an eager young man with a lot of energy who was trying to experience all he could.

I found that every three or four days, I would have to take a day of rest and spend most of the day sleeping. This also worked out quite well as between naps I could visit NPS friends and was usually rested enough to join Badger employees in the Lodge Pub as they restored electrolytes lost during the day's work. After that I would retreat to my private room and store up some more winks to last through the long MOP shift ahead.

I managed my sleeping and skiing schedule fairly well until one day I was awakened at thirty minutes after midnight by Mather District Ranger Tommy Tucker. Was I on MOP? Was I planning on coming to work? Yes. Yes. When I realized what time it was, chagrin and remorse woke me instantly and apologies were stammered. I had failed to set the alarm clock. Tommy was very understanding, gracious, and forgiving.

I remember the first vehicle stop I made on MOP. It was a quiet two o'clock in the morning when the only other vehicle on the road besides mine went sailing through a stop sign at relatively high speed. Without having rehearsed or thought through the scenario, I immediately flipped on my vehicle's red light. The offending driver reacted promptly, slammed on his brakes, and pulled over to the side of the deserted road.

At that time each valley patrol car had a holstered handgun, extra ammunition, and a pair of handcuffs locked in the vehicle's glove compartment and a four-cell flashlight lying on the front seat. When I had gotten into the vehicle that night, I had unlocked the glove compartment, checked the handgun to see if it was loaded—it was—and checked the flashlight—it worked.

As I got out of my patrol car to contact the driver of the stopped vehicle, I took the handgun out of the glove compartment and put it into my front pocket where it fit comfortably without being apparent. So far so good. I took the flashlight off the front seat and approached the car.

The driver was very polite and even apologetic; he knew the stop sign was there but hadn't seen me and thought it would be all right to run the stop sign since there was no other traffic. I asked for and received his driver's license. It was valid, and I copied the pertinent information into my NPS notebook. I gave the license back and told the driver I was giving him a warning for excessive speed and for running through a stop sign. He thanked me for not issuing him a citation.

So ended my first nighttime car stop. In more than 36 years as a permanent park ranger, I never made a nighttime car stop without a firearm on my person. At that time the agency emphasized low-key law enforcement contacts and was very anti-firearms so my precautions were unusual. I still have in my memorabilia (better known as saved junk) that NPS notebook filled with drivers' names, addresses, descriptions, and license expiration dates. These names represent the only records on file of the many drivers to whom I issued warnings. Little did they know that many of them received warnings because I didn't know how to issue a citation. NPS law enforcement was somewhat simpler in those days.

I continued to make periodic car stops as I worked a variety of shifts that winter. I found as the days grew longer that I could kill two birds with one stone toward the end of a MOP shift: I would park visibly as if I were monitoring traffic approaching a junction. Folks would slow down, stop completely at the junction stop sign, and then continue on to work. In the meantime, with the brim of my Stetson braced against the window, my head would be upright and erect while my eyes could be shut and resting. It was almost like having your cake and eating it, too.

At this time, there was parking space for about a dozen vehicles in front of the Yosemite Lodge registration and just off the lodge access road. One space was clearly marked, "For Ranger Patrol Vehicles Only." On either side of this handy parking were larger but less convenient parking areas. Often the patrol vehicle space was taken by personal vehicles whose drivers chose the posted parking space rather than walk fifty or so yards to either of the roomier parking areas. When I was on patrol and ran into this situation, I made it a habit to double park, in such a way that the offending vehicle was blocked inside the lot. If the driver was still there after I had finished my business, I would identify the driver and give him/her a warning for parking in a posted area. Many of the usurpers were NPS employees not on government business. I contacted a couple of them more than once.

One busy Sunday I was assigned to Badger ski hill duty along with several other rangers from the valley. That afternoon my boss, Mather District Ranger Tommy Tucker, said he was headed back to the valley by himself and asked me to ride down with him. I agreed, flattered to be asked and there was always a good chance to learn something just being around Tommy. As we headed down the hill, I wondered if Tommy had something on his mind. As I soon found out, he did. After some talk about the day's events, Tommy said, "I hear you've been making quite a few car stops."

That proved to be the introduction to a far-reaching, thought-provoking conversation that I have replayed and reflected on many times over the years. After hesitating, I said something to the effect that I only made car stops when I saw something that should be addressed; I wasn't trying to find excuses to stop people. Then I asked him why he was asking?

Tommy said he had heard from a number of people that I

could be overly aggressive; I tended to talk down to people; and at times I had been officious. Some of these folks seemed to think I was too worried about the letter of the law rather than safety and the reasonable intent of the law. He went on to say that a lot of people remembered Dad, and some of them felt my demeanor reflected unfavorably on him. I was stunned and mortified and sat in silence trying to let it all sink in. I was particularly dismayed over how my actions may have reflected on Dad.

After a time, I finally spoke, asking Tommy if he thought I should quit making car stops altogether. "Not at all," was Tommy's answer, "but remember the offense isn't against you. You need to let people know why you are stopping them but don't lecture them, don't talk down to them. Pay attention to what is happening, but be more conversational. Don't be aloof or standoffish. You need people to pay attention to what you are saying, so don't let your demeanor give them reason to shut you out." Tommy spoke conversationally but convincingly. If I had a word-for-word transcript of what Tommy said that day I am convinced it would win a Pulitzer Prize for defining sensitive, effective, low-key law enforcement.

Tommy's message had a profound and lasting effect on me. I thought more carefully about what I was trying to accomplish. From that day on I analyzed every public contact I made to determine how I could have done a better job. Years later, when I became a supervisory ranger responsible for training others, I integrated Tommy's advice with my own experience and training. I relayed Tommy's advice to inexperienced rangers: Pay attention; don't talk down to the people you contact; communicate, don't preach; and don't take the offense personally. My personal additions: When you issue a citation, make the person more inclined to assist you as if he were the only witness to your getting the snot beat out of you. Remember who you are and what you stand for.

Looking ahead toward summer, Dad suggested I ask to be considered for a front country assignment. Since I had settled on a career with the NPS, he felt I needed to develop a broader background to make myself more competitive for a permanent position. I hesitated since backcountry and wilderness were the primary focus of my interests.

At the same time I could see the validity of Dad's suggestion, especially for getting a permanent appointment. So I approached Herb Ewing, who said he would discuss it with the chief ranger. In due time Herb told me I would be assigned to Tuolumne Meadows for the summer. I was happy since a lot of fine backcountry could be accessed from the meadows.

In the meantime I was enjoying the arrival of spring in the valley as I worked a variety of shifts, a lot of MOP, some day patrol, and a few front desk shifts in the ranger office. I grew in confidence and assurance on road patrol just as I had grown comfortable with backcountry horse patrol. One challenging task was contacting employee groups at beach parties. It was the MOP ranger's duty to check the several beaches on the Merced River for which fire permits had been issued. Fires had to be out at one a.m. While some groups were cooperative and understanding, a few would test the patience of Job.

One group I contacted early on had quite a messy site and was quite loud. When I asked them to put out their fire as was required by their permit, they objected that it was still early. The loudest mouth of the party said if I wanted the campfire out now I might have to call some more rangers. I took a deep breath with my mind going into high gear and my eyes focused intently on the speaker who wouldn't look me in the eyes. My mind skipped back to Dad and how he would deal with this confrontation.

I followed an example of his that I remembered and very quietly said to the group that tonight it was my job to check and make sure the campfire was out by one a.m. I said I didn't intend to wake up off-duty rangers and cause them to lose sleep just to help me do a job I should be able to do by myself.

One individual was more vocal than his peers. He appeared quite nonplused when I asked if I could talk to him in private. I asked him to consider a few things: they wouldn't like it if another group had left the beach as messy for them as it was now; this was no way to show respect for Yosemite; and they should take more pride in the division they worked for.

I spoke very quietly and only to him. He seemed to listen and said if I would say the same thing to the group, he would do his best to see it was cleaned up when I stopped back later. I told those at the fire ring that we had a lot in common, especially in choosing to work in Yosemite; Yosemite deserved to be treated better than as a garbage can. I said I had other places to check and would stop back in an hour to see how things were going.

When I returned the fire was out, and the place was as close to pristine as it could be with a fire ring and a half dozen couples scattered about visiting quietly. One individual came up and thanked me for the way I had handled the situation. Sometimes you get lucky, but it pays to have good mentors and role models. You never can have too many of the good ones.

About the middle of June I transferred to Tuolumne Meadows for the summer. The tent I shared with Bob Hartung was standard Yosemite seasonal quarters—two canvas wall tents mounted back to back on permanent wood floors and frames. The back tent housed two pairs of bunks, dressers, metal wall-lockers, folding chairs, and a bedside stand between the bunks.

The front tent contained a wood stove, a sink, a refrigerator, and a standard-sized picnic table. There were between six and eight such tents to house seasonal naturalists and rangers, which were located around a community shower and restroom tent. In front of the tent complex were two wood frame and shake buildings housing the two permanent rangers. The smaller one was for Assistant District Ranger Chet Miller. Chet was married and had a teenage son who mostly stayed in the valley at quarters Chet kept there. Herb Ewing, his wife Ruth, and son Bobby lived in the larger frame building.

Bob Hartung and I were referred to as "utility" rangers since we did a wide variety of jobs—road patrol, backcountry patrol (foot and horseback), chores, as well as "other duties as assigned." We did not regularly work either the campground or the entrance station although we would patrol those areas and would facilitate those operations as needed.

The patrol vehicle was a Ford Thunderbird station wagon with a prominent red light and a top-mounted siren. It was the hottest vehicle I had driven up to that time and could cover the country. The top-mounted siren was really an attention getter as compared to the usual low-key, under-the-hood-mounted sirens, which you often had to put your ear to the hood to hear. I learned a lot about sirens, marked vehicles, and the public response to them. I found that the tap-tap of the horn was usually a better attention getter, and drivers would recognize the patrol vehicle and respond appropriately. Sirens often caused drivers to slam on their brakes and stop in the middle of the road rather than simply pull over. Without specific instructions and guidelines I did my own research. I would park visibly at the end of the 25 mph zone in front of the Tuolumne store where people would usually go through at 45 mph plus. I gave numerous warnings for speed.

I hiked on my days off, covering a lot of country on trail and off trail. One of my hiking companions was Roger Hendrickson, Doc Sturm's new assistant. We had many interesting hikes. In addition to hiking, I spent many hours rock climbing. Wayne Merry was a permanent ranger working in the valley. A couple of years earlier he had been on the four-man climbing team that made the first ascent of the face of El Capitan. For a time that summer, Wayne and I had the same days off, and because of my interest in improving my technical climbing skills, Wayne would come up from the valley and meet me.

For practice, Wayne had us go through the protocol of climbing roped up and on belay. I learned a lot as we climbed higher and higher on a peak. The trip down was usually routine, with more learned each foot of the way. When we went "off-belay" at the bottom, Wayne returned to the valley, carrying my profuse thanks.

One lesson I learned that summer resulted from trying to pack a difficult load on a round-backed mule with no withers. "Don't try it" was the lesson, but as usual I found out why the hard way. Herb, Ruth, and Bobby had gone on a weeklong backcountry trip/patrol and had taken all the stock except one husky, nondescript, quasi-talented, black gelding about 16 hands tall.

Beside the extra large AH brand on his left hip, this horse's most notable characteristic was his penchant for going absolutely ballistic whenever he got a pack horse's lead rope under his tail. He would clamp down his tail on it and start bucking, lunging, farting, and whirling in fine imitation of Midnight and the other legendary rodeo bucking horses. In polite circles, the black horse was referred to as Alexander Hotshot because of his large AH brand. In less circumspect company he was commonly referred to as Ass Hole.

A few days after Herb and company left on their trip, a chunky, round-backed sorrel mule showed up at our barn. It turned out to be a trail crew mule that had been left at the trail crew barn a couple miles down the road. The trail crew packer, Bob Barrett, had left him behind when he took the rest of the string into the backcountry. Lonesome and with time on his hands, the mule went looking for companionship. We put him in the corral with Alexander Hotshot. When his days off came up, Chet Miller left Tuolumne for the valley to spend time with his son. Bob Hartung was in charge of what was left of Tuolumne's ranger operation, and the scene was set for another epic adventure.

We got word that a guest at Vogelsang High Sierra Camp had suffered a heart attack while fishing and died. Bob and I called Vogelsang and talked to an excited staff person who said they thought the person might still be alive. He had been lying there an hour and was still quite warm! I left to catch the black horse that was grazing in front of the station. Bob got more information and called the valley to let them know what was happening and to get advice.

I caught AH, jumped on him bareback, thumped him on the ribs, and we were soon heading for the barn at a high lope. AH slipped on the pavement and almost went down as we crossed the road. Hell of a way to start a rescue I thought, but the black horse recovered, and we finished the trip to the barn at a gallop. Eight or nine interpreters, wives, and kids had gathered at the barn to see what was happening and to offer their assistance. They jumped back as AH slid to a stop just in time to avoid crashing into the corral fence. Relieved to have made the ride intact, I jumped off the black horse as if I always came in from the meadow that way.

While Bob went to the trail crew barn to get the pack-saddle and gear for the red mule, I saddled AH, caught the red mule, and brought the wheeled Stokes litter to the corral. I found the two wooden, home constructed "D" shaped devices designed to let you carry the wheeled litter on a pack animal. (The flat side of the "D" rested on the pack boxes while the litter sat on the arched side of the "D" just above the sawbucks of the saddle.)

Bob returned with the red mule's tack and reported that Bob Barrett was back in the area and would be up shortly to lend a hand. Bob and I packed the wheeled Stokes onto the red mule and snugged it down tightly. Since I was ready to go, I took off on the horse with the mule, and Hartung and Barrett were to follow and catch up. It was full dark as I crossed the road and headed for Vogelsang. To AH's credit, he settled down to a good, steady pace. I was paranoid about keeping the mule's lead rope away from the black horse's tail. As time passed, and we covered the miles, things were going so good that I began to get a nagging feeling something wasn't totally right.

I finally realized that in the dark I had missed a junction, and we were on the trail to Emeric Lake, not Vogelsang High Sierra Camp. Shit! What to do now? Just then the moon came out of the clouds, and for the first time that evening I could clearly see the profiles of the mountains. I decided to continue as I was going and then head cross-country for Vogelsang Peak and the camp, hoping not to run into any insurmountable obstacles on the way. After a couple of minor adventures we reached a location where I could see a glow of light, and in a short time the glow materialized into a Coleman lantern sitting on the hitch rack in front of the Vogelsang cook tent. I was elated to have made it and, looking back at my mule and the wheeled litter, everything seemed to be intact. Barrett and Hartung arrived shortly after. So far, so good.

WE TIED OUR CRITTERS AND WENT TO CHECK ON THE FISHER-man. No doubt about it, he was dead. He was lying on a slab of granite that had absorbed the day's sunlight. That kept the body from cooling too rapidly and prompted our night ride to Vogelsang. Judging from his outfit and gear—expensive, well cared for, and well used—he must have been an avid fisherman. For such an individual to pass while fishing in Yosemite's high sierra was probably not a bad way to go. One could easily speculate he was at peace.

Not so for the three of us who had just ridden up from Tuolumne. We placed the deceased in a body bag and strapped him into the Stokes litter. Bob Barrett took the wheel from the litter and put it on his pack mule. We adjusted the saddle on my mule and tightened the cinches on his saddle. The mule was as round backed as a barrel from neck to rump and had no discernible withers. He was much more suited to pulling a plow or a wagon than he was to packing a load, but we put the Stokes litter on him and started for Tuolumne. We were hardly out of sight of the high sierra camp before Hartung called out that the pack was slipping to the right side. Damn! We stopped, straightened the load, found a rock to try to balance the load, and started out again.

After traveling less than half a mile, the pack once again started to shift, this time to the left. Again we stopped, adjusted the pack, and added more rocks. We repeated this procedure many times as we went down the trail, and then we experienced the mother of all wrecks. The load and saddle tipped completely over and the mule started bucking, pulling the lead rope out of my hand. He bucked out from under the litter and dragged the deceased a ways. Bucking away from the litter, he ran and bucked in circles around the boulder strewn meadow with the pack saddle under his belly. I tried to head off the bucking mule to no avail: AH was not a cutting horse.

Bob Hartung bailed off his horse and grabbed the trailing end of the lash rope. The mule dragged Bob easily. Bob braced himself against a boulder, yelling "Whoa, you SOB! Whoa!" As if he were offended at being called an SOB, the mule dragged Bob to the next boulder. At last the mule stopped, and Bob said "I stopped him!" Bob and I debate this to this day. I claim the mule just changed his mind and stopped of his own accord. Either way we cleaned up the mess and re-saddled the round-backed mule. Finally we decided to reattach the wheel to the litter and wheel the body to Tuolumne Meadows. What a grind. Though we were both in good shape, we were pooped, dehydrated, and glad for a rest when we got there. Chet Miller, back from his days off in the valley, met us at the camp and took the body. Bob Barrett took the horses and mules home, dropping AH at our barn as he went by.

Michael Adams, manager of the Tuolumne Meadows High Sierra Camp, invited Bob and me in for refreshments. We consumed copious amounts of ice water, juice, and sliced fruit. I ate so much diced cantaloupe that I embarrassed myself, but it was so cool, sweet, and thirst quenching that I kept eating long after Bob quit.

Almost 50 years later, as I try to recall things past, I am

both amazed and depressed. Amazed by the detail and intensity with which I am able to recall some things; depressed by the vagueness and lack of detail of other events. For the most part, it is the dates and often the sequence of happenings that have grown fuzzy or disappeared altogether. Some events, though shy of detail and background, I remember with enthusiasm and a sense of accomplishment.

The next major event of my 1960 season was the Merced Lake Fire, which started during a series of lightning strikes on September 2. Initially there were 32 fires park wide. One fire started across the river from Merced Lake Ranger Station and about half way up to the base of Mount Clark. Herb sent Bob and me to the Merced Lake Fire, and since helicopters were in high demand, he sent us the old fashioned way—on horseback.

Bob and I arrived at Merced Lake Ranger Station in the early afternoon when the fire was kicking up a good column of smoke. We were unpacking our tools, rations, and gear when Clyde Lockwood showed up. He was a permanent ranger stationed at Merced Lake that summer. His wife, Shar Spranger, was away from Merced Lake as the fire started. Clyde had been scouting the fire and had come back to use the phone to report fire size and weather conditions.

We took care of the horses while Clyde called the Fire Cache to update them on the fire, which he estimated to be around 20 acres. Just as we were starting out, Bob Barr, a lean, wiry, all muscle and sinew, middle-aged, and long-time trail crew member, joined us. He had been baby-sitting the trail crew camp while they all had gone into the valley for a break during a resupply. Since the other fires had started, they had been detained in the valley to help. Barr was wearing his hard hat, had a canteen slung over his shoulder, a lunch wrapped in a jacket around his waist, and was carrying a fire shovel and a finely tuned, double-bitted axe.

We found an easy way across Merced River and made our way to the fire, arriving around three in the afternoon. The fire was a going concern. We spread out along the downhill side and started digging line, following Barr's example. He was a precise, methodical, no motion wasted, line-digging machine. We worked steadily until eight or nine and decided to go down to the ranger station for the night, which would allow us to update the fire cache by phone. Bob Barr opted to stay as he didn't believe in leaving a fire until it was out.

We got to the cabin at dark, started a fire in the wood stove and took showers. Clyde talked to the Fire Cache, updating them and requesting additional help. They said the whole park was short of help but would see what was available. They said we could eat our fire meals at the Merced Lake High Sierra Camp as long as it was open. The next morning we got to the fire in good time, checked on Bob Barr and gave him a fire ration for breakfast, and started digging line. Barr was a really rugged individual, able to survive, even thrive with a minimum of comforts. At night he would sleep next to the fire without a sleeping bag, blankets, air mattress, or pad. To be able to breathe, he would dig a hole in the ground near where he rested his head. Stretching out, he would place his head over or in the hole to breathe the cleaner, dense air that settled there, since the less-dense smoke would rise upwards. That little technique gave him room to breathe.

About mid-morning a helicopter flew over, circled a few times, and then approached us. Out from the helicopter came a roll of toilet paper, the loose end fluttering and streaming to mark the spot where the toilet paper landed. On retrieving it, I found a message jammed in the center of the roll. It said, "Fire

looks good/NW line needs improving/radio us your needs//
sgd.//Betts, Fire Cache." After discussing our needs, Clyde
climbed the ridge overlooking Merced Lake where the radio had
an almost straight shot into the valley. Clyde told the Fire Cache
our fire had grown to an estimated 35 to 40 acres and still growing, and we desperately needed more manpower and rations.

The Fire Cache responded that they would do what they
could, but the park's biggest concern was the Mt. Gibson Fire
in the Mather District, which was several hundred acres and
growing. I also seem to remember a fire around Bridalveil
Falls that was visible from the valley floor. It was pretty clear
that we would be second best if we were competing with a
Tommy Tucker-managed fire or a fire that was visible from
the valley. We were out of sight, out of mind. We had all the
resources we were going to get.

On the tenth of September, it started to rain. Once again,
Mother Nature accomplished what man had been unable to
do—put an end to the fire season. We never got the help
we needed for the fire. Bob Hartung and I rode back to Tuolumne on a damp trail with no dust but with a number of
stories to tell. The vast majority of the rangers in the park had
been on the Gibson fire, and they pointedly let me know the
Mt. Gibson fire was the major Yosemite happening of 1960.
Merced Lake? What happened there?

I didn't have very much time to enjoy the Indian summer
at Tuolumne before I was faced with a big conundrum. I
was offered a permanent ranger position. It wasn't in Yosemite but in Bryce Canyon National Park, Utah. The offer was
complicated by the fact that the Curry Company had asked
me to be in charge of the ski patrol that winter. While I was
not excited by the added responsibility, I did want to ski and
had accepted their offer.

Decisions. I asked Dad's advice, and he said I needed to decide on my own since I was the one most affected. He said I should realize there were more NPS areas east of the Mississippi than there were west of the Mississippi, and my next offer could well be less attractive. Several people suggested I talk to Yosemite's new Assistant Chief Ranger Wayne Howe. Wayne had been Bryce's first chief ranger after it ceased being administered by Zion National Park. He carefully listened to my concerns and then spoke enthusiastically of his former park. While not as big as Yosemite, Bryce Canyon was very diverse and had a lot of challenges, which would present opportunities to learn.

Wayne said I would learn more about the other divisions because I would be working more closely with them, and it would look much better on my resume to have worked in several parks whenever I applied for a supervisory job. I listened attentively and with amazing restraint for that period of my life. I didn't say what was in my mind—that I was much more interested in learning about being a ranger than learning about other divisions. Nor did I say that I was not interested in being a supervisor; I just wanted to be a ranger.

I shook hands, thanked him for his time, and went for a long brooding walk. Little did I realize how this decision would affect the rest of my life. I walked to the barn and looked at the mules and horses until a couple of them came over to see if I had a treat. I walked up the route between the residence area and the corrals to the Yosemite Falls Trail, recognizing a few rocks I had dropped there after using them to balance my pack loads coming from Merced Lake in previous years. I walked to the falls, almost devoid of water, and to John Muir's cabin site, brooding, daydreaming, and speculating. By the time I got back to my car I had decided to accept the Bryce Canyon job. It was a decision made by the mind, not by the heart.

I worked in Tuolumne until the end of September. I was reporting to Bryce on October 20. Friends congratulated me for getting a permanent ranger job and slapped me on the back, but I glumly focused on what I would be missing, rather than being thankful for what I had already experienced. I went home for two weeks and sorted through my possessions. Mom pampered me, and I ate well. Then it was time to pack up and go. Right before I left, Dad gave me a nickel-plated Colt .380 semi-automatic pistol, which had been given to him as a "traveling" gun when he transferred from Yosemite to the Blue Ridge Parkway in 1946.

Dad said not to rely on it too much; it was more important to avoid problems by paying attention to what was going on around you. Don't think of the gun as support for getting out of a problem, he said. He told me I might come upon a deputy sheriff or highway patrolman who would need help on an isolated section of highway. He had always felt that if that happened to him, he would want to be able to do more than just be a good witness. But, he said, I would have to make up my own mind about that.

It was time to leave. Mom hugged and kissed me; Dad gave me a massive, arm-encircling embrace; and their oldest (and only) son drove onto 19th Avenue, headed for the Oakland Bay Bridge, then Yosemite, over Tioga Pass, and eventually to Bryce Canyon. Upon passing through Yosemite's Arch Rock Entrance Station, I slowed down and began paying attention to the rocks, trees, landscape, and scenery. My destination for the evening was Tioga Pass, but I wanted to take one last turn around the valley. I had already said my good-byes to friends and acquaintances and wasn't looking to repeat them. Saying "good-byes" had never been one of my easier tasks.

I just wanted to enjoy the scenery one more time and pay my respects to the places I had enjoyed for so many years. I drove up the south side of the valley, past Bridalveil Fall, through the Old Village, and beyond Camp Curry to Happy Isles. Turning around at the Happy Isles parking area, I was once again awe-struck by the sheer majesty of Half Dome. There was no traffic, so like a tourist, I stopped in the middle of the road and got out of my car to enjoy the view. When my vision swept to the steep, sometimes almost sheer exposure of Clouds Rest's north face, I shook my head in amazement to think I had ridden George onto that face on a ledge not nearly as wide as my VW bug.

Thinking of George, I drove by Indian Cave to Ahwahnee Meadows and the spot where George had made his dramatic car stop. I smiled, recalling the look on the driver's face as George magnificently reared up. I continued, still smiling, and made a quick turn around the NPS residence area, acknowledging each house my family had lived in, and then headed past Yosemite Lodge for Tuolumne Meadows and Tioga Pass. I relished the scenery and thought about George and my other four-legged friends and all they had taught me in the last four years.

From George I learned horses could become true partners if you let them, and Coyote and Socks taught me the value of patience and consistency. Bar Heart taught me that good-looking blonde females, with stunning bodies (mares, that is) can easily compete with their male counterparts. By contrast, Lady/Babe let me know that you should expect the unexpected and never get complacent. Cumulatively, they taught me that horses were like people, and each was an individual that should be evaluated only on his/her own actions.

By the time I got to Tioga Pass the weather had clouded over and it had become dark. Ferdinand greeted me ebulliently and predicted snow before morning. Once inside, he started the fire he had so carefully laid in the fireplace. As Ferdinand and I refreshed ourselves with cold beer that I supplied, the fire produced some great coals on which he grilled to perfection two steaks that he provided. It was an enjoyable evening highlighted by a fine supper and good conversation.

In the morning there was an inch of wet snow and more was rapidly falling. Were the Fates trying to tell me something? If so, I was too far committed to change course now. After a cup of coffee, I helped Ferdinand sweep snow and open the station early. I dusted off my VW, loaded my sleeping bag and overnight kit into the car, shook hands with Ferdinand and thanked him for his hospitality, and then headed down the road toward Bryce Canyon and destiny. The road was slick and treacherous for the first few miles, and it took all my attention and slow traveling to stay on the road. Finally snow turned to rain.

The farther I drove, the less time I spent thinking of Yosemite and the more I spent wondering about the future. I stopped for the night in Mesquite, Arizona, got a motel room, showered and went across the street for supper. I ordered a beer and after checking the menu, ordered a T-bone steak, rare. It cost $4.00, and up to that point it was the most I had paid for a meal.

Up early I continued on, driving through Zion National Park, impressed by the colorful Yosemite-like cliffs, and then breakfast of ham and eggs at Hatch, Utah. At Panguitch, Utah, I dragged Main Street a couple times. Not particularly impressed, I noted the hospital's location and looked over the

Emergency Room entrance. I bought two weeks of groceries and headed for Bryce.

Chapter 11

A Love Affair with Guns

BRYCE CANYON COULD NOT HAVE BEEN MORE DIFFERENT than Yosemite. Being in California, Yosemite was free flowing, liberal, and forgiving. Bryce, being in Utah, was quite the opposite. The Mormon Church was pervasive in its influence on thought, activity, and operations, both public and private. While this presence had mostly positive aspects, it nonetheless contributed to a "them" and "us" atmosphere that was felt more acutely by those with families and kids in school than it was by single people. My first few weeks were a real mixture of ups and downs, yeas and boos.

Bryce had about sixteen year-around employees, and unlike Yosemite, which had exclusive federal jurisdiction, Bryce Canyon had only proprietary jurisdiction, which is basically the same right a landowner has. In order to enforce laws other than park regulations, park rangers were commissioned as deputy sheriffs in the two counties that contained the park. I later learned that this jurisdictional issue caused real problems. Shortly after my arrival, there was a tri-county law enforcement meeting in Panguitch. In conjunction with the meeting, the FBI gave a firearms demonstration at a local range to promote the training opportunities they offered. As part of the program, an agent ran about twenty of us through two handgun courses.

Much to my surprise, I received the top scores in both exercises even though I used a NPS handgun I had never fired. I attributed the finish not so much to expertise on my part but to the other participants' lack of interest and/or lack of training. Skill at arms is only a minor facet in the law enforcement repertoire. However, in police circles, the value given firearms competence seems to rank far ahead of other important qualities. I mention this because of its influence on a future event—it prompted the purchase of my first handgun. Sometime earlier, I had come to the conclusion that a nickel-plated .380, semi-automatic pistol just didn't cut it as a primary defense/duty weapon.

After much debate with myself, reading and brooding, I decided on a Smith and Wesson, Model 19, .357 Combat magnum with a four-inch barrel, target hammer, and target trigger. Chief Ranger Stan Broman signed a statement saying I would be using it as a duty weapon so I got it at a "police" price, which was less than the over-the-counter price. It was a beautiful, precision piece of equipment with clean lines, bright blue finish, and crisp "out of the box" trigger pull. If it wasn't love at first sight, it was at least a very deep attachment.

I started down the slippery slope to becoming a firearms enthusiast, or as some call it, a "gun-nut." The chief ranger didn't help me avoid this when he gave me his two-year collection of assorted gun magazines, which I read with the eagerness of a newly pubescent teenage boy reading "girly" magazines. Like the fashion-conscious woman who buys a new purse and then has to purchase a whole new outfit to go with it, I had to select a holster for my Combat magnum and a belt to carry it on, and how I was going to carry extra ammunition, etc. More reading, brooding, and introspection helped me pass the long fall and winter evenings at Bryce without television. Hours upon hours were spent dry firing, drawing the weapon (after I decided on a holster), and developing gun-handling exercises. This occupied a major part of almost every evening and was time well spent in the long run.

As life settled down to a quiet routine I missed Yosemite more but concentrated on learning about Bryce and the country around it, including southern Utah and northern Arizona. I usually manned the visitor center information desk on Saturday and Sunday. Quiet duty, not many visitors, and lots of time to read. My other three days on duty were quiet as well: I checked the boundary for hunters, patrolled roads, and did chores.

Early in my tenure at Bryce the chief ranger decided to send me to the 1961 spring session of the NPS Training Center in Yosemite (aka Kowski College, for the training center director Frank Kowski). I showed up a couple of days early, picked a choice bunk at the Ranger Club dorm, renewed acquaintances, and had fine days of skiing at Badger Pass.

I was in a very good mood as things settled down to a routine of up early and breakfast at the Yosemite Lodge cafeteria where there was usually time to visit with ski friends, instructors for the training courses, or fellow classmates. Going to class was no problem—subjects were usually interesting, often well taught, and almost always evoked good class participation. I so enjoyed being in Yosemite.

Before returning to Utah I took the few days of annual leave and visited Mom and Dad in San Francisco where Mom pampered me with my favorite meals. A friend of Dad's who had been a firearms enthusiast and a consummate hand-loader had passed away, and Dad had bought all his reloading equipment from the widow. When I returned to Bryce I had several boxes of reloading equipment, accessories, powder, and lead. It turned out the Bryce chief ranger was an avid hand loader, and in short order he built a stand for the reloading tool, set everything up to reload, gave me a demo, and had me reloading. It took awhile to catch on, but in time I could load 200 rounds of .38 Special ammunition in an evening.

I worked hard to make good law enforcement cases, but too often the county attorney declined to prosecute. Everyone at Bryce was puzzled and annoyed by the decisions. Then a local maintenance worker explained that the Morman church hoped to work with the persons arrested and try to rehabilitate them, and the church felt this would be impossible to do if the accused were in jail.

Although I had Yosemite on my mind and felt that Bryce was sleepy hollow by comparison, the reality was that I learned a lot. At work, much of my time was spent on evening patrol (three or four in the afternoon until midnight or 1 a.m.). I became more comfortable with front country operations and more confident in a patrol vehicle. Recalling times riding with Dad, I soon developed better habits of patrol—checking the vehicle's equipment before starting shift, keeping the gas tank topped off, parking backed in to simplify prompt response, etc. I studied and refined my car stop procedure—preplanning location, minimizing pre-stop activity in order to maintain focus, and appearing open and relaxed while remaining in control and alert.

On nights I did late campground checks or night patrol, the .357 was a comfortable presence in my front pants pocket. In a nighttime quasi-felony stop when backup was thirty miles and a long half hour away, the magnum's mere presence gave me the confidence to overcome my inexperience and lack of training. The gun stayed hidden and was never displayed, but it helped make my voice commands convincing enough to gain the necessary cooperation.

My drive to become accomplished with a handgun came from watching Dad through the years, and my goal was to become as proficient as he was. I also believed that one should be as competent as possible with all the tools of his trade.

Many of my early memories revolve around my dad's guns. As with any American boy who worshipped his father, I was fascinated with the various firearms he had. One incident occurred when I was five. While Dad was a park ranger in Yosemite, my folks were hosting a potluck at our home in the valley. Some twenty folks were milling around our dining room, living room, and kitchen and enjoying pre-dinner drinks and conversation.

Three of Dad's friends were joking around and giving him a good-natured hard time. After one comment, Dad said in mock seriousness, "I don't have to take this anymore! Gerald, go get my gun!" Not many saw me leave the room. They all saw me come back.

I had gone into my parent's bedroom, opened Dad's closet door, and dragged the bench from Mom's vanity dresser into the closet. I took a stool from the corner, put it on the bench, climbed atop both, and retrieved Dad's gun from the highest shelf in the closet. It was a Colt Model 1911 semi-auto pistol in .38 Super. Dad stored it with the magazine full and the chamber empty. Earlier he had told me never to touch the gun unless he was present, and I promised I would not. But just now he had told me to get it, so I thought it must be okay.

I re-entered the living room, gun in hand. I held it by its grip, barrel toward the floor, away from me, and not pointing at anyone. All conversation stopped. The only sound was ice cubes clinking in glasses held by nervous guests.

Dad knelt down and accepted the gun. He took me in his 6'4" hug, his muscled arms snug but gentle around my shoulders, as he whispered to me alone, "Thank you, son, you did just right. You handled it just the right way. Thank you. C'mon, let's put it away for tonight."

In the summer of 1941, I observed numerous events I didn't fully appreciate until years later. We had moved 35 miles from the valley to Wawona where Dad was the district ranger. Despite the National Park Service's anti-gun sentiment at that time, Dad was ahead of his time and very proactive. He was not the least bit shy about practicing with his handgun right next to Wawona Ranger Station. There was a 200-man CCC camp at Wawona. Dad would often be practicing as truck loads of them were returning to Camp Wawona after a day building trails, cutting brush, constructing stone walls, and generally saving Yosemite much as the U.S. Cavalry had done several generations earlier

While the enrollees were all volunteers and usually caused little trouble, some of them periodically got drunk and disorderly in the valley. That never happened at Wawona where Dad was at times the only ranger on duty. One day Dad walked out of the Wawona General Store just as a group of CCC enrollees were walking in. May Gordon, the postmistress and store manager, smiled later when she told Dad the conversation she overheard: "Boy, I'd never mess with him. He's a big son of a bitch," said the first enrollee. "Yeah, and he's always practicing with that damn gun of his," his companion responded.

Years later, Bill Jordan, a retired Border Patrol officer, wrote "No Second Place Winner" in which he commented on the impact firearms proficiency can have in law enforcement. Jordan said, "...the confidence inspired by your knowledge of what you can do with a gun if necessary is bound to be reflected in your bearing. It is a confidence that cannot be counterfeited. It will enable you to go through many a tough spot with a poise and presence of mind, which may avert the actual opening of hostilities."

Dad understood this 20-plus years before Bill Jordan's book, and he also knew a person's reputation can be disquieting to potential adversaries. I always tried to be there when Dad was shooting. Usually there was an opportunity for me to shoot a few rounds. Concentrate though I did, I was a slow learner and despaired of ever being as good with a gun as Dad.

Dad's coolness, competence, poise, and proficiency made an indelible impression on my young mind and memory. Despite a few imperfections, such as colorful vocabulary and a sometimes-irascible temper, it is unlikely I could have had a better role model both as a person and as a ranger. The themes of "think," "look around you," "pay attention" were often repeated and soon became a part of me—my mantra in fact, although at that time I had yet to even hear the word.

Winter was long, days were short, activity minimal at Bryce Canyon, and with no TV to interrupt, I passed many long evening reading, thumbing through gun magazines, and dry firing, dry firing, dry firing. Sometimes I would dry fire while reading. I finished each dry fire session with a half dozen sequences of total concentration on correct sight picture and good technique. Then I carefully wiped my fingerprints off the bright blue of the revolver's finish, reloaded with live ammunition, holstered it, and put it away. I would make sure it was out of sight so I wouldn't be tempted to pick the gun up for just one more trigger pull and inadvertently pop off a live round. Luckily, with careful protocols, I never had an unintentional discharge. Maybe I should say, "Thank God for big favors."

In pursuit of firearms proficiency, I went to every police pistol competition and training I could. When I transferred to Yellowstone National Park, I continued going to police pistol competitions in the three-state area around Yellowstone and even to California. I was surprised at the number of competitors who said they didn't realize park rangers were law enforcement officers. Nor does park management realize this, I would think to myself.

Chapter 12

Never Look Back

AFTER WORK THE DAY BEFORE MY DAYS OFF DURING THE WIN-
ter at Bryce Canyon, I'd drive north, get a motel in Sandy,
and drive up to Alta Ski Area the next morning in time to be
one of the first on the ski hill. I wanted to be a solid, competent skier regardless of the terrain and comfortable in powder, crud, or nicely groomed slopes. In my years of downhill
skiing I never quite reached that goal but certainly had fun
trying.

As winter drifted into spring, I began to take short trips
when the weather was favorable. Early in April I had three
days off and a good weather forecast, so I decided to go to the
South Rim of the Grand Canyon. I visited all the viewpoints
along the South Rim Drive and was impressed once again by
the Grand Canyon's majesty. Stopping at the visitor center,
I met Jim McKown, a permanent ranger who was resigning
his job at Grand Canyon to seek a seasonal position in Yellowstone. Because of my attachment to Yosemite, I could
understand why someone would be drawn to Yellowstone.
Nonetheless, as hard as it was to get a permanent position, it
impressed me that McKown would resign to become a Yellowstone seasonal. I would run into Jim again a couple of
years later.

I also met Chief Ranger Lynn Coffin who asked how I enjoyed Grand Canyon. Very much, very impressive, I said. We visited for awhile, and I asked to be remembered to Bud Estey, Grand Canyon's assistant chief ranger, who had been the Lake Area ranger in Yellowstone in 1952 when I was the Pelican Cone Lookout. After I had been back at Bryce for a few weeks, I got a big surprise—I was offered a North Rim ranger position at Grand Canyon. I'll be damned! Everyone thought it was a great opportunity, but I worried about how it might affect getting to Yosemite. Since there were no vacant positions in Yosemite that I was qualified to fill, it meant that I had to wait another year before thinking of Yosemite. (At this time, policy dictated you remain in your new job at least one year before transferring to another park.)

I spent a day or so brooding and vacillating. Fret and stew, stew and fret; phone calls home, talk to Dad. Bottom line—it was my decision to make; my life to live; no sense burdening anyone else for advice. I decided on Grand Canyon and started repacking numerous half-unpacked boxes stored in closets and hidden under the bed. I told Mom and Dad, and they responded, "Go with enthusiasm, and don't look back. Yosemite will happen if it is meant to be."

I arrived in Grand Canyon National Park in May 1962 where I was a ranger on the North Rim. Summers were spent clearing fire roads, fighting forest fires, working hard, and learning a lot. When snow closed the North Rim, I moved to the South Rim and filled in for rangers on their days off and did a variety of miscellaneous chores, read, and visited with whoever came by. Those were relaxed times, quite the contrast to the park's busy, hectic summers and to Yosemite's year-round activities.

Occasionally I crossed paths with Jim Bailey, the ranger

in charge of the Havasupai area at the west end of the park. He had a federal firearms license and was usually trying to peddle one gun or another. I enjoyed handling whatever gun or guns he was offering at the moment. At that time he was overstocked with Smith and Wesson .44 magnum revolvers and said he would make me a good deal on one. He was sure I would enjoy its power and accuracy and claimed I would be prepared for just about anything in North America, etc., etc.

I looked over the guns, dry fired them, and finally told Jim I wasn't in the market for a bigger, more powerful gun. I said my Smith and Wesson .357 Combat magnum was enough gun for me, and I needed to master it before going to something bigger. Jim really wanted to sell a gun, and before he left I had the price down to $100 but had made no commitments. At the end of my shift the following day, Jim showed up with his guns and accessories. He came right to the point, asking, "Do you have $100 on you?" I pulled my wallet out, opened it, showing him three or four $100 bills, several twenties, and other bills. "Shit," he said. "Give me $100. Take whichever .44 you want. I'll order the reloading dies and get them to you as soon as they come in." I chose the Smith and Wesson .44 magnum with a four-inch barrel.

While I was adding to my arsenal, the National Park Service continued its ambivalence about firearms. Statements were made such as, "There is little need in the NPS to carry firearms." As part of this ambivalence, the NPS did not require training. Back in 1957 when I signed up for my first seasonal ranger position in Yosemite, I asked if I could check out a handgun for the summer in case I might have to put down an injured horse. No problem. They had me sign out for a .38 Special Smith and Wesson revolver with no more concern than if I were checking out a tape measure. No one asked if I could shoot or even if I was familiar with a handgun.

I did not particularly want Jim Bailey's .44, but it was one of the best bargains I ever made and the gun served me well the first day I shot it. I have sometimes wondered what I would have done without it when I transferred from Grand Canyon to Yellowstone. During my first ten years in Yellowstone when I was heavily involved in bear management, the .44's presence on my hip added to my poise and helped me to think calmly and clearly in many stressful bear situations.

Chapter 13

On-the-Job Training for Canyon Rescues

WHEN I TRANSFERRED TO YELLOWSTONE IN 1964, MY JOB became much more complex. As the Canyon sub-district ranger, I was first in command in an area known for visitors' fatal falls into the Grand Canyon of the Yellowstone. Because of conflicts between bears and people in the Canyon Campground, we trapped, drugged, and relocated bears. We also had to deal with the normal ranger duties, including fires, heart attacks, and automobile accidents.

I spent four years at Canyon. Similarly to my four years of college, I knew just about enough when I graduated to make the decisions I had to make when I started. I began my tenure without sufficient experience, but as each season progressed I learned more about the operation and more about canyon rescue. During each of my first two seasons a visitor fell into the canyon and died, and each was followed by a complicated body recovery. Less serious than fatal falls, but nonetheless challenging and educational, were the visitors who became stranded while climbing in the canyon. Each episode required a costly and potentially dangerous rescue, which consumed the time of people from all NPS divisions.

Canyon's ranger staff consisted of two permanent rangers supplemented by ten seasonal rangers who were mostly schoolteachers on summer break. This ranger staff handled each recovery expeditiously, and we succeeded not because of great rescue techniques but because we weren't intimidated by what we didn't know. It was our job and what we hired out to do. So we did it, and we learned.

Close cooperation of the other NPS divisions stationed at Canyon was a major part of every success. Maintenance Supervisor Ted Jump was in his mid-sixties, white haired, and deliberate in his movements. Mild mannered and slow talking, Ted knew his area and job thoroughly, and his subordinates respected him completely. George Downing, a Denver schoolteacher and long-time senior seasonal, was in charge of the Canyon Interpretive Division. He imbued his staff with a love of Yellowstone, the importance of interpretation, and the value of interdivisional cooperation.

When we got word someone was stranded in the canyon, routine operations came to a halt. Maintenance workers supplied manpower for hauling and lifting, and they directed traffic as needed. Uniformed interpreters kept sightseers away from the operation, explained what was happening to the witnessing public, and let them know it was very dangerous as well as illegal to climb in the Canyon between the brink of the Upper Falls and One Mile Hole. This stretch includes the steepest, sheerest, and most dramatic portions of the Grand Canyon of the Yellowstone.

Rangers scrambled to get ropes and rescue equipment to the site, size up the situation, and establish belay and anchor points. Off-duty rangers were called in to help. One ranger stayed free of the rescue operation to handle other calls that might come in. Adjacent districts were notified and asked to extend their patrols into our area. When everything was ready a ranger would rappel down to the stranded individual and secure him onto the belay rope, and then the person was raised. During my tenure at Canyon I assumed this role— partly because I was the most experienced of the Canyon crew and partly because I did not like to ask anyone to do something I wouldn't do.

When the rescue was completed the illegal canyon intruder was issued a citation that required a mandatory appearance before U.S. Magistrate James W. Brown at park headquarters. Judge Brown, as he was referred to, held court in his office, which furnished ample room for his desk, an easy chair, and an impressive array of law books behind his desk. It became quite crowded with the addition of a half dozen straight back chairs for the defendants and their legal counsel, and for the citing ranger and a ranger who acted as prosecutor.

Brown's office was in his residence, a classic stone house that dated back to the days when the U. S. Cavalry patrolled Yellowstone. Located near the lower end of the Mammoth Terraces, it was close to the site of McCartney's "Hotel" where in 1877, Nez Perce warriors, retreating through the park, shot a visitor as he stepped out of the hotel's front door. Judge Brown was a crusty, independent soul who had his own ideas of what the fine should be regardless how time consuming, expensive, or dangerous the rescue was.

With a decided penchant for lecturing rangers as frequently as he did the violators, Brown's standard fine for climbing in the canyon was $15. While $15 was worth more in 1966 than it is today, it was hardly fair compensation for the time a ranger spent dodging falling rocks while in the canyon. Nor did I think it was reasonable compensation for the six to ten employees it took away from their regular work. In my slightly prejudiced point of view, it was certainly not sufficient to repay a field ranger for the angst suffered from spending a half-day at park headquarters filling court responsibilities.

Not all my trips down into the Canyon were to retrieve people; some were made to retrieve "things" people had dropped. One day we received a frantic request from two young ladies from France. They were very attractive, slender, and well-endowed, and they spoke fluent English with a delightful accent. It would have been difficult for any healthy American male to refuse them anything in his power to give.

One of the young ladies had dropped her purse and it had slid to the canyon rim, over the rim, down a sheer two-hundred-foot wall, and onto a long, steep slope that ended in the Yellowstone River. The purse had opened and scattered its contents, including both of their passports, $3,500 in traveler's checks, $455 in cash, and an address book with the names, addresses, and phone numbers of their friends, sponsors, and contacts in the United States. Considering such valuables, public service retrieval seemed appropriate whether the person who dropped the purse was young, old, homely, handsome, grouchy, or gracious.

I felt this was a good time to try out a recently acquired piece of climbing equipment—a pair of Jumar ascenders, which are lightweight aluminum frames about ten inches long, four inches wide, and a couple of inches thick. The climbing rope is threaded around the Jumar, which can be slid up the rope when the Jumar does not bear weight. When weight is applied, a ratchet in the Jumar locks the device in place on the rope and it can be used as a step. I was familiar with Jumars from my time in Yosemite but was not adept in their use.

Several Canyon rangers and I gathered our climbing gear and drove to the site. We set up our anchor and belay points, and I rappelled down to retrieve the valuables. It was a routine trip down with rock fall being modest and not as terrifying as some trips in the canyon. By maintaining tension on my ropes I was able to stay upright and move around the area sloping to the river.

In short order I found the purse and most of the contents—success beyond my wildest expectations. I climbed back to the base of the 200-foot drop and prepared to Jumar up to the rim. Then reality gave me a perspective. I unhooked from the rappel rope but stayed on belay. I had planned to use the rappel rope to Jumar up and to keep the belay as an additional safety, but as is often the case, practice does not always keep pace with theory. The system didn't work for me; I needed three hands and arms and had only two.

After a half hour of frustrating, sweat-producing effort managing the ropes, I had to ask Ted Jump for assistance, and I was mortified. Previously when Ted's crew had pulled me out of the canyon it had been a joint operation to rescue a visitor or to recover a body. This time it was due to my own ineptness and miscalculation. Ted temporarily stopped a couple of jobs and within half an hour had six men on site. They and the two rangers on the rim easily pulled me up and out. I arrived on top relieved, safe and sound, but very embarrassed by my ineptness with the Jumars. I thanked Ted profusely as he left with his crew.

The French ladies were ecstatic and offered to pay us for our efforts. My reply was "absolutely not, thank you." By this time I had regained a bit of composure and a slight semblance of humor. The French president Charles de Gaulle had recently been quite anti-American in his rhetoric. This prompted me to say, "I hope President de Gaulle appreciates the effort our government made to return French property."

"We don't know what Charles de Gaulle thinks, but we appreciate what you did," they answered in unison as they both gave me a hug and polite, appreciative smooches on my cheek. Being a late bloomer in my relations with the opposite sex, my first response was to blush, stammer, experience an accelerated heart rate, and feel a rise in temperature. Sometime later I re-read the NPS policy on receiving gratuities from park visitors. It said something to the effect that any gifts received should be returned. I had missed a golden opportunity; I could have returned those kisses. So ended my first effort at international relations.

Canyon rescue attempts were almost never joking matters. During this period, a boy fell into the canyon between Grandview Point and the junction of the North Rim Drive and the Canyon Village Road. Erosion through the millennium had formed a bowl-shaped cliff out of the decomposed rhyolite lava rock of the canyon. The sixty-degree slope of the bowl started ten to twenty feet below the rim. It then funneled down six- to eight-hundred vertical feet to a final drop of two-hundred feet into the whitewater rapids of the Yellowstone River.

The fallen boy was lodged precariously against one of the rock outcroppings two hundred feet above the river. I decided I would rappel to the victim, and rangers Bud Ross and Pat Moran would bring the Stokes rescue litter down on my rappel rope after I had secured the victim. We quickly reviewed the plan, the rigging, and the procedure. While we were operating short of equipment, training, and experience, there was no reluctance to do the job. We shared a quiet confidence that Canyon rangers could accomplish whatever was necessary.

Tension mounted as we made our final preparations. I

thought I had prepared for this moment almost my whole life. Little did I realize as I dropped over the edge how unprepared I really was. Raised in Yosemite National Park, I had listened to climbing and rescue stories as early as I could recall. While going to law school in San Francisco I attended Sierra Club climbing sessions open to the public, and as a seasonal ranger in Yosemite I climbed with experienced rangers.

When the National Park Service Training Center in Yosemite held rescue sessions I attended whenever I could. I always volunteered to be the victim—not only did I get to experience how it felt from the victim's point of view, I also got to observe the whole operation from start to finish. I didn't think I would ever become a real climber but felt I was at least a good novice rescuer mostly because of my interest in knots and packing.

As I rappelled into the canyon, I was reminded how Yellowstone's decomposed rhyolite lava differed from Yosemite's granite. The weight of the rappel rope alone would dislodge rocks and scree, which seemed to be coming by me at supersonic speed. Pebbles rattling off my aluminum hardhat made me thankful that they weren't bigger. By the time I reached the victim, I was sweating profusely, as much from the emotional strain of dodging rocks as from physical exertion, but I was too late. Bruised, battered, and dust covered, the 16-year-old boy was already dead. With the majority of his life ahead of him, an enthusiastic misstep had ended it prematurely, 600 feet down in the Grand Canyon of the Yellowstone.

I got a sling around the body and secured it to the rappel rope. I signaled the rim that it was not a rescue but a body recovery. Ross and Moran traded first aid gear and blankets for a body bag and started down with the Stokes litter. Then my problems began in earnest. If rock fall had been a serious concern when I came down, it was terrifying now as all sizes of rocks were knocked loose and came streaking toward me like falling stars. I couldn't decide which was better—to watch the progress of the litter crew and dodge the rocks I saw hurtling towards me, or to hide behind the rock outcropping, cowering, head down and unable to see anything. I tried both options. When the others arrived, we placed our young victim in the body bag, secured him in the Stokes litter, and raised him back to the rim.

Older, wiser, more experienced, and retired now, I am still impressed by the hard-charging, odds-defying energy of youth. Those were simpler times in 1964. When you put on the uniform, you became a ranger and learned the job by doing it. No prior certification was required other than to have an able body and the desire to do the job. During my first four years in Yellowstone I recovered two bodies and more than a half dozen live subjects from the Canyon of the Yellowstone. Some of the rescues lasted a few hours, but one took a large part of two days and another lasted from dawn to dusk. On one occasion I had to dodge rocks for almost two tense, stressful hours.

But the scariest rescue was over and done in less than fifteen minutes. In Class A uniform, including Stetson and tie, I hardly broke a sweat and didn't even get my shiny boots dusty. On an otherwise fine early fall day, I was out and about to see and be seen. I drove out of Canyon Village, reached the North Rim Drive junction, and then turned left to drive to Inspiration Point. There was only one car parked there, and I almost didn't stop, not wanting to intrude on the car's occupants' solitary enjoyment of the canyon. But since the specific purpose of my patrol was to contact people, I stopped and got out.

Inspiration Point juts over the Canyon rim and offers a spectacular view of the Canyon and the Yellowstone River several hundred feet below. It is located well below the parking area and is reached by a series of cement steps that drop steeply for about 100 yards to the point. The steps go past several landings on which benches are built beside and perpendicular to the trail for sightseers to rest when climbing up or down. A four-foot high, two-rail iron pipe fence lines the steps and landings.

I was enjoying the fresh morning air as I started down the steps to the viewpoint. Two women were sitting on the bench nearest the view point, their backs to the Canyon, visiting, while a young girl about four years old was close by, playing with a doll. The women were focused on each other. The little girl appeared content playing with her doll, alternately putting it down and picking it up. In defensive-shooting circles, my state of mind would be referred to as Condition Yellow—relaxed but aware of your surroundings.

The little girl, content in her world with her doll, placed it on the cement foundation that rimmed the bench alcove. Out of the corner of my eye I noticed the little girl stoop down to pick up the doll, and as she reached for it, she accidentally knocked the doll off the cement foundation and onto the steeply sloping wall of the canyon. The doll slid a short distance and came to rest a few feet down the slope. The resourceful little girl knelt down and reached under the lower rail of the pipe fence, but the doll was beyond her reach. The women remained absorbed in their conversation.

I CONTINUED WALKING BUT WAS NOW SOMEWHERE BETWEEN Condition Yellow and Condition Orange (when you focus more intently on a general area). I was now watching the two women, the little girl, the nearby doll, and the steep slope on which the doll lay. The slope was around seventy-degrees for 20 yards and then dropped several hundred feet straight down to the Yellowstone River.

I was fully in Condition Orange as I watched the little girl tug on the skirt of the woman seated nearest to her to get the woman's attention. The woman was still engrossed in conversation. I couldn't hear what she said, but her body language indicated it was something like "Darling, it isn't polite to interrupt when adults are talking. I'll be with you in just a minute." I was now striding rapidly down the steps. The little girl turned away from the woman and looked intently at her doll. I started running as I saw the little girl duck between the cement foundation and the bottom rail of the pipe fence.

Condition Red, intense focus, fully alert, all arrived like a shot of epinephrine straight into my heart. I took the steps two at a time and may well have taken the last five in a single leap. I grabbed the top railing of the fence and vaulted over it just as the little girl slipped and started sliding down the slope on her butt, toward the cliff.

As my feet hit the ground I reached out and grabbed the hem of the little girl's skirt with my left hand a nano-second before it slid beyond my grasp. The little girl cried out, startled by the sudden stop. Her mother jumped up from the bench as I pulled the girl up to me, lifted her up, and handed her over the railing to the mother. "Watch her!" I snapped. "I have been," the mother replied. I gave her a brief, dirty look, thinking but not saying, "Bullshit, lady."

The doll, looking helpless and innocent, laid on its back a step below me. I realized the situation wouldn't be over until the little girl had her doll back so I took a deep breath, let go of the railing, and took a cautious step to the doll, slowly bending down and picking it up. I made it back to the railing, climbed over, and handed the doll to the woman holding the sobbing child in her arms. Neither woman met my eyes as I said, "Watch her more closely from now on." I walked away without waiting for a response.

When I got back to my vehicle, I dropped onto the driver's seat and trembled for five minutes. Brain throbbing and pulse racing, I relived the incident, interrupted by flashes of "what ifs"— what if I had gone to Grand View first…what if I had not stopped…what if I had gotten there a few seconds later… what if I had lost my footing when I reached for the doll…? I spent the rest of the day avoiding people. Several years later I told the story to a group of friends. "Just another day in the life of a ranger," one said as I finished the story. "More like fifteen minutes," I replied. "I couldn't have taken a whole day of that."

Then again, there *were* more days "of that," as with the Marita Eilers's incident.

Chapter 14

A Fateful Visit for Three German Women

MARITA EILERS, A TWENTY-THREE YEAR-OLD GERMAN WOMAN, was touring the western United States in the fall of 1965. She and her two traveling companions, both young German women like Marita, stayed overnight in Gardiner, Montana, the night of October 31st. They registered in a small hotel overlooking Park Street and told the proprietor they wanted to visit Yellowstone the next day. Being familiar with Yellowstone, the hotel proprietor knew that Yellowstone usually closed the roads for the winter on October 31st. He called park management and found out the roads were being left open because there had been so little snow. The roads were bare and dry. He was told his guests needed to be self-sufficient and prepared since there was no gas available and no facilities open. After breakfast, with lunches packed and their car topped off with gas, the three German women started their tour of Yellowstone.

Weeks before the travel season had been extended, the chief ranger had called an "all rangers meeting" to critique the summer's operation. This was scheduled in Mammoth, park headquarters and was to start at 9 a.m. on November 1st. I was in my second year as Canyon sub-district ranger. Not being partial to meetings, I told my supervisor, South

District Ranger Bob Morey, that I thought it was a bad idea to have every ranger in Mammoth when visitors were touring the park. I even volunteered to miss the meeting and go on patrol, but Bob said the chief wanted all the rangers at the meeting. "Besides," Bob replied, "There shouldn't be that much traffic, and maintenance has crews working in each area. They'll let us know if we're needed."

Being a good soldier, I dutifully showed up in Mammoth. I enjoyed catching up with the rangers from other sections of the park whom I had not seen since the spring ranger conference. The meeting was routine and covered nothing memorable. Then in mid-afternoon, we got word that a woman had fallen into the canyon and was unconscious or dead. No one had been able to reach her to find out. Morey and I immediately left for Canyon in separate vehicles. Traffic was light; there was no need for red lights or sirens and while Bob went to the accident scene, I went to the rescue cache for ropes, rescue gear, first aid equipment, and a body bag—just in case.

The incident had occurred at Lookout Point on the North Rim of the Grand Canyon of the Yellowstone. From the parking area, a wide paved trail with rock steps and rock railing went a hundred yards to Lookout Point, where one got a magnificent view of the Canyon and Yellowstone River, almost a thousand feet below. A narrower, paved trail branched off to the right a short distance down the Lookout Point Trail and led to Red Rock Point about an eighth of a mile away and a few hundred feet above the river.

I met Morey about half way to Red Rock Point where he was talking with two young women. Lookout Point had been the ladies' first view of the canyon, and they had all been thrilled and awed by the view. When they started for Red Rock Point, Marita ran ahead of her friends. When she reached a side canyon, Marita called back to the others, "Oh, this is so beautiful. I want to get closer." They told her to wait, but Marita stepped off the trail and started down the steep slope toward the rim of the side canyon. The footing on the soft sedimentary deposit looked stable but it was akin to walking on ball bearings. Her friends said Marita slid, skidded, and almost glissaded down the slope, and when she hit the edge, she plunged head first into the side canyon.

I checked the rest of the trail, and it was apparent the best access to the side canyon was the route Marita had taken. When I got to the point, I was told by a maintenance worker, "She hasn't moved in two hours." A couple of hundred feet below us, the German girl lay stretched out on the floor of the side canyon, face down. Her head and left arm hung over the edge of the side canyon, above the open maw of the main canyon.

I hurried back to where Marita had gone off the trail. Ted Jump was talking with the two women. They had stopped crying, and Jump decided to take them to his residence where they could be with his wife, Tilly. I thought that was a great idea as Tilly was a Montana farmwoman who was as outgoing as Ted was reserved.

Above the trail were several substantial lodgepole pines. I used three of them to make an anchor for the ropes—one to rappel from and one to assist the person who would belay me. I had two 300-foot and several 150-foot climbing ropes, miscellaneous slings, and a variety of carabiners and hardware. I tied a 300-foot rope into the anchor and threw it down the slope as my rappel rope. Morey and one of Ted's crew who said he had belayed once before were working on the belay station with the other 300-foot rope.

I loaded a pack with two 150-foot climbing ropes, a first aid kit, two portable bottles of oxygen, extra climbing gear, and a body bag. The last item was the only one I thought I would need. I tied a sling rope diaper seat around myself and hooked it into the rappel rope. I shouldered the pack, snugged it tight and put on a state-of-the-art climbing helmet. It was the only such helmet in Yellowstone and had been purchased the previous October with "end of the year funds" because of the number of canyon rescues we had.

Little did I know how important that helmet would be to me. I took a couple of deep breaths, mentally phrased a silent prayer, and made eye contact with both Morey and my belayer. They nodded, and I stepped back and started rappelling. It was a jerky and uneven trip down due the treacherous footing, knocking rocks and scree loose, trying to get slack from my overly conscientious belayer, and trying to ignore my growing stress. I stopped at the rim of the side canyon and, after sizing up what lay ahead and catching my breath, I dropped over the edge and made it to the bottom. With my feet on the solid floor of the side canyon, I unhooked from the rappel rope and started carefully and slowly down the steep slope toward the main canyon, often dodging rocks knocked loose by my belay rope.

Continuing carefully to Marita, I knelt next to her motionless body and looked for any sign of life: none. I called her name several times, not really expecting a response and got none. She lay partially over the edge of the side canyon and precariously close to tipping into the main canyon. While I usually wasn't bothered by heights, I was unsure of the ground's stability where I was kneeling and felt reluctant to lean too far out. I asked the belayer for "tension." When I felt pressure on my waist, I inched closer to Marita and grabbed her left shoulder to stabilize her body's location and pulled her right arm as close and parallel to her torso as I could.

Kneeling by her shoulders, I yelled "TENSION," took a deep breath, leaned out over her and grabbed her left elbow with my left hand. With my right, I got a solid hold of her hair to keep her neck in line with her body as I heaved myself backwards and rolled her onto her back. This put her body on the relatively stable surface of the side canyon floor.

As my breathing returned to normal, I examined her for signs of life and found none. No pulse, no sign of breathing, and her eyes were glazed over. There was a prominent depression in her skull over her left eyebrow, but I noted that even in death, Marita Eilers was a strikingly attractive woman. I checked again for signs of life and again found none. I called to Bob Morey, "Individual is 10-7." In radio protocols, "10-7" means "Out of Service." As I used it, it was a somewhat gentler way to say "deceased."

Daylight doesn't last long in November, and it was starting to get dark as I rolled Marita into the body bag and secured it. It was almost fully dark by the time I dragged her to the rappel landing. I knew the body would stiffen with rigor mortis by morning, but I felt it would be easier, safer, and more practical to haul the stiffened body up in the body bag rather than to complicate the operation with a Stokes rescue litter. It also made sense to wait until morning and daylight to haul out the body, and I suggested this to Morey.

"Are you sure she's dead?" was Bob's response. I unzipped the body bag and checked everything I knew to check. "Yes." "We need to do it tonight," was Bob's immediate response. I paled at the prospect as we had already pressed our luck too far. "If we do it tonight, Bob, I'll have to come up and get a Stokes litter and that's too dangerous in the dark." "Are you sure she's dead?" Once again I checked everything, and said "Yes, she's dead." "Okay, if you're sure she's dead." "I'm sure." While they re-rigged the rappel rope to haul me out, I made sure Marita was laid out straight. Now it was fully dark.

I was on belay when a rock the size of my head fell from about twenty feet and hit me square on top of my climbing helmet. The impact knocked me down a foot or so. If I hadn't been on belay with tension, the blow would have knocked me tumbling down the side canyon, racing the rock to the main canyon. If the rock had hit a hand, arm, or shoulder, I'm sure it would have broken the bone. As it was, I only had a sore neck for a few days.

I was relieved when I got to the trail and went "off belay." Several of Ted's crew touched my shoulder as they passed, and I thanked each one for his efforts. Bob once again asked me privately if I was sure she was dead. "Yes," I answered unequivocally, and we agreed to return at seven in the morning. At home, I drank a beer, took a shower as hot as I could stand until the tank was out of hot water, had another beer, ate something and went to bed emotionally and physically exhausted. The next morning my neck was stiff and sore, but I was at Lookout Point by 7 a.m.

It was a cool twenty degrees and foggy. I wore a winter jacket and insulated gloves and was barely comfortable. Ted's crew was already there, bundled up and hunched over, their hands in their pockets when they weren't passing a thermos of coffee around. Bob and I exchanged greetings, and our breath vapors added to the density of the fog surrounding us. At the rescue site, I checked the rigging and was soon dropping into the side canyon. At the bottom, I took off my gloves and walked over to the body bag, dragging my belay rope with me.

When I reached out to move the body bag, *it felt warm!* *My heart raced.* I hyperventilated and trembled. Had I left an injured, live person out overnight? I was sweating; I was chilled, all at the same time. My hand was trembling so frantically I could hardly grasp the zipper. When I finally got the bag unzipped, Marita's glazed-over eyes stared at me exactly as they had the last time I saw her. Her features remained pale and covered with dust. There was no pulse. No breathing. No sign of life. No different than last night—except her body was stiff and straight. I had been silent and motionless so long that Morey called down, "Jerry, are you okay?" "Yeah, okay," was my muffled reply as the fog lifted a bit and visibility improved.

For the first time I noticed the ground under the bag was wet. There was a slight stream of water running down the canyon wall, and the water was warm. A thermal feature on the rim that I had not noticed yesterday apparently overflowed during the night. The water had warmed the bottom of the bag. I was so relieved that I hardly remember the rest of the day. The evacuation of the body without having to use the Stokes litter was uncomplicated and almost routine, and we were done by mid-morning. We turned the body over to the representative of a Livingston, Montana, mortuary that Marita's parents had contracted to ship their daughter's body back to Germany.

I never told Morey why I was silent so long after going off rappel. It was quite some time before I told anyone what had happened. I continued to be haunted by the fear that in my zeal to keep an evacuation simple, I could have left an injured person out overnight, unattended. The panic I experienced after feeling the warmth of the body bag stayed with me for years. It resurfaced frequently in my dreams (nightmares?). My dad used to say, "When you've had a bad experience, you have to tell the story again and again until you get enough comfort to make up for the misery you had experiencing it." He was right, as usual. I guess that's why I'm retelling the story here.

Chapter 15

Barney Sanders's Tie (or, A Not-So-Good Day in Yellowstone)

IN THE SPRING OF 1968, I RETURNED FROM A THOROFARE SKI patrol with Rangers Tom Milligan and Terry Danforth to find I had been offered the job of North District Ranger in Grand Teton National Park. It would be a promotion in title and pay—as well as a transfer out of Yellowstone. In the eyes of many, I was on the fast track to NPS success. From my perspective, success was being a good ranger, not a highly paid administrator, and after reflection, I turned down the job.

In my effort to get back to Yosemite I had accepted the Canyon Sub-District job before I was ready and I did not want to make the same mistake again. Besides, I wanted to stay in Yellowstone. I was given an appointment to meet with Superintendent John McLaughlin who told me I was jeopardizing my NPS career by turning down the Teton job. When I persisted, the superintendent placed a letter in my personnel file saying he had counseled me about the consequences of turning down the Teton offer. It was one of the most significant decisions I ever made.

I wound up working in Yellowstone for thirty-two years. I had to retire in 1995 because of newly mandated age requirements. My only regret was that I didn't have another thirty-two years to work there. I will leave it to others to comment on whether I was ever a good ranger.

Instead of going to Teton, I became the (Yellowstone) Lake sub-district ranger in the spring of 1968 and remained in that position through the fall of 1975. Not only did I adapt to Yellowstone, it became the center of my universe. Yosemite was my first love as it was a wonderful place to grow up and a great place to learn the ranger's trade. It will always rank high in my heart, mind, and soul.

But more and more I listened to the voices of Yellowstone—the distant crying of loons on remote lakes, sandhill cranes challenging me when I rode too close to their nests, the bugling of elk in the fall, and the guttural grunting of bull bison during the rut.

Yosemite reminded me of a stunningly beautiful sixteen-year-old girl: what you saw was what you got. By contrast, Yellowstone was an attractive, mature woman with a depth that you continually tried to fathom, but you would never know all you wanted—or even fully understand what you knew.

The years at Canyon taught me a lot and set standards for growth and development that I seldom equaled and never surpassed in my subsequent twenty-eight years in Yellowstone. I arrived at Canyon a novice in canyon rescue; I left a journeyman. When I came to Canyon I had seen a total of one grizzly bear; I left a practiced, experienced, and careful trapper/handler of both black bears and grizzlies.

At Lake I worked with Barney Sanders, who for several years had been a seasonal park ranger. In the winters, Barney was a teacher and a wrestling coach in the Fort Morgan, Colorado, school system. A muscular man in his early to mid-fifties, Barney always reported for duty looking sharp in his meticulously clean uniform. Barney's real name was Clarence, which he detested. However, thanks to Yellowstone's personnel office, which lacked a sense of humor and didn't acknowledge nicknames, Barney's nametag labeled him Clarence E. Sanders.

On one early summer day, Sanders had the 6 a.m. to 3 p.m. road patrol shift. Characteristically, this shift started in the Fishing Bridge campground where the ranger counted and recorded the number of tent and trailer campers. Like any bureaucracy, the NPS placed great value on collecting and keeping statistics. Upon entering the campground, Barney checked the bear trap set by the previous night's patrol. The trap door was down, indicating there could be something in the trap.

Barney cautiously peeked around to look through the vented front gate. From the back of the trap a huge grizzly charged and slammed into the gate. The large culvert trap shook and vibrated like a kite in a crosswind. The angry bear blew snot and saliva through the vents as he repeatedly bit and clawed them. At first rush Barney jerked back but not before his meticulously clean tie was covered with bear slobber. He hurried back to Lake Ranger Station, traded his station wagon for a pickup with a towing hitch, and then hauled the trap with the still irate grizzly to the Lake Incinerator area.

He was locking the gate to the incinerator behind him when the Communication (Comm) Center called "Lake Patrol." Barney answered and was told the Lake Hospital ambulance was responding to Fishing Bridge Campground for a possible heart attack and requested ranger assistance. Barney raced to the campground and arrived almost simultaneously with the hospital's ambulance. Barney's luck did not improve as the patient turned out to be a huge middle-aged man who was a challenge to lift. Barney was positioned at the man's shoulder, and as he and three others responded to a nurse's command to lift on three, his tie suffered yet another insult. It was sprayed with the partially digested contents of the man's last meal.

Shortly after coming on duty, I was at the incinerator checking the trapped grizzly and trying to determine the bear's sex, weight, and identity so we could decide what to do with it. On the radio, I heard Old Faithful patrol notify the Comm Center that he had the subjects of an APB (All Points Bulletin) under surveillance, and there was not enough manpower on duty to contact the subjects. He said he would follow the suspect vehicle until sufficient manpower gathered to make a safe stop.

The APB was for five (three male, two female) hippie-type, Vietnam war protesters who had bombed a University of Wisconsin lab allegedly involved in war-related research. The bomb had detonated on the weekend when no one was supposed to be in the lab. However, the blast killed a lab technician and considerably damaged the building. The suspects were considered armed and dangerous and were driving a dark colored, older model, four-door sedan with outdated Wisconsin license plates. Extreme caution was advised. I listened only half attentively to the radio traffic as I was more interested in trying to read the ear tags on the trapped grizzly.

My attention locked in on the radio transmissions when the suspects were reported headed toward Lake rather than leaving the park through the South Entrance. I dug into my daypack for my .357 revolver, extra ammunition, and handcuffs, and strung them on my belt as I told the Comm Center I was heading south. I asked Old Faithful and Grant Village patrols to continue north out of sight to make sure the suspects didn't double back. A little later Barney said he was southbound from Lake in his patrol car.

I crossed paths with the suspect vehicle at Arnica Creek and tried not to arouse their suspicion by staring but noticed the seating arrangement and how much the vehicle and its occupants matched the APB. As soon as they were out of sight, I U-turned and followed them while trying to come up with a plan. Their actions cut short my deliberations.

The suspects pulled off the road at "Hard Road To Travel" overlook, a quarter-mile-long parking area where travelers access Yellowstone Lake. My options suddenly went from many down to just two—make immediate contact or not. The suspect car had pulled into the south end of the parking area, and everyone was still inside the car. A couple of vehicle lengths north were three visitor cars with a number of people, including young kids, standing around talking and enjoying the view. I had only a second to make a decision as I was certain the suspects knew they had been spotted and were being monitored. Although a less than ideal situation for a contact, I decided that if I could keep the suspects in their car until back-up arrived, it might be safer for the visitors nearby. There would be less chance for them to get involved, hurt, or be taken hostage.

Decision made, right or wrong, I rapidly accelerated toward the suspect vehicle and turned on my top-mounted revolving red light and siren to focus attention and warn the visitors something non-routine was happening. I advised Comm Center that I was making contact with the suspects. I slammed on my vehicle's brakes and stopped partially in front of them so they couldn't accelerate away but would have to back-up first. I bailed out of my vehicle, drew my

.357 as I ran around the back of it, and charged toward the suspects. In a loud and, I hoped, commanding voice, I said "I'm a federal law enforcement officer. DON'T MOVE! DO EXACTLY AS I SAY, OR I'LL SHOOT!" I stopped beside the driver, close enough to see inside the vehicle and keep all five occupants in view. The windows were rolled down which made communication easier. I held my .357 in a two-handed grip, pointed at the suspects, moving from individual to individual. All eyes and attention were focused on me—or maybe it was on the muzzle of the .357.

I REPEATED THAT I WAS A FEDERAL LAW ENFORCEMENT OFFICER and would shoot anyone who moved without my permission. Since I had their attention, I said they strongly resembled people wanted for serious felonies involving death and major property damage and were reported to be armed and dangerous. I added that if they weren't the wanted persons, I would apologize for the harsh treatment and for pointing a gun at them, but in the meantime for their safety they should do exactly what I told them. I was relieved when they were cooperative and even more relieved hearing sirens coming rapidly closer both from the north and south.

Barney arrived first and pulled behind the Wisconsin car, jumped out of his vehicle with a shotgun, racked a round into the chamber, and covered the passenger side. When Grant and Old Faithful patrols arrived we got the individuals out of their car one at a time, handcuffed them, frisked them, and sat them down in the parking lot. We notified the Comm Center and Law Enforcement Office, who told us to take them to Lake Ranger Station and fingerprint them. Jim Protto, the assistant law enforcement officer, was headed there. When Protto compared these prints with the prints reproduced on the wanted posters, none matched. These were not the people who were wanted. The Comm Center ran record checks on all of the individuals, and there were no warrants outstanding, only speeding tickets and parking tickets. Even the outdated license plate was resolved when we found new plates sent to the driver/owner by the Wisconsin Department of Motor Vehicles on the front seat of the car. They just hadn't gotten around to putting them on.

So I did what I said I would do when I first contacted them—I apologized. They said they understood. The driver added they were going to visit more national parks and asked if I could I give them a note explaining they weren't bad guys—kind of a Monopoly get-out-of-jail-free pass. I told them I couldn't do that but suggested they get shaves and haircuts so they looked more like the pictures on their driver's licenses and less like the wanted posters. The driver said they would get the plates on right away, but he wasn't so sure about the shaves and haircuts. We shook hands, and they departed.

When we had first brought the Wisconsin folks into the ranger station, Barney had rushed to the front office to phone the Comm Center with the information to run checks on. Next to the front office was the public contact room where a park aide was behind the information desk talking to several concession employees. One of the employees was complaining loudly about a parking ticket. He went on and on in a loud, demanding voice. The young, first-year park aide tried repeatedly to explain, but the irate employee was on a self-righteous rampage.

When he finished with the Comm Center, Barney stepped into the public contact room to help the park aide. On seeing Barney, the complainant yelled, "That's the ranger that's

National Park Service ranger Gerald Mernin holds his nine-month-old son, Jerry, in Yosemite National Park, 1933.

Seasonal ranger Jerry Mernin at Yosemite's Tioga Pass entrance station, 1959.

Jerry Mernin on George, his partner on many Yosemite adventures.

Jerry Mernin (right) assists on a helicopter relocation of a grizzly bear in Yellowstone. Mernin was heavily involved in the park's bear management in the 1960s and 1970s.

Jerry Mernin stands by a bear trap in Yellowstone's Canyon area, mid-1960s.

*Yellowstone rangers, circa 1980: Front row, left to right: Dunbar Susong, Bechler Area Ranger; Dave Mihalic, Old Faithful District Ranger; Tom Hobbs, Chief Park Ranger, Mammoth; Norm Bishop, Resource Management Specialist, Mammoth; Bob Mahn, Lake Area Ranger. Second row: Tom Black, Emergency and Air Operations Specialist, Mammoth; Terry Danforth, North District Ranger, Mammoth; Stu Orgill, West Entrance Ranger; John Donaldson, South Entrance Ranger; Bob Mihan, Law Enforcement Officer, Mammoth; Randy Fehr, Mammoth Area Ranger; Duane McClure, Grant Village Area Ranger. Third row: Doug Barnard, West District Ranger, Madison; Tim Blank, Lake District Ranger: Jim Sweaney, Supervisory Forestry Technician, Mammoth; Marv Miller, Northeast Area Ranger; Helen McMullin, Staff Assistant, Mammoth; Dale Nuss, Forestry, Bear and Fire Management Specialist, Mammoth; Judy Kuncl, Madison Area Ranger; **Jerry Mernin,** South District Ranger, South Entrance; John Lounsbury, Canyon District Ranger*

Jerry Mernin and Scott overlooking part of the South District in Yellowstone.

Jerry Mernin, riding Dusty, leads Jet, Max, and the mule Ike past Turret Peak and Table Mountain in Yellowstone's backcountry.

After retiring, Jerry Mernin continued to patrol Yellowstone's backcountry as a volunteer. Here he enters the Fern Lake Patrol Cabin.

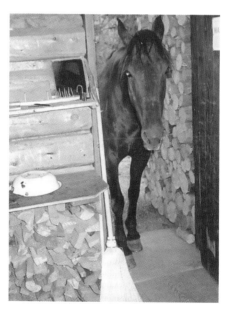

Rosita stands in a cabin doorway. Horses and mules were often Jerry Mernin's only companions at the backcountry cabins.

Cindy Ferguson on top of Avalanche Peak in Yellowstone a few months prior to her marriage to Jerry Mernin in December 1971.

Jerry Mernin and dog Ross in Yellowstone, circa 1980. (James Fain photo)

Jerry and Cindy Mernin in 2006. (Tom Ovanin photo)

Jerry Mernin (in front) and fellow rangers patrol the Yellowstone boundary, 1987. (JAMES FAIN PHOTO)

During the 2012 memorial ceremony in Yellowstone to honor Jerry Mernin's life and career, backcountry ranger Jackie Hampson led a pack horse carrying Mernin's gear and a saddle horse with Mernin's boots reversed in the stirrups. (TOM OVANIN PHOTO)

Jerry Mernin and Scott, Yellowstone National Park. (James Fain photo)

costing me money! Why does one guy get a warning and another have to pay for parking in the same area? Can you explain that, *Clarence*!?"

I don't know if it was the residual adrenalin from the car stop, cumulative irritation from listening to the complainant's manner, or a spike of adrenalin from being called Clarence. Barney reached across the counter, grabbed the complaining employee by his jacket, and lifted him off his feet. Almost eyeball to eyeball with the complainant, he whispered between clenched teeth, "I can't explain it." Barney put the individual down and walked out of the room. He apparently took a deep breath or two because by the time he told me of the incident, he was quite calm and very apologetic for causing me yet another problem on a day like this.

It had been easier to explain to five people why I had threatened to shoot them than it was to soothe the bruised ego of the one complainant. When I brought him into my office, I explained the circumstances that might lead to one person getting a warning and another person getting a citation, but I said I would not invalidate the citation. I tried to explain how the buildup of stress and adrenalin during a serious law enforcement contact could affect someone's behavior. I apologized for his mistreatment and told him, as Sanders's supervisor, I would do everything in my power to see it didn't happen again. When that did not satisfy him, I gave him the name and address of the chief ranger and told him that was his next level of recourse.

When I returned to the back office, I told Barney that I guessed we both had had better days. He agreed. I thanked him for his good work and quick response during the car stop. I looked at my watch—it was 2:45 p.m. Barney was scheduled to go off duty at 3 p.m. so I told him to take the rest of the day off. "But I haven't taken the campground count," he replied. "Don't worry," I said. "We'll use yesterday's figures." "Well, all right," was Barney's response. "I do need to clean my tie."

Chapter 16

Changing Times Arrive in Yellowstone

IN THE LATE 1960S AND EARLY 1970S THE COUNTRY WAS UN-
dergoing dramatic changes in attitude. People were protesting the Vietnam War and questioning, even defying, the
government and any authority. Men were growing long
hair and beards. Women were wearing mini-skirts, peasant
dresses, and flowers in their hair. The country was experiencing a sexual revolution. During this period, Yellowstone's
superintendent, chief ranger, and south district ranger were
all World War II veterans. While their generation had yet to
be proclaimed the "greatest" generation, all three managers
had definite ideas on how "their park" should be run. They
did not accept disrespect and defiance of the government or
the park. Nor did they tolerate shoddy appearance or conduct
in their employees.

I was Lake sub-district ranger during much of this period. Early on I experienced how their version of "my way or
the highway" worked. A Lake area seasonal ranger, who was
highly regarded, returned for his fourth season. He had just
finished two years with the Peace Corps, and he arrived with
fresh enthusiasm, eager to get back to work. Not only did he
now have a broader work experience, he had long hair and a
ponytail to go with it.

His first exchange with Dale Nuss, the South District ranger who was also my boss, went something like this.

South District Ranger, shaking hands: "Hi. Good to see you again. When are you going to get a haircut?"

Seasonal: "Hi, Dale. It's good to see you, too. I wasn't planning to get a haircut any time soon. I was hoping to keep it the way it is."

SDR: "You know better than that. You're not going to work in my district looking like that, and you won't work any place in Yellowstone until you get a haircut."

S: "But, Dale, other parks allow hair this long. And the Supreme Court has said that long hair was no reason to deny a person a job."

SDR: "I don't care what other parks do, and the Supreme Court doesn't run Yellowstone! Get your hair cut or be in my office at four-thirty, Friday afternoon."

The seasonal didn't get his haircut. Since I was his immediate supervisor, I was summoned to the South District Office on Friday afternoon as well. We arrived at almost the same time. When we were seated, the district ranger handed the seasonal his termination papers. When the man protested, Dale Nuss insisted.

This particular incident ended well. The seasonal ranger got a suitable haircut and was a valuable asset that summer. He later got a permanent position in another park and had an eminently successful NPS career. Some years later he was appointed acting superintendent of Yellowstone for six months. In this capacity, he made some difficult, politically unpopular decisions that benefited the park. And while in Yellowstone, he made it a point to visit the long-since-retired district ranger who had almost fired him. So ended the first wave of Lake's long hair sagas.

If I thought the regulation of long hair was draconian, it paled when compared to management's efforts to enforce the rule that "members of the opposite sex are not allowed in bachelor quarters." Originally it was written to cover barracks and bunkhouse situations, but then management expanded the rule's interpretation to cover all single employees in any government housing. As an unmarried, career NPS employee assigned to my own private, one-bedroom apartment attached to the Lake Ranger Station, I could not have female visitors. Nor could the superintendent's secretary—a forty-year-old single woman living in her own house at park headquarters—have male visitors. Shades of George Orwell's *1984!* She and I had a lot to commiserate about when we ran into each other.

As shortsighted, inappropriate, and illegal as I thought the rule to be, I ignored it rather than make an issue of it. I was so busy trying to save the world, the park, and my sub-district that I didn't have time for other crusades. Grizzly bears in campgrounds came first, and patrolling the backcountry was far more important. But you can't dodge fate forever, and one day I was called to the district ranger's office and informed of the inappropriate conduct of one of my seasonal rangers. He had driven quite rapidly through the Lake government residence area one evening, parked in front of his girlfriend's apartment, gone in, and had not come out until the next morning. Several park wives observed this breech and had been offended. The district ranger told me to see that that this conduct wasn't repeated.

As soon as my misguided seasonal came on duty the next day we sat down and had what I hoped was a perspective-giving conversation. I listened to his version of the incident; the young lady he visited was his fiancée. I discussed image, appearances, the need for discretion, and the importance of scrupulously obeying the laws we were charged with enforcing. He said he understood, and I thought the matter was settled.

The next day I was again summoned to the district ranger's office. It was the same complaint, same employee, and same park wives. While he had driven up slowly and had not sounded his horn to announce his presence, my boss said that he had not been adequately discreet. Through a series of my questions and the district ranger's abrupt answers, I discovered that "adequate discretion" was not achieved by the seasonal ranger waiting until after dark and quietly entering through the front door. Nor was it accomplished by quietly entering through the back door after dark. Apparently it could only be attained by quietly crawling in through the back window after dark and crawling out the same window before daylight the next morning. Ripley, of "Believe It Or Not" fame, was fond of saying "Truth is stranger than fiction, and a thousand times more interesting!"

"That's bullshit," was my response on hearing this definition of discretion.

"That's the way it is," was my boss's response.

Fortunately, neither of us had to repeat his opinions or definitions. The next day one of the subjects of consternation accepted a permanent job in another park, and the other individual resigned to follow. While the Lake uniformed divisions were now short two positions, we were able to devote our energy and efforts to the important tasks at hand—such as checking hair length.

Some might infer that I didn't hold these managers in very high regard. To the contrary, I felt they performed the bulk of their responsibilities quite capably. While I disagreed with some of their attitudes and actions, each did things I admired. It was like the flip side of the coin.

In 1970 the chief ranger more than redeemed himself in my mind when I shot a charging grizzly bear in the midst of a couple dozen employees and park visitors. It was a situation I should not have let happen. In this case circumstances conspired against me when I made a series of bad decisions.

I had tranquilized a sow grizzly bear that had caused problems in the Fishing Bridge RV Park. The bear was in a trap but was to be relocated by helicopter. As soon as we dragged her out of the trap and her limp body hit the ground, she jumped to her feet and lunged at me. The spectators that I shouldn't have allowed to gather in the first place, gasped, screamed, and scattered as I emptied my .44 magnum into the bear at point blank range. She dropped dead at my feet, but I was mortified I had let matters erupt into a fiasco and horrified that I had killed a female grizzly of cub-producing age.

The district ranger was out of the area, so I called the chief ranger and explained in unvarnished detail what had happened. "Don't worry," he said. "I know you well enough to be confident that you did what you had to as safely as it could be done." His response lifted the weight of a thousand anvils from my shoulders. I was even more relieved when we found out that the sow was not lactating.

Late the following fall, the superintendent enhanced his image in my view more by his conduct than by words. A visitor party entered the park through the South Entrance and stopped to enjoy the view in Lewis River Canyon. A young man of the party went beyond the barricade and was jumping from rock formation to rock formation when he fell about forty feet, and after tumbling another fifty feet, was still alive.

Two South Entrance rangers entered the canyon a quarter mile north and picked their way un-roped to the victim. I responded from Lake, Ranger Gil Hall came from Canyon, and a ranger arrived from Grant Village. This late in the season, there were no other protection staff in the district. Shortly after I arrived, we decided that the safest and most expedient rescue would be a direct descent with a Stokes litter, followed by a direct lift of the victim.

The Grant Village ranger kept traffic moving. Gil, who had rescue experience in Yosemite, and I set up the necessary anchor and rigging for me to take the litter down. We were about ready to go when an imposing uniformed figure pushed through the onlookers and spoke to me. It was the park superintendent. "Jerry, sorry to interrupt, but I wanted you to know I'm in the area and available. You're in charge. Tell me what you want me to do." My response was "Keep traffic moving and when we get the victim loaded, we'll want you to get eight or ten strong men to raise us using this rope."

"You got it. Good luck," was the superintendent's response. The recovery went smoothly thanks in no small part to his help. The South Entrance rangers took the injured man to Jackson, and the superintendent helped us pack our gear and clear the area. He thanked us for a job well done, then continued his trip. I thought a lot more of him for his support at that operation than I ever did for his efforts to keep members of the opposite sex out of bachelor quarters.

In late May 1971, a series of events conspired to put me personally in conflict with the "members of the opposite sex in bachelor quarters" manifesto. With lots of snow still present, only limited facilities were open to the public. Some of Yellowstone's more impressive snowstorms occur in the spring, and on one particular morning I awoke to eight inches of new snow on the ground with more rapidly falling. Fortified by a solitary cup of coffee, I was out by 6 a.m. checking roads, relaying information to our Comm Center, and getting plow crews started. After the wild weather in the morning, the snow slacked off and the plow crews returned to quarters.

In the early afternoon I went home for a bite to eat and more coffee. I made some phone calls and listened to the park radio for road and weather conditions around the park. Little did I realize as I savored that second cup of coffee, my life was about to change forever.

I was getting into my vehicle to check the roads again when two cars entered the plowed out parking area behind Lake Ranger Station. The lead car was driven by an attractive young woman. Two more attractive women were in the second car. A thought flashed through my mind, "There's trouble for someone."

The first young lady rolled down her window and said, flicking her eye lashes over her bright blue eyes, "We're nurses looking for the Lake Hospital. We're supposed to report to work there." I told them I didn't think there was anyone there, but I would check. Did they want to come in for a cup of coffee while I called Dr. Fox in Mammoth? Being a semi-trained investigator, a student of body language, and a law enforcement officer capable of utilizing his peripheral vision, I had already picked out the nurse I thought was most attractive. She was the one with the straight, shoulder-length, dark hair wearing lavender-tinted dark glasses.

We went into my bare-walled, Spartan kitchen with its sink full of dirty dishes, snow melt on the floor, paperwork and magazines on the kitchen table and counter, along with a NPS base station radio. I found out they were Leslie, Kathy, and Cindy (with the tinted glasses). While they took chairs around the kitchen table, I made coffee and called Dr. Fox in Mammoth to let him know that three of his nurses had arrived.

It turned out Dr. Fox wasn't expecting the ladies until tomorrow; there was no one at Lake Hospital nor was the heat and water on; but he had a place for them to stay at Mammoth. After they found out Mammoth was more than fifty miles away, they were three unhappy nurses. They had come from Wall, South Dakota, that day and weren't interested in more driving on snowy roads. After I explained the complete lack of facilities in the Lake area, one of them asked if there was a place to stay at Lake Ranger Station. "We would be happy to exchange housekeeping chores for a place to stay rather than drive fifty miles."

It so happened that the two-bedroom front quarters of the Lake Ranger Station were set-up with rations and sleeping bags for winter ski patrols. It would be an ideal place for the nurses to stay, and it could use a good cleaning. However, a seasonal ranger had arrived a few days earlier and needed a place to stay until he was assigned his regular quarters. He currently was in West Yellowstone getting groceries and had said he wasn't sure if he would be back that night or the next.

I was in a quandary. I would certainly have a more enjoyable time visiting with three attractive women than I would eating a can of beans by myself and finishing the western novel I was reading. The way my luck was running, however, the seasonal ranger would show up to spend the night and the district ranger would stop by first thing in the morning for a visit. So the three nurses drove to Mammoth.

The next day I thoroughly cleaned my kitchen and then, under the guise of registering the ladies' cars for employee passes, I stopped by the hospital. They were back and busily cleaning the hospital in preparation for opening. Counting on the fact there wasn't much happening around Lake after work, I asked them over for coffee and Sara Lee pound cake that evening. Their subsequent visit confirmed that Cindy, the nurse with the tinted glasses, was not only the most attractive, she was also the most interesting.

Our first date consisted of driving to Cody through spectacular Sunlight Basin and having dinner at Cassie's, a former brothel now a famous steak house. While in Cody I had to do two weeks of laundry. There's nothing like an hour in a Laundromat washing dirty clothes to mix a touch of reality into an otherwise romantic evening. When the summer ended, Cindy returned to Baltimore to find a job. We kept in touch with frequent phone calls. When I said I would be driving to Asheville, North Carolina, to visit my folks, Cindy said she hadn't found a job that interested her and offered to fly out and drive back with me if I could drop her at her parents' home in Baltimore. I was excited at the prospect.

We had a pleasant three weeks at Lake Ranger Station before we headed east. Since it was mid-November and only a skeleton crew remained, Cindy got to meet the Lake winterkeepers but didn't meet (or offend) any of the wives in the government residence area. One evening in my bare-walled Spartan kitchen, now cleaned to Cindy's strict emergency room standards, I asked her to marry me. She agreed. We got a marriage license in Bozeman, Montana, and I bought her a snow machine. We went back east and met both sets of parents.

When we returned to Montana, Ranger Terry Danforth and his wife Mary were our witnesses for our marriage at Holy Rosary Church in Bozeman on December 18, 1971.

Terry said he had heard the chief ranger wanted the district ranger to tell Mernin to get rid of his "Dolly." I'm glad I didn't have to, and more importantly, I'm glad my "Dolly" hasn't gotten rid of me during the forty years since then. She certainly has had reason to do so. I look back on that second cup of coffee as the most fortunate cup of my life. Even if it was just *instant* coffee.

Chapter 17

Bear in the Bathroom

TO BE HONEST, I HAVE MY SHARE OF IDIOSYNCRASIES AND even a few downright character deficiencies, such as procrastination. However, when it comes to virtue and good character I claim to be the equal of (maybe superior to) any male I know in one realm of major significance: I always lower the toilet seat. It wasn't always this way, and I can clearly remember the precise moment of my conversion.

Cindy and I had been married two years and were living in the back quarters of the Lake Ranger Station. It was basically a one-bedroom apartment with the kitchen window looking into the parking lot. The bathroom window opened onto an enclosed porch that served as the entry to a seasonal apartment on the east and to our kitchen on the west.

This porch was about 15 to 18 feet long and about eight to ten feet wide. The bottom half of the porch was enclosed by one inch boards; windows formed the top half. On the porch was a wood box, a sizeable stack of stove wood, fire extinguishers, axes, snow shovels, and brooms. It also contained a three-year collection of empty Rainier Ale bottles waiting to be recycled. There was a box or two of outdated cabin rations with some of the cans quite rusty.

On that cold night in late October, the Lake area was mostly deserted of people. With patches of snow on the ground, bears were frantically searching for their last food before hibernation. Our quarters were not intended for winter occupation and were heated only by an oil heater in the living room.

At midnight Cindy and I were asleep in our warm bed when we were awakened by a loud crash on the porch, followed by the rolling and tumbling of bottles. Bolting upright, I jumped out of bed, grabbed the bedside flashlight, and was fumbling for my .44 in my daypack next to the bed. Cindy was awake and sitting up in bed with the covers wrapped around her. She was closer to the source of the noise than I and kept asking, "What is it? What is it? What is it?"

I finally had both my .44 and flashlight in hand. Barefooted and in my regular bed attire of shorts and t-shirt, I was as cold and trembling as a well digger's proverbial ass in the Klondike. I reached inside the bathroom door, switched on the light, and got an immediate response from the porch. A grizzly bear snorted and charged the bathroom window, huffing and blowing snot and saliva. Its teeth clacking and masticating, it hit the window with enough force to shove it open even farther than it had been. Bottles kept rolling and getting stepped on in the porch area. I immediately shut off the light, closed the door, and moved quickly away.

I hurried to the kitchen window, wanting to keep sight of the bear that had retreated outside to the parking lot. I was still barefoot, shivering, and in my underwear as I asked Cindy to bring me the extra .44 ammunition from my daypack. As Cindy came to the kitchen with the extra ammunition, she was talking rapidly, asking where the bear was, telling me what she was going to do if the bear got in, and asking me what I was going to do.

With one of the most ill-considered statements of my life, I told her to shut-up and sit down in the next room. I couldn't pay attention to her and the bear at the same time, and right now I needed to pay attention to the bear. I regretted my words as soon as I said them, but words once spoken can't be changed. Cindy shoved the extra ammunition into my hand, whipped around, and left the room without saying a word.

Totally chagrined but still pumping adrenalin, I studied the parking lot. It was illuminated by the dull glow of a security light, and I could see the bear was a sow grizzly with a cub-of-the year. They were classic silver-tip grizzlies, both beautiful specimens, apparently unmarked, unblemished, and in good condition.

During this lull I went in the bedroom and quickly dressed. Feeling a little more composed and comfortable, I turned on the kitchen light. The sow instantly charged, hitting the north wall and the window so hard that the building shook as if it had been rammed by a front-end loader. It may have been heightened alertness or just stress-induced imagination, but I swear I saw the window glass bend from the force of her nose!

The sow whirled and ran back to the cub to make sure he was all right, and then she charged again, hitting the windows and wall once more. Amazingly none of the windows broke. She checked all the windows on the north side, sniffing them, and pushing them with her nose. She would not go away.

I watched her from the shadows in the living room, holding my .44 with a two-handed, double action grip, aiming at her all the time she was pushing against the windows. If she broke into the kitchen I was sure I could kill her before she injured Cindy or me. I simply did not want to have to kill her, and I did not want to fire the .44 magnum in the close confines of the kitchen.

Finally the sow and cub laid down together at the far end

of the parking lot, and I turned off the kitchen light. It was around 1:30 a.m. and I wanted to make amends to my bride. Now that my stress had subsided, I felt very remorseful and went into the other room. Cindy was seated in the far corner smoking a cigarette. She had her arms folded across her chest and was fully dressed, including wool cap, zipped-up down coat, and heavy gloves.

I tried to be positive and upbeat as I told Cindy there were two bears, and one of them was a really cute cub of the year, and she could take a look if she wanted. She looked straight ahead and answered emphatically, spitting out a puff of smoke with every word, "I don't want to see the little son-of-a bitch!" I knew I was going to have to do more than just be positive and upbeat.

I went into the other room and called Dale Nuss, the South District Ranger. When Dale arrived we looked over the damage. The sow had torn off the siding next to the porch door, entered, and then rooted through the Rainier Ale bottles. We made a plan and while Dale went to the utility area to get a bear trap, I went to the station and got the drug kit and CO_2 capture rifle. I made up two different drug doses for the sow so I would have a choice after I made an analysis of her weight. I also made up a follow-up dose just in case. Dale left the trap at the less lighted end of the parking lot, but we didn't set it. We didn't want to take a chance of trapping the cub and then having to deal with a super-irritated grizzly mother in the dark.

When and if the bear came back in the daylight, I was to notify Dale and try to tranquilize the bear. A patrol ranger was scheduled to come on duty at 7 a.m., and Dale was to notify him to stay in the area and wait for my call. Dale went home, and Cindy and I went back to bed.

As soon as I was sound asleep the bear returned. She woke us up by sorting through the bottles and cans of outdated cabin rations. Again I was up, barefoot in the cold, dressed only in my underwear and carrying my .44. This time I tried pounding on the door to see if that noise would scare her away—it didn't. She charged the door, hitting it with such force that the whole building shook. Finally she and her cub departed.

Enough of this nonsense, I thought. So I prepared for what I hoped would be the final episode. I went into the bathroom, opened the window overlooking the porch just one inch more so I could fit through the barrel of the capture rifle. I turned off the bathroom light to see if there was enough ambient light from the outside security lamp to sight the capture rifle, and there was. I relieved my bladder and returned to the bedroom in the dark.

Cindy was already in bed again. I carefully leaned the capture rifle against the bookcase on my side of the bed. Then, fully dressed except for my boots, and with my .44 on my right hip, the NPS radio on my left, and extra ammunition in between, I carefully crawled into bed, trying not to disturb Cindy.

I had barely stretched out and gone to sleep when I heard the most terrifying, blood-curdling screech I had ever heard! As I came fully awake, I realized I was standing on the bed with my flashlight in one hand, the .44 in the other, and both pointing in the direction of the scream, ready for action.

The bathroom door was open, and Cindy's side of the bed was empty. In rapid order I learned that Cindy had gotten up to go to the bathroom. In the dark she sat down on the ice-cold porcelain of the commode because I had forgotten to put down the toilet seat. The resulting yell, on a night filled with bears, was one I will never forget, and I never, ever made this mistake again. For a time I was so sensitive to this matter that I would check the commodes in public rest rooms to make sure the seats were down.

By 8 a.m. that morning, I had succeeded in shooting the bear with the drug Sucostrin, and we loaded the sow and cub into the trap. We later released the mom and cub at Pebble Creek, near the north boundary of the park.

Whenever I reflect on this episode, I am surprised our marriage survived the night. Cindy remembers it as the time she was almost blown off her own commode by a .44 magnum.

Chapter 18

Patrol Cabin Etiquette

WHEN PARK SERVICE EMPLOYEES FROM A VARIETY OF DIFFERent parks get together, the conversation inevitably drifts to how much things have changed. We discuss how complicated and complex things are now compared to how simple and straightforward they used to be, and someone will eventually lament that rangers spend too much time in front of a computer screen. Inevitably someone will say, "Rangers just aren't what they used to be!" When I hear this my answer has often been, "Bullshit! Yellowstone still has rangers who can do anything any park ranger ever did, plus they can use a computer to their advantage."

My response is influenced by three factors: the heritage and memory of Yellowstone's early rangers, the presence of a widespread system of backcountry patrol cabins, and how the traditions are kept alive and fresh by the continued use of the cabins. When the Army pulled out of Yellowstone National Park in 1918, it left Fort Yellowstone with all its buildings to the National Park Service, the agency created to manage the nation's national parks. This transfer included patrol cabins the Army had built in the backcountry.

During the winter, Army scouts used the cabins during long ski patrols into the backcountry to check on the wildlife, watch for poachers, and shovel the cabin roofs to prevent collapse from snow loads. One of those winter travelers was Harry Trischman. After being raised in Yellowstone, Trischman became an Army scout in 1909 at the age of twenty three. When the Army left, he became a Yellowstone ranger and later a buffalo keeper, and in the process became a Yellowstone icon. When he died he left behind a legend, many good stories about his exploits, and a knob bearing his name five miles west of Shoshone Lake on the Continental Divide.

I first heard of Harry Trischman when I arrived in Yellowstone and was on a Thorofare ski patrol in 1964. Although I was an avid downhill skier, I had done almost no cross-country skiing. Less than a month after arriving in the park, I was following Bob Morey and Ranger Ed Widmer across the frozen surface of Yellowstone Lake heading to Park Point Patrol Cabin, the first stop on an 18-day ski patrol. Since arriving in Yellowstone I had been given a crash course in cross-country skiing and waxing by a variety of rangers. I was using a pair of borrowed eight-foot-long Strand, "Yellowstone Special" skis made of solid hickory. Each ski weighed eight to ten pounds and was designed for heavy breaking of snow, not racing.

Heading toward Park Point, we fell into a routine: The lead skier broke trail for fifteen minutes, then stepped aside to let the number two man break trail. Skier one dropped back to the "overdrive" position and was able to relax on the trail packed by the previous two skiers. This routine allowed us to share equally in the vicissitudes and the enjoyment of the day's travel. At Park Point, Bob was disappointed with the cabin's condition. He said that quite often the cabins closer to civilization were not as well cared for as the remote cabins. That night cabin chores were rotated much as breaking trail was—one person cooked, another did the dishes, while the third dried the dishes and put them away. The following day two of us moved up the ladder of responsibility while the cook dropped back to the "overdrive" position and dried dishes.

Morey was an excellent cabin cook and produced outstanding sourdough pancakes. Widmer was a competent journeyman chef. We suffered when it was my turn to cook as my idea of a gourmet cabin meal was mixing three cans together for supper and not burning the pancakes or bacon at breakfast. I did have redeeming features, however. I carried a quart of 150-proof Lemonhart Rum and made hot buttered rums after we got the cabin opened up and were re-hydrating before supper. And, since I owned a Smith and Wesson Chief's Special five-shot revolver with a two-inch barrel, I carried the only gun in the group. Morey figured there should be at least one firearm on the patrol in the rare event we found someone with a trap line in the park.

Bob was a good storyteller, and while we skied along he made us aware of a lot of park happenings and lore of previous ski patrols. As we approached Cabin Creek Patrol Cabin on a heavily wooded stretch of trail, he told his first Harry Trischman story. Apparently Harry would pick up the pace in certain locations and actively seek out landmarks until he located a particular tree. Skiing to that tree he would reach through the tree limbs and retrieve a bottle of whiskey. After taking a healthy pull on the bottle to fortify his inner person, Harry would offer his partner the same opportunity. When suitably refreshed, Harry replaced the bottle and continued the trip with added vigor. The story impressed me partly because of the planning and effort it took to make it happen.

When I opened the door to the Cabin Creek cabin, it was so spotless and squared away that I stepped back and wiped my feet. Morey came up and said, "Now that's the way a cabin ought to look!" Everything was neat and orderly, the floor and windows spotless, rafters and walls free of dust and cobwebs, the wood stove clean and recently blackened, and the table and chairs were laid on edge so mice couldn't walk across them. The blankets and bedding were neatly folded and hung on a "blanket pole" suspended from the rafters with folds facing the door; sheet blankets were on top of the bedding; and each mattress laid across its own pile of bedding. With the bedding hung this way, the user would flop a mattress onto a cot, spread and tuck in the sheet blankets, and finally lay out the blankets he needed for the night. When done correctly, it was definitely a user-friendly system.

Bob Wood had been the Thorofare patrol ranger during the previous fall's hunting season and had been responsible for stocking Thorofare, Cabin Creek, and Fox Creek patrol cabins, and he had done an impressive job. The cabins were neat, orderly, meticulously kept, and Spartan. For the rest of my time in Yellowstone, I used Bob's example to define how a cabin should be left.

As Morey, Widmer, and I left Cabin Creek for Thorofare, I continued to upgrade my learning curve, including a painful lesson while crossing Mountain Creek. We were skiing in the open, facing a howling, snow-whipping wind on a socked-in, cheerless, twenty-below-zero day when a snow bridge collapsed under me and plunged my left foot and ski into Mountain Creek's bone-chilling waters.

I flopped and scrambled violently like a panicked fish out of water, until I made it out of the creek onto the deep and unpacked snow of the bank, dragging my ski with me even though it had an extra quarter ton of ice, slush, and snow sticking to it.

Morey and Widmer packed an area for me to stand while I kicked off my ski, got an ice scraper from my wax kit and started scraping. It was painfully slow and miserably cold work, but we finally got the ski bottom free of ice. Despite increasingly numb hands I managed to get a layer of paraffin on the ski base, get my ski on, and start following Bob and Ed down the trail. My hands never completely warmed up until later that evening after we made it to Thorofare and found another Bob Wood-squared-away cabin. That night we toasted Bob Wood and Harry Trischman with hot buttered rums—more than once.

The following day we skied past Bridger Lake to the Forest Service cabin at Hawks Rest and returned by the Wyoming Game and Fish Cabin located on the park's boundary a mile south of Thorofare Station. We saw no one and no sign of recent human use. Back at Thorofare we shoveled roofs and melted snow for bath water. Before leaving Thorofare we hooked in tandem several automobile batteries used to power the station's radio and made a brief check-in with park headquarters. At that time there were no hand-held radios in the park so we were not any better than our predecessors in being able to get assistance or to talk to headquarters. We were better off than the old timers who skied in pairs since there were three of us—one to stay with the injured party if one were hurt and one to ski out to get help.

Fox Creek Patrol Cabin was another Bob Wood tour de force example of how to leave a patrol cabin. As soon as we arrived we dumped our packs and started shoveling the roof to get a head start on the next day's task. The following day we skied to the top of Big Game Ridge. It was a stormy, overcast, heavy breaking day. I learned that after two days' travel on cross-country skis into remote backcountry, you're on your own. Even with communications (which we didn't have), the weather most often would deny helicopter use, even if one were available. It just doesn't pay to fall with a heavy pack, as it can be hard on equipment as well as the body.

Morey cracked a ski tip on a tree he body checked. Widmer sprained an ankle on the last hill dropping into the Snake River but was able to limp the last mile to the cabin. I stayed upright by dragging my poles, an ignominious technique for one wanting to become a deep powder skier. Going for the gusto was one thing on a commercial ski hill manned by a state-of-the-art ski patrol, but it was quite another on Big Game Ridge. Bob wrapped his ski tip with duct tape and made it out by skiing in the number two spot; he couldn't chance the weakened tip with deep breaking. Widmer wrapped his ankle with an Ace bandage and toughed out the rest of the trip.

Over the next decade I went on more than a dozen Thorofare ski patrols, including two years where I made two Thorofare ski trips, checking the country, checking wildlife, shoveling cabin roofs. I used my Strands on four Thorofare trips. They were the same make/model Harry Trischman used, but I never skied as far as Harry or tried to drink as much. I did stock my patrol cabins with a personal, no expense to the government, supply of beer and plenty of tomato juice to mix with it—a healthy way to restore your electrolytes at the end of a good day's ski patrol.

Today, Yellowstone rangers still ski to the backcountry cabins to shovel roofs, check on wildlife, and check other winter users. They have better and more advanced equipment, the benefit of the experiences of their predecessors, and more reasons to escape the burden of bureaucracy. Just as the national park idea may be America's best conservation idea, the patrol cabins remain one of the Army's best contributions to Yellowstone. They encourage rangers to get away from computers. The cabins remind them that the heart of Yellowstone is not found at the headquarters building nor at any of the developed areas. It can only be approached by trails on foot, horseback, or skis.

Chapter 19

God Bless Park Rangers' Wives

THE WORD SERENDIPITY (FINDING SOMETHING GOOD ACCI-dentally) has been around for more than 250 years, according to Webster's *New World Dictionary*. Another bit of trivia tells us that the saying "It's an ill wind that blows no good for some-one" has been quoted for a couple hundred years longer than that. A somewhat impromptu visit by President Gerald Ford to Yellowstone in the summer of 1976 combined portions of both sentiments for a number of people—including me.

At the time I was the Snake River sub-district ranger, and John Townsley, who was noted for his "my way or the high-way" management style, was superintendent. When he want-ed something done, his M.O. was to order rather than ask that it be done. I got along with him better than many of my peers. We both had been raised in Yosemite and were second-generation NPS employees. His father was a chief ranger in Yosemite. My biggest advantage, however, was that I lived 90 miles from headquarters and rarely saw the man.

The superintendent had a dignitary trip set up through "my" area starting at Heart Lake Trailhead and finishing a week later at Trail Creek on the Southeast Arm of Yellow-stone Lake. After a week's trip traveling through great coun-try, along with good food and good company, the superintendent hoped the trip's deep-pocket participants would see fit to make a big contribution to The National Park Foundation. Funds gathered by the foundation could then be distributed to individual parks for special projects or additional services over and above what that park's regularly allotted bare-bones budget could afford.

I had been told my presence on the trip was not needed. However, I was to make sure the patrol cabins were available and that they were in good shape. For the most part, I was happy not to have to deal with a group of rich people who were getting special treatment. Coming from a more egalitarian background, I felt everyone should be treated the same. Then Yellowstone got word that President Gerald Ford would be visiting in a week to deliver a major environmental speech at Old Faithful. President Ford had worked in Yellowstone in 1936. While former seasonal rangers regularly visited Yellowstone, this was the first one to return as President of the United States.

This notice set off a flurry of planning. Ford's visit demanded the superintendent's presence at Old Faithful, and this meant the postponement or cancellation of his backcountry trip with his potential big donors. Obviously an ill wind for some, but it did blow some good. I was in Mammoth for a court case when I heard the superintendent wanted to see me right away. "Oh shit, what now?" was the first thought to flash through my mind. When I got to his office, Townsley greeted me warmly. It didn't appear as if I was there to get chewed out.

The superintendent came right to the point. "I guess you're aware the president's visit has interrupted my backcountry trip?" He had tried unsuccessfully to reschedule it after President Ford's visit. "I'd like you to take my place and lead the trip. Can you do that?" If a hummingbird's feather had fluttered into me, it would have knocked me over, I was so surprised. I cleared my throat to answer, but Townsley continued, "Bill Huffman has the food ordered and the menu laid out down to what wine to serve with the hors d'oeuvres each evening, but he has to stay out to handle communications at Old Faithful. I'm counting on you to fill in for us...."

"I can do it all, no problem," I finally answered. "Except I'm no cook...if your guests can handle the cooking chores, I can do the rest." "I wouldn't want to burden them with that," was his answer. "Then I can ask my wife Cindy to do the cooking," I said. "She's a great cook and knows her way around the patrol cabins. She's a nurse, she's good with stock...she can help with the packing if it's necessary." This was my attempt to avoid the fiasco of having to cook.

"This is supposed to be a male-only trip. All the wives wanted to go along...we had to limit it to men only, or the trip would have gotten out of hand," Townsley said. "And Jim Hotchkiss (in charge of Yellowstone's horse operation) will be along to do the packing." "If I tried to cook, it would be a waste of Huffman's good food," I answered. "My idea of gourmet cooking is to heat three different kinds of cans in the same pot at the same time."

On hearing that, the superintendent relented. "Bring Cindy. I'll try to explain it to the wives." When I got home, I found Cindy surprisingly receptive. She thought it might be interesting. I heaved a sigh of relief. Once again Cindy joined the generations of park rangers' wives who had accepted drudge work to help their husbands with their jobs and to help the NPS operate effectively—all for no pay other than nice sunsets and the satisfaction of a job well done. May God bless all park rangers' wives, past, present, and future.

August 27, the day the dignitary trip was to begin, started badly. In the early morning mist and darkness the stock truck carrying the trip's horses and mules overturned going around the sharp turn near Mud Volcano. Six of eight head were injured. Hotchkiss had to scramble to find replacement stock, triage and treat the injured, get the stock truck right side up, and get to Heart Lake Trailhead in a timely fashion. Delayed by phone calls about the rollover and horse substitution, Cindy and I arrived late at the trailhead with our horses and gear. There we met Townsley and his guests who were already there with wives and families. Townsley introduced us to John Bryant, executive secretary of the National Park Foundation, and to National Park Foundation board members Ernie Cockrell and Homer Luther.

Homer Luther was a husky, fortyish businessman, an avid photographer, outdoorsman, and fan of Yellowstone. Not quite as tall as his companions, he wore a weathered, broad-brimmed Hoss Cartwright-style Western hat. He was an experienced rider. John Bryant was in his late thirties, a tall, quiet but friendly, Ivy League-appearing individual. He said he had ridden only twice before. Ernie Cockrell was from Texas with an oil and ranching background. Somewhere in his forties, tanned, slender and pleasant, he could pass as a character actor in the movie "Giant." He had brought his own saddle, which was a good sign.

When our guests-to-be and their wives were introduced to Cindy, they met a tanned, attractive, athletic, self-assured woman in her late twenties. About five-feet four-inches tall, with short, straight, dark hair, she wore horn-rimmed glasses that gave her a business-like demeanor quite in contrast to the red, heart-shaped patches stitched on the rear of her faded blue jeans. I noticed the wives showed an increased interest in Cindy when they realized she was to accompany us on the trip. I smiled and kept my head down.

After getting a traditional Snake River start (off by the crack of noon) we had a flawless trip to Heart Lake. Our guests were perfectly matched to their horses and seemed to enjoy them. The packs rode well, and it was a beautiful early fall day. We arrived at 4 p.m. and found that Chuck Lee, the Heart Lake Ranger, had left the cabin totally squared away and in great shape. Our guests were impressed with the area and the cabin and seemed excited to be there. Not at all the pampered people I expected, they wanted to help with everything.

They had fishing gear and were enthused when I said a canoe was available. I told them they had to wear life jackets when out on the lake. By this point I felt comfortable speaking candidly to our special guests. I explained that the life jacket alone might not save them if they capsized and had to stay in cold water too long. "But," I said, "In a worst case scenario, life jackets made bodies easier for searchers to spot and recover." They wore their life vests.

Our guests were pumped when they saw how good the fishing was. They caught and released a 26½-inch, a 24-inch, and numerous smaller cutthroat trout. They were happy campers when they returned for hors d'oeuvres and wine. While the boys were fishing and Hotchkiss and I were feeding and caring for stock, Cindy had gone through Huffman's grocery supply. In charge of the park radio shop and telecommunications, Bill Huffman was well known in Yellowstone as a backcountry cook. He characteristically had fresh lettuce and sourdough pancakes with real maple syrup on the fifth day of a backcountry trip.

Supper was T-bone steaks, corn on the cob, green salad with a choice of dressings, and an appropriate wine selected by Huffman. Everyone gave Cindy's efforts rave reviews, and I passed their compliments on to the superintendent when I next saw him. I didn't tell him his guests hauled water and did the dishes as well. Patrol cabin life runs smoother when cabin chores are equally shared by all the beneficiaries. One partially thawed steak was left over. Cindy wrapped it carefully, selected a bottle of wine, and stored them in the root cellar with a note to Chuck Lee thanking him for the use of his ship-shape cabin.

The next day lingering fog and mist lifted dramatically to the call of loons on the south side of the Lake. A cow and calf moose grazed in the meadow by the cabin, and our horses were still here. What more could one ask for? After Cindy produced a breakfast of sausage, hash browns, and eggs, we spent a leisurely morning. Fishing was good but didn't match yesterday's size. Everyone helped with the cabin chores and pitched in to get Hotchkiss, Cindy, and the mules headed to the Harebell.

Our guests and I headed up Mount Sheridan to the fire lookout. It turned out to be a great trip. The higher we got on the mountain the more spectacular were the views highlighting Yellowstone's diversity. On the top the guests were as enthused as students at a high school pep rally before homecoming game and were truly in awe of Yellowstone. Jim McKown, previously in Grand Canyon and now the fire lookout, was a gracious host. He invited us into his spotless, everything-in-its-place, lookout with its 360-degree view. He showed the guests how to use the fire finder and took pictures with each of the guests' cameras of the four of us lined up smiling happily. Then we left him to his solitude with our thanks and a bottle of wine. We headed down to the lake and south to Harebell Patrol Cabin.

While Heart Lake had been an opulent, two-room cabin where we all were able to sleep inside, Harebell was a one-room cabin where our guests had to pitch tents. When we got the mules unpacked, Cindy went right to cooking. Our guests alternately helped Hotchkiss and Cindy or fished in Harebell Creek for the many small ones hiding in the cascades. In time we enjoyed a meal of fried chicken, mashed potatoes, and green salad. The next day we went over Big Game Ridge to Fox Creek Patrol Cabin. About the time President Ford was giving his address at Old Faithful, we were on top of Big Game Ridge, looking across at Mt. Sheridan and down at Heart Lake.

The views from Big Game Ridge stretch for miles in every direction. Our guests snapped so many pictures that I felt Kodak would be able to declare a stock dividend. The trail went by stands of white bark pine; past clear, ice-cold springs flowing abundantly out of the hillside; and down into a series of high mountain meadows that were intersected by patches of timber. The trail also crossed a thermal area with quiet, variegated shades of color and a natural salt lick that caused a confluence of game trails. We crossed the lush Snake River bottoms and rode through willows to the river. The fishermen in the group were excited to watch trout fleeing upstream and down to escape the approaching horses. We let the horses drink their fill, then splashed across the Snake, and rode the last half mile to Fox Creek Patrol Cabin, our home for the night. It had been a day that provided both guides and guests with a deeper appreciation of Yellowstone.

The next morning we were up early, ate breakfast, and, with great help from our distinguished guests, got on the trail much earlier than on previous days. We had more than twenty miles to get to our destination. After a steep, six-mile climb to the Continental Divide, we rode through sparse timber to an overlook that provided a sweeping view of Yellowstone Lake and many mountains beyond. While the horses' breathing settled back to normal after the climb, our eyes swept the scenery, and one by one we focused on the first minuscule but square intrusion into our wilderness psyche. The distinctive yellow walls of the Lake Hotel, about two days' travel away, reminded us of the other reality we would soon face.

I overheard guests lamenting, "Hate for this to end…no hurry to get back…." When we broke out of the timber and onto the beach of the Southeast Arm of Yellowstone Lake where the boat dock, Trail Creek Cabin and barn were located, the afternoon breeze had kicked up modest whitecaps on the lake. Trail Creek Cabin is a square log cabin with about the same square footage as the Heart Lake Cabin. Originally built as a fire cache in the 1940s in response to a series of large fires on Two Ocean Plateau, it had been used as a patrol cabin for many years.

Hotchkiss and I had to take the stock about a mile back to find good grass while Cindy prepared a ham dinner. The boys had amazing fishing off the dock and farther out with a canoe. Our last supper was delicious but subdued both because of our long day and because the good trip was about to end. It was somewhat like reading a good book—you're anxious to experience what's next, but you don't want the book to end.

After a leisurely breakfast and dishes the next morning, a NPS patrol boat appeared on the horizon. Not shy about speaking her mind, Cindy said, "There goes the neighborhood." I smiled as our three guests all agreed wholeheartedly. Accompanied by two canoes, the patrol boat came slowly through the hand-propelled zone and tied up at the dock. Townsley, Huffman, and NPS Director Gary Everhart arrived by canoe. Two former Yellowstone superintendents of the 1960s, Lon Garrison and John McLaughlin, came on the patrol boat as did an opulent supply of food and beverage. We definitely were not going to go hungry or thirsty.

We hauled food and baggage to the cabin, the patrol boat departed, and Huffman busied himself organizing. At noon, we had gourmet sandwiches and a choice of beverages from an iced cooler. I was reminded of an old saying—never suffer in the land of plenty! No one at Trail Creek suffered that day, for sure. The rest of the day was spent visiting, schmoozing, and talking of President Ford's speech and visit. I told the superintendent of our trip so far and how well his guests enjoyed the country and Cindy's cooking. Meanwhile Cindy helped Huffman produce an outstanding steak dinner. The next morning Huffman whipped up superb, individual omelets with the skill and grace of a Spanish matador in the bullring. I was honored with the first one.

Then it was over—both the breakfast and the trip. As we saddled the stock and made up packs I reflected on the past week. Rather than being an ill wind, President Ford's visit turned out to be a lucky wind for me. I couldn't think of better ways to spend my time than riding a good horse in good country, and I ate exceptionally well to boot. While I still didn't care much for the idea of giving rich, well-connected people special treatment, I could see its benefit to the NPS. A week's ride in the backcountry had transformed our three guests from that category into close personal friends with a shared love of Yellowstone.

In the late morning the NPS patrol boat again tied up at the dock. The superintendent and everyone else climbed aboard and headed out to rejoin wives and families. Hotchkiss, Cindy, and I started our long ride out to Heart Lake

Trailhead, leading three empty saddle horses and carrying the memory of our trip.

I don't know if the National Park Foundation ever got the big donations from our friends. Later that year Cindy and I got a photo album with several dozen pictures to remind us of the trip. It included pictures of Cindy's heart-patched jeans and the picture McKown took of us on Sheridan. With the album was a note that read in part, "I hope these pictures bring back as many pleasant memories for you as they do for us. Ernie, John and I will never forget the great trip." It was signed Luther, and after thirty-five years, the album still brings back pleasant memories. Here's to good winds, good wives, and serendipity. I'll drink to them any time.

Ford's was not the only presidential visit in the late 1970s.

Chapter 20

The Day the President Rode My Horse

DESPITE GROWING UP IN FISHING COUNTRY WHERE SOME OF my heroes were avid fishermen, I am not a fisherman. I have spent most of my working life in a world-class fishing area. Just because I don't fish doesn't mean that I don't enjoy going along on another person's fishing trip. The most memorable was President Jimmy Carter's fishing excursion to Yellowstone Lake's South Arm in August of 1978.

At that time I was the Snake River District Ranger and my area of responsibility extended from the middle one third of Yellowstone's south boundary north to Pumice Point. It included West Thumb, Flat Mountain Arm, and the South Arm of Yellowstone Lake. Since the president was fishing "my" part of the lake, it was only natural for me to be involved. When a sitting president goes fishing it involves a lot more than one man picking up his fishing rod and walking down to some stream or lake. His schedulers, planners, handlers, image-makers, and the Secret Service all have a say in every move he makes or thinks of making. From the initial planning process to the president's return home, the trickle-down effect alters the routine of every place the president passes through or visits.

This was especially true when John Townsley was superintendent. He was a big man with big ideas and the energy and attitude to see them through. During Townsley's tenure, the visiting dignitaries included patrons who might contribute big bucks to park projects, congressmen and senators who could influence the park's budget or image, and presidents of the United States and their staffs. Townsley didn't like routine operations to interfere with his efforts to show the best of Yellowstone to his special guests.

In preparation for the president's visit, an advance Secret Service team checked all the areas the presidential party planned to visit. They also met with local law enforcement personnel and many of the area rangers. As the plan evolved, the Carter party would helicopter into the hand-propelled zone of the South Arm, land at a campsite that had been closed for the president's visit, fish a few hours, and then helicopter to Old Faithful for an early afternoon tour, photo opportunity, and speech. Ranger Joe Fowler and I were told to be at the campsite on horseback. Our task was to provide perimeter security, to decorate (look "rangerly"), and to watch for grizzly bears, which were known to frequent the area.

However, I had conflicting responsibilities. Before the president's itinerary had been finalized, I had scheduled an appreciation dinner for a Student Conservation Association (SCA) high school group doing trail work in my district. I had planned to meet them when they emerged from the wilderness with root beer floats, followed the next day by a hamburger dinner.

With the help of rangers Roger Rudolph and Joe Fowler, we figured out a plan so I could fulfill all of my responsibilities. After I rode in with Joe, Roger would pick me up in a Bertram-25 patrol boat, get me out for the SCA dinner, and get me back the following morning prior to President Carter's arrival. (Roger was to be part of the perimeter security team.) Joe would take my horse to the Trail Creek Patrol Cabin, the cabin closest to the picnic site, for the night.

I met Joe at Heart Lake Trailhead the morning before the president's fishing trip. We had two horses: Eli, a husky, sixteen hands, experienced, brown Heinz-57-Variety horse for Joe. Earlier that year I had lost Dusty, the horse I had ridden since I had arrived in Yellowstone. As a replacement I was trying out Eb, a slender, solid, unflappable, medium-sized sorrel that was a journeyman mountain horse. He was a good ride, but he wouldn't amount to a tick bite on Dusty's hindquarters. Our choice of horses turned out to be fortuitous.

After Joe and I had ridden twenty miles to the presidential fishing spot, Roger picked me up mid-afternoon, and I made it to Snake River in time to be tardy host to the student crew after my wife Cindy had done most (all) of the work. The group enjoyed their evening, and we enjoyed their energy and enthusiasm.

After a short night's sleep in my own bed, I met Roger back at Lake, and he gave me a boat ride to the South Arm fishing site where I was to meet Joe Fowler and my horse. When Roger and Barry Mathias (a back-up boat ranger who was to be with Roger all day) dropped me off, everything indicated it was going to be a perfect day on the lake. The morning's freshness and the sound of lake ripples quietly slapping the sand of the shore were hardly interrupted by the well-tuned hum of Roger's boat engine. The sun rising over the Absaroka Mountains burned off the last of the lake's morning mist. Happy to be alive, I enjoyed the moment. When Barry handed me two rifles in heavy leather scabbards, I was reminded that I had a bigger agenda than just enjoying the South Arm scenery.

While I wasn't overly worried about people or bears in our

perimeter security responsibilities, I was glad we had the rifles. They would be slung vertically from the saddle horns, therefore readily available and out of our way but highly visible. I briefly wondered what the superintendent would say since he had definite opinions about firearms. He preferred no visible weapons, but if rangers felt they were necessary, the firearms should be carried in a low-key manner. I decided utility and function were more important than low-key aesthetics, even when the latter were the superintendent's wishes. Besides, he probably wouldn't even see them.

I looked over the area and was surprised to see two tents set up near the helispot. It turned out to be Sandi Fowler (Joe's wife) and Karl Striby, two members of Yellowstone's helitack crew. They had been flown in by a military support helicopter the previous afternoon, along with a Mark III fire pump and other equipment. Their task was to provide fire protection for the helispot.

A little later Joe arrived with Eli and Eb. He too had a short night on a patrol cabin cot and not his own bed. He got up at 4 a.m. to take care of the horses, button up the cabin, ride eight miles, and find his way here through off-trail downfall. Joe and I rode several widening circles through the timber behind the meadow that encircled the helispot and fishing site, checking for anything abnormal or that might pose a threat to the president's party. It was routine Yellowstone forest/meadow interface terrain. There were several grizzly bear day beds, but none showed recent use. We rode out of the timber onto the upper meadow, selected a vantage point in the sun, dismounted and let our horses graze. I was about to comment on the hurry-up and wait syndrome in government operations when we heard the distinctive whop-whop-whop of a large helicopter.

Marine Helicopter II came into view a few minutes later, made a couple of exploratory circles around the area, and landed as directed by Sandi and Striby. The pilot let the engine idle awhile to cool down, then the hatch opened and several Marines exited and checked the area. They strung a cable and hooked it to an antennae they installed uphill from the site, and within five minutes of landing they were talking by phone to Washington, D.C., on a secure channel that was as clear as any Ma Bell could provide to her highest paying customers.

Joe and I rode up to the helicopter to introduce ourselves and let them know our job. The Marine in charge was happy to see us and said, "Everything's on schedule. Our only worry is grizzly bears, and I'm glad you guys are here to take care of them." While they probably had enough firepower aboard to neutralize a force twenty to thirty times their size, they seemed happy to have two rangers on horseback to keep grizzly bears from bothering them. It made me smile as we rode away.

The park's contract helicopter, an Alouette III, landed next. The superintendent and assistant superintendent were aboard as was the park's photographer and the president's fishing guide, a seasonal interpreter from the John D. Rockefeller Memorial Parkway (between Yellowstone and Grand Teton). Townsley's wife Elaine was also on board and brought a sumptuous lunch for the Carter party.

I let the superintendent know we were there and then went back to where I was out of the way but could keep track of what was going on. We didn't wait long. When Marine Helicopter I landed with the president, Rosalynn, Amy, and staff, there was a flurry of activity getting them down to the lakeshore, fitted with life vests, and into canoes. Two canoes of

Secret Service Agents launched first and stayed on the outer perimeter to guard against any interlopers.

Amy and a secret service agent were in a canoe with Ranger John Scott, who formerly had been a Yellowstone Lake fishing guide. Mrs. Carter and her secret service agent went with another ranger who also had been a Yellowstone Lake fishing guide. The president and the superintendent were in a third canoe with President Carter's fishing guide.

North of them, out of sight, were four NPS patrol boats on standby. The crews of Marine I and II remained at ready, while other people who had come watched the President's party or lounged on the beach and meadow. Joe and I and our horses were up slope, making sure grizzly bears didn't crash the fishing party.

The Carter family had barely begun fishing when Amy caught a fish—a nice 20-inch cutthroat. She held it up for others to see and got a quiet round of oohs, ahs, and applause from the others. Scott carefully unhooked the fish and released it back into the lake. Then Amy caught another fish. Mrs. Carter caught a fish almost simultaneously. Mrs. Carter caught her second fish, and Amy caught a fish, then still another fish. Mrs. Carter caught a fish and then Amy, Amy, Amy!

So it went for about a half hour. I observed apprehension and tension mounting in the group watching the fishing party. Judging from the body language, some seemed to be holding their breath while others seemed to be hyperventilating. Then the president caught a fish! A sigh of relief swept through the onlookers, and everyone seemed to relax. All was once again right in the world (or at least in the South Arm).

It turned out that the president's out-of-town guide had gotten separated from his tackle box and was limited in what he could do. And he didn't know the lake nearly as well as the local fishing guides who accompanied Amy and Mrs. Carter. When they got back on shore they relaxed, sat down for lunch, and seemed in a fine mood. Joe and I continued our vigil, and then I saw the superintendent stand and gesture for me to come down. I thumped Eb a couple times to get his attention and started that way, arriving at a fast trot.

When I got there Townsley asked me, "Jerry, would you mind if President Carter rode your horse?" "Not at all," was my answer as I dismounted. For the first time I was glad I was riding Eb. It is difficult to deny a request to let the president of the United States ride an NPS horse assigned to you. Had I been riding Dusty, my answer may well have been different. Thanks to Eb I avoided this dilemma.

The superintendent continued, "I have a picture of my father and President Teddy Roosevelt on horseback taken when Roosevelt visited Yosemite in 1905. I'd like to have my picture taken riding with President Carter." I waved for Joe to come down, then I took the rifle off my saddle and handed it to the assistant superintendent who was standing nearby. I checked Eb's cinch and led him around so the president had the advantage of climbing aboard from the uphill side. To his credit the president took the reins and climbed on Eb without a problem. While not a particularly graceful effort, it was certainly not the first time the president had mounted a horse. I looped Eb's lead rope around the saddle horn as the president got as comfortable in the saddle as he was going to get. The stirrups were a little long for him, but being a gracious gentleman, he made do as they were.

Joe arrived and handed Eli over to Townsley. While the superintendent had his share of critics, even the most vocal admitted he was a competent horseman. Townsley climbed on Eli and brought him alongside Eb and the president. The superintendent was quite a bit taller than Joe, so he had to ride with his knees doubled up since, in the interest of time and schedule, he didn't want to have the stirrups adjusted. Together they made several passes up and down the meadow, as the park photographer dutifully documented the occasion. The superintendent riding with his stirrups too short and the president riding with his stirrups too long were recorded for posterity.

Mrs. Townsley made polite conversation with Mrs. Carter, saying, "The president looks comfortable on a horse." "Oh, yes," Mrs. Carter answered in her fine Southern accent, "He's an accomplished horseman." I would say he was an accomplished gentleman and an adequate horseman. When the photo op concluded, they returned our horses, thanked us, and finished their lunch. We retrieved our rifles and continued our grizzly bear watch.

It was time to leave. The Carters thanked Mrs. Townsley for the fine lunch and started up the hill. The helicopters fired up and Joe and I went to the lunch site with Mrs. Townsley, who was leaving on one of the patrol boats. She thoughtfully offered us the extra food. While our horses grazed at the end of their lead ropes, Joe and I wolfed down a delicious lunch. The carrot cake was especially good, and I asked Mrs. Townsley if she would part with the recipe. She agreed and mailed the recipe to Cindy, who still has it and often uses it. When the patrol boat arrived, we helped Mrs. Townsley aboard and then rode out to Heart Lake Trailhead and home. The meadow so recently alive with activity seemed to heave a sigh of relief as we rode off.

Once on the trail I reflected on the last two days' events and decided it wasn't all bad duty being a bit player on a dignitary's fishing trip. Nevertheless, I preferred joining Cindy on her trips each April 1st when the Snake River outside of Yellowstone opened to fishing. We would ski or snowshoe a half mile south of our residence to her favorite fishing hole, where she fished and I enjoyed the snow-free river's edge. After fishing long enough to catch two, 18 to 20-inch cutthroats, she cleaned them, and we skied or snowshoed home. While I read and relaxed, Cindy created a super-fine bacon, egg, toast, and cutthroat trout breakfast. That was my idea of how to enjoy someone else's fishing trip, and to celebrate the impending end of winter at Yellowstone's South Entrance.

Chapter 21

Paying Tuition at the School of Hard Knocks

THE MORE TIME YOU SPEND IN YELLOWSTONE'S BACKCOUN-
try on horseback, ski patrols, or presidential fishing trips, the
greater opportunity there is for a "special challenge." I don't
know if the saying, "Save something for the bivouac," is widespread outside of Yellowstone. But when rangers, day-hikers,
riders, or cross-country skiers in the park are finishing up
lunch on the trail and putting away leftovers, it is commonly
heard. The comment is a half-joking, friendly reminder with
a touch of gallows humor, often pronounced by someone
who has been there and done that. In this context, "bivouac"
refers to an unplanned and unexpected night out on the trail
after failing to get to the planned destination.

During all my years in Yellowstone, misadventure led me
to bivouac twice. The first time was in the winter of 1967
when two companions and I attempted to ski from Fawn Pass
to Sportsman Lake cross country, rather than take a marked
trail because it was longer. We didn't make it due to heavy
breaking in deep snow; a snow storm that added more snow
depth, darkened the sky, and hid the sun most of the day; and
my inept navigation efforts. We went east instead of north at
a crucial point and spent a minimally comfortable night biv-
ouacked on the upper reaches of Reece Creek instead of bask-

ing in the comfort of the Sportsman Lake Patrol Cabin. You could call this paying tuition in the college of hard knocks.

Some 34 years later I experienced my second dose of bivouacking when I attempted to ride from Lamar Ranger Station across the Mirror Plateau to Fern Lake Cabin in a rainstorm. Apparently I was still an inept cross-country navigator. This happened after I had retired and was spending summers as a backcountry volunteer working out of Fern Lake Patrol Cabin. As a backcountry volunteer I helped clear trails, contacted campers and day hikers, and evaluated horse outfitters who guided the public in the backcountry. In between chores I was free to rest or explore.

The horse they assigned me was Scott, a 16-hands sorrel, Missouri Foxtrotter. I had ridden him in my last decade as a ranger, from 1986 when the park purchased him until I retired in 1995. In my opinion, Scott was the best all-around backcountry horse the park owned. He was smooth to ride, a durable traveler, and he wasn't afraid of grizzly bears—an acquaintance had watched Scott join a mule and together chase a two year-old grizzly out of the Lake horse pasture.

When Ranger Patty Bean and I were in Pelican Valley on a trail-clearing hitch, we saw two wolves as we passed the outlet of Tern Lake. We watched them awhile, then went on to Fern Lake Cabin. We were aware that a pack of ten to twelve wolves, referred to as Mollie's Pack, was in this area. The National Park Service had reintroduced wolves to the park in 1995, the year that I retired. On our third night at Fern cabin, Patty woke me at one in the morning. I had been sleeping soundly after two hard days of trail clearing, but as I slowly came awake I could hear wolves howling all around us. The howling sounded so close that at first I thought they were on the porch.

Instead they were a hundred yards away—where we had our horses picketed. It sounded as if there were wolves howling on three sides of the horses! Patty spoke abruptly and earnestly, "We gotta get down there." "Wait," I said. "Let me wake up a bit. They may be just passing through." "I'm going down now," was her immediate response as she strapped on her duty belt. "Light the lanterns, and I'll be right with you," I said, getting out of my warm sleeping bag and throwing on my clothes as quickly as I could.

We left one lantern burning inside the front window, and Ranger Bean led the way from the cabin carrying the second lantern. She was wearing her duty belt with a canister of bear spray and a flashlight attached. I followed and had my fanny pack with a fresh can of bear spray and an extra mini flashlight inside. I carried three horse halters, the cabin flashlight, and a pocket full of treats for the horses. Between the frequent wolf howls I could hear the bell on Stillwater, the packhorse that I had let run free knowing he would stay close to the picketed horses. The howls were so intense and pervasive that I had a brief image of a troika being chased by a huge pack of wolves across Russia's steppes.

We found the horses clustered together. Scott was facing the pitch dark void in the direction of the howls, pawing the ground with his un-picketed hoof. Shibida, Patty's horse, was trembling and seemed much relieved at our arrival. Stillwater, ordinarily somewhat of a loner, was standing between the picketed horses. When we came up, he moved toward us as if seeking body contact with humans to ward off the evil spirits. Petting, treats, and our presence calmed the horses. The wolf howls continued as loud as coyotes on steroids but kept getting farther away.

Wolf howls, while mystic and impressive to humans, tend

to be disquieting, even terrifying to horses because of genes passed down for generations from times long ago when these predators roamed widely across the continent. The volume and distance of howls can be especially deceptive at night. They were awfully close to our boys, and I could understand why the horses were upset. While horses and rangers were the actual intruders in this instance, I found the presence of these reintroduced cousins of the land's original owners disconcerting.

I was worried about how we could successfully get along with our canine neighbors in the weeks and months to come. As we led our boys back to the cabin for what was left of the night, I also wondered what to tell horse outfitters and the public. Ranger Bean was evidently pondering some of the same questions, and a few days later, when she returned to the front country, she contacted and questioned several wolf experts. They said we should be bold with wolves and make them apprehensive about hanging around a cabin or camp. They suggested chasing wolves while on horseback, which would make them wary of horses rather than thinking of a horse as a meal to take down. It would help convince the horses that wolves were nothing to fear and could be intimidated simply by a horse's size.

At this time of year, the Mirror Plateau was great summer range for herds of bison and elk and dozens of deer. The wolves were apparently enroute to check out this smorgasbord of food. Rising a couple thousand feet above the Lamar Valley to the north and Pelican Valley on the south, Mirror Plateau is the headwaters of about twelve named creeks and countless unnamed ones. It is divided by several prominent drainages going in almost every direction, and it houses several large sweeping basins of grass, numerous ponds, and one named lake—Mirror Lake. The Mirror Plateau is about fifteen miles long and four to six miles wide.

For several summers while working out of Fern Lake Cabin, I had explored the southern end of the Mirror. I had followed marked but long abandoned NPS trails from Mirror Lake to the headwaters of Pelican Creek. I had also followed several possible 1877 Nez Perce retreat routes up Raven and other creeks and felt relatively comfortable on the south third of the Mirror. I had yet to cross the north end and ride out to Lamar Ranger Station.

My opportunity came at the end of a Fern Lake shift in the latter part of August. I had my car shuttled from Lake to Lamar Ranger Station. A ranger on a day patrol in Pelican Valley took my packhorse back to Lake for me so Scott and I were ready to cross the Mirror. We went directly to the Specimen Creek Trail and once on the trail made good time. We interrupted several bunches of elk bedded down in the timber for their mid-day siestas. Bison were into their rut, and we went around several bunches with the bulls making loud guttural snorts and grunts.

My horse and I followed the trail down to the valley and headed straight for Lamar Ranger Station, also known as the Buffalo Ranch. As soon as he sighted the Lamar barn Scott figured that was where his next oats were coming from. All I had to do was keep my feet in the stirrups as the red horse splashed across the Lamar River under the watchful scopes and telephoto lenses of three car loads of wolf watchers from the Yellowstone Association Institute located at the Buffalo Ranch.

After taking care of my horse, I left him in the corral and headed to Bozeman and home for rest, recovery, and Rainier Ales. After four days of Cindy's good food I was ready to head back over the Mirror to Fern Lake. However, it was overcast and raining with more rain showers predicted. After dithering awhile I decided to go to Lamar and decide there. The weather was better at Lamar—overcast, low ceiling, and light drizzle. Scott was glad to see me and get his pan of oats. It was later than I had intended to start, but I decided to go anyway despite the forecast of more rain.

We headed for the mouth of Chalcedony Creek, which is the more direct way onto the Mirror. Everything smelled new and clean in the damp morning air. I had my slicker on and was wearing my "shotgun chaps" partly to keep my clothes from absorbing moisture and partly for good luck—the idea being, if you are prepared for bad weather, it is less likely to occur.

The stiff climb up Chalcedony Creek took longer than I anticipated. It was already a lot later than I hoped, considering where I was and how far I still had to go. I tried to keep on route and not get diverted into any side drainages no matter how interesting they might appear. But by side-hilling around, instead of going over high points, I got sucked into the Deep Creek drainage quite a distance before I realized my mistake. This was not the time to explore and I rode back out.

Paying more attention to the beauty of my surroundings than to navigation, I repeated this diversion on other drainages. Then the late afternoon thundershowers materialized, and I had to wait out lightning strikes on the ridge in front of me. After two or three additional misadventures, it dawned on me that the sun had gone down. I figured I should find a good bivouac site while I still has some daylight. The chagrin and embarrassment over having to bivouac would be the same whether it was a comfortable site or a haphazard one, but there could be a lot less physical suffering if I picked a good location.

I found a group of large fir trees growing so close together that their canopies joined. The soil beneath was still dry despite the fairly heavy rain. There was a good supply of dead and dry wood, and the open area nearby had enough grass to keep Scott happy for a year.

I tied Scott and then raced the oncoming darkness to collect enough dry wood to keep a large fire going all night if necessary. As full darkness arrived I unsaddled Scott under the fir canopy and led him out to graze. While he grazed, I turned on my hand-held radio and listened as various backcountry parties checked in with the park's Comm Center. When there was a lull, I called in, identified myself, and said, "Just checking in. Everything's fine." They acknowledged.

I let my friend eat for an hour and then tied him close to where I would bed down. I ate a granola bar and had a drink of water for supper. Then I spread the saddle blankets to serve as a pad, put my saddle at the head of my impromptu mattress, wrapped my slicker around me and laid down. Using my saddle as a pillow just like they did in many a Western song and movie, I promptly fell sound asleep.

I don't know if I slept five minutes, an hour, or half an hour, but I came abruptly awake and aware of another presence. My senses focused, I heard again the sound that must have awakened me. It was a nearby grunt and snort—or was it a growl? My pulse raced even as I stayed motionless, and my breathing was minimal and quiet. The sound was repeated and was definitely a grunt, followed closely by the stomp of a foot that seemed to express irritation.

I could see Scott's silhouette against the sky. He was standing at attention, ears alert, and focused on something in back of me.

I heard more grunting (growling?) and more foot stomping. There was also a second presence. My flashlight and fanny pack with a can of bear spray were close by my head, but I didn't want to move and irritate whatever was there. Then I realized it was a bull bison, likely two of them, grunting and stomping. My bivouac site had intruded on their bed-ground, which explained why the ground was so trampled. For a second I was relieved it was not a grizzly, but then I realized it wasn't good to piss off a 1,800-pound bull bison either. I continued to lie still as the grunting got farther away. Scott relaxed, but there was no more sleep for me, and I spent the remainder of the night moving just enough to stay comfortable. Fortunately, it wasn't too cold.

When daylight finally arrived I grazed Scott for an hour and then headed out to find where I had gone astray. Riding was great, the country beautiful and interesting, but I didn't find what I was looking for. I saw almost everything except the route to Mirror Lake. It was partly because I spent too much time admiring the scenery and not enough time seriously navigating. There was much more country to see than I had imagined.

Not wanting to bivouac another night, I had resolved to head back the way I had come if I was not on the right path by noon. However, when noon arrived, the siren song of adventure took me down the Opal Creek drainage. I hoped it would be shorter and quicker to Lamar Ranger Station rather than heading back up the way we had come. When we dropped onto the bench above the Lamar River, it was choked with downfall from the '88 fires, as Mike Ross had warned me. I led Scott through the maze of downed trees to the river, and I dismounted to lead my red horse up that steep pitch.

I got a head start up the steep incline and tugged on the rope to get Scott going. He lunged up the pitch past me and reached the top, pulling the lead rope out of my hand. Shit, I thought, he'll be at Lamar way ahead of me. But, like the true professional he was, he waited for me, and we arrived at Lamar together. It pays to ride a good horse.

Retrospective: I crossed the Mirror four times after my bivouac but never found the site of my misadventure. Somewhere on the Mirror Plateau, sheltered by a canopy of several mature fir trees, lies a pile of dead wood big enough to fuel a substantial fire all night long. If you ever stumble across it, let me know where it is.

Chapter 22

My Introduction to Yellowstone Bears

WHEN I TRANSFERRED TO YELLOWSTONE IN 1964, MY IMME-diate supervisor asked me what I knew about bears. I replied that I had been raised in Yosemite with black bears and had seen one grizzly. He said I would have to learn fast since one of my responsibilities was to minimize bear problems, and there were a lot of bears at Canyon. Canyon was also head-quarters for the Craighead Grizzly Bear Study Team.

Jack Hughes, an experienced Yellowstone ranger, was as-signed to Canyon with me. He had Yellowstone bear experi-ence, and he had a good rapport with the Craighead broth-ers, John and Frank, who had been conducting grizzly bear research in Yellowstone since 1959. Canyon campground had around 400 sites, about half of which were in the older section and had the old style attempt at a bear-proof garbage can. This was basically a can in a vault in the ground, cov-ered by a lid and accessed by pressing a pedal that raised the lid. They were ineffective: Some bears apparently figured out how to operate the lid within five minutes of when the first can was installed. The new section of the campground had around 200 campsites, which had the current, usually effec-tive, style of bear-proof can. This consisted of a heavy-duty can resting on a concrete platform. The can was covered by a heavy sheet metal lid mounted on a pipe set in the platform. These were expensive but for the most part kept bears out of the garbage.

At this early date there were no food storage regulations, and coolers were left on picnic tables and on the ground. Gleeful bears raided these coolers and defied most attempts to chase them away. It was not uncommon to see bears in the campground in broad daylight. It was also common to see black bears and grizzlies feeding from the same garbage can or overturned cooler.

One day during this era I counted seven different grizzlies and five different black bears in the Canyon Campground over a four-hour span of time (late afternoon to dark). If this were to happen today, it would make the front page of most major newspapers. The majority of the activity was nocturnal, but daylight raids, especially by black bears, were not uncommon. Blacks caused most of the damage and tended to be bolder. Grizzlies tended to be shyer and more secretive, but both species ate well in the campground.

During this time period, on-duty rangers showed up at the ranger station first thing in the morning to fill out bear damage reports from the previous night's activity in the campground. The visitors' attitudes varied widely from extreme ire to good humor. Some felt the story they had to tell was well worth the loss. Others wanted immediate compensation and/or wanted to sue the government and/or wanted to punch someone out.

One lady was apologetic for bothering us when she reported a slight tear from a tooth bite in a sleeping bag. Her three-year-old daughter had been sleeping on the ground in the bag when the lady and her husband, awakened by their daughter's crying, saw a bear dragging away the sleeping bag with their daughter in it. They scared the bear away by banging on pots and pans. The daughter was uninjured and went right back to sleep. The lady said the tear was hardly worth mentioning, but she thought she should let us know about it anyway. Didn't she know that her daughter could have been killed?

You don't work around bears for very long without developing a deep appreciation for their individuality, smarts, and capabilities. Contrary to their sometimes clown-like appearances, bears have amazing memories, a super quick ability to learn, outstanding perceptions, and speed, agility, and dexterity. They are among Mother Nature's most impressive and complex creatures. When you think they don't see you or aren't paying attention to you, you are usually wrong.

Most people fail to comprehend a bear's sheer strength, and accurately estimating their size or weight is an art few folks ever master. There is a saying that the bear's size depends on whether it is daylight or dark, whether the bear is coming toward you or going away, and whether you are inside or outside.

And that's just a beginning. Bears pay attention to nuances. They recognize marked patrol vehicles and the NPS uniform, and they can be warned by the merest glance. All summer I responded to situations where a bear couldn't be scared off by campers only to quickly disappear when it saw me approach. Late in the season I went to the campground on such a report and found a 200-pound grizzly in possession of a sumptuous cooler near a picnic table. About 75 people were gathered, some as close as 20 to 25 yards of the bear.

I started walking between the people and the bear, asking the people to move back. This was long before bear spray, and I had begun carrying my .357 magnum revolver when involved in bear matters. I still don't know why the bear decided to take exception to my presence and charge. People ran, some yelling and some screaming. I stood my ground and drew my .357, cocked it, and with a two-handed grip tried to get a sight picture on the charging bear's bobbing head. When the bear was about five to eight yards away and had not hesitated, I pulled the trigger.

The bear stopped, turned, and started retreating. When it was broadside I shot it again, this time aiming at the heart. That was all I had time for before the bear disappeared. I was using .357 factory ammunition, 158 grain, solid point, semi-wad cutters. We looked for the bear for several hours with no success. I called Bob Morey and told him the story, and to my great surprise I didn't get chewed out. Morey listened and told me to search until dark, to warn as many people as we could, and to check the campground frequently.

This incident changed my protocols for carrying firearms in bear country. After analyzing my experience, I decided if I ever had to shoot another bear, I would shoot for bone to render the bear less mobile. I also resolved that I would finish the job on the spot, shooting as fast as I could shoot accurately, as many times as necessary, to drop the bear then and there. I started carrying my more powerful .44 magnum revolver all the time in my increasingly heavy daypack. When I responded to bear situations, I wore the .44 with at least 12 extra rounds. I resolved that never again would I have to look for a bear I had wounded, and I did not make this error again. However, on three occasions I did have to look for bears that other people had wounded.

The bear I shot showed up dead sometime later alongside the road. Canyon maintenance found him and hauled the carcass to the Trout Creek Dump and left him there to feed his former compatriots. The Craighead Grizzly Bear Study Team spent almost every evening at the dump to census grizzlies as they came in to feed on the day's collected garbage. One of the research assistants told me about the bear, and I was very relieved to find that the situation had been resolved, but at the same time I was extremely mortified by how it came about.

We often set culvert traps on the fringe of the campground to try to capture some of the nuisance bears. By park protocol, when we trapped one we could not take it out of our district. So we would take a bear to the district boundary, point the trap toward our neighbor's territory, and release the bear. The neighbor would do the same with their problem bears. Rarely did a bear beat us home, but most would usually show up a short time later. Hardly even a temporary solution, this method sometimes provided a brief respite from a particular bear.

Each bear trapper had his own formula for success, and many were creative and innovative. Some bears were elusive while some seemed to be trap junkies. Seclusion and a natural approach to the trap helped, and chances for success were higher if the trap was low to the ground and stable. Squeaky-clean traps versus real garbage-can-style traps were a heated debate.

Favorite bait was also a hot topic. Just about everything was used, from garbage to road kill, from rotten meat to fish guts, from over-ripe fruit to canned fruit and any combination of the above. I had good success with blueberry and peach pies, but these were not always available. You had to have good rapport with concession cooks to get stale, left over, or burned pies.

If you trapped a grizzly, you showed it to the Craighead researchers in case they might want to make it a part of their study. If you trapped a grizzly that was tagged by them you would notify them, and they would usually take the trapped bear to Trout Creek to weigh it and rework it. This was an interesting, time consuming process. First they would tranquilize the bear, then take measurements (girth, length, leg lengths, paw width, etc.), weigh the bear, make a plaster cast of a foot and/or make a soft mold of its mouth and bite size. They would also tattoo an ID number on the bear's inner lip.

The team would check and record the ear tags, which were all numbered but were different colors and shapes. From a distance you could identify a bear by documenting the shape, color, and location of its tags. But like reading a cattle brand, reading the color codes on a marked grizzly was not easy for the uninitiated. For example, a round (yellow, red or blue) tag could be on the top or the bottom of the ear, and it could be facing forward, or it could be facing back. They also used other tag shapes—triangular, square, etc. An almost infinite number of combinations were possible.

If you got the correct combination of tags or if you got the number on a tag, you could identify an individual bear. From the Craighead records you could get a lot of information about the bear including sex, weight, age, trapping history, and miscellaneous other interesting tidbits. While they weren't casual about handing out information, they were happy to supply field people like me with any information I requested.

Somewhere in this era (late 1950s to early 1960s) the tranquilizer Sucostrin became available for rangers to use. It was a neuro-muscular blocking agent used by veterinarians to immobilize animals. While immobilized, the animal was still conscious and aware of what was happening to and around him. Sucostrin, in the doses used on bears, would be fatal if injected in a human, so it was not used casually or incautiously. For our purposes the drug was administered to a trapped bear by means of a syringe mounted on the end of a jab stick. With a reasonable dose in the muscle, the bear would go down in one to five minutes. The first part of the bear to react would be the hind legs, then incapacitation would move to the fore part of the body, with the bear last losing control of its head.

The bear would be immobile for ten to twenty minutes, depending on the bear's age and condition. During this time the bear could be tagged, checked, or moved to another trap. A follow-up dose could be given to gain more time, but follow-up doses were administered judiciously since it was possible to overdose and lose an animal. When a bear recovered from the drug effects, the use of its head came back first, then the neck, shoulders and front feet, and finally the hind legs. Outside stimulus could provoke a startled response and greatly accelerate this process, much to the surprise of the individual handling the bear.

At this time there was only one CO_2 capture rifle in the park, and it was kept in the management biologist's office. It was capable of shooting cylindrical aluminum darts. Inside the dart was a rubber plunger activated by an impact charge. This charge detonated on contact with a solid object, plunging the liquid drug into the target. That is, if the dart stayed in the target (bear) rather than bouncing off. All in all, there was a lot of witchcraft, a.k.a. dumb luck, in delivering a successful dose to a bear.

These were interesting and innovative times with a lot less structure than in later years. For instance, folks had used a bow and arrow to deliver the Sucostrin to capture a bear that would not be trapped. (The point was cut off the arrow; the rubber plunger from a syringe was glued in its place. The syringe was filled with the desired dose, the arrow with the rubber plunger was carefully inserted into the syringe, and the innovator was ready for adventure.) Most of our lessons came through experience, many of them by bad experiences.

Jack Hughes was familiar with the equipment. He had used it previously and was able to borrow the CO_2 rifle and drugging kit. Jack gave me an orientation on the intricacies of the drug kit and setting up a drugging operation. We sighted in the CO_2 rifle and waited until evening. We went out after supper and in a short time found our first candidate. After a maneuver or two Jack got a shot off. The dart hit the bear in the rear, and the bear took off to get away from us, the source of the pain in his rump. Now a bear can go quite a distance in one minute, so later we found it was better to shoot from cover so the bear did not associate us with the thump in its rear and did not feel the need to run so far away. We tagged the bear and released it at Trout Creek the following day.

Then Jack was away from Canyon for days off. There was still an abundance of bear activity in the campground, and I got the Sucostrin from the refrigerator and cruised the campground. There were good candidates for removal everywhere. I loaded a dart for a particular black bear, got a good hit on the bear, and then waited a couple minutes to give the drug time to work. With the help of a couple of off-duty seasonal rangers, I found the bear, tagged it, and we dragged him to a waiting trap. The bear died of an overdose. Glum times for me. Then the same result for the second black bear I stalked and shot. Shit! This was no way to manage bears.

After seriously reducing my estimate of the third black

bear's weight, I managed to dart it and get it to the trap. And the bear lived! I felt relieved. When Jack got back to the residence area late that night, I had just pulled in with one black bear in the trap and two dead black bears in the bed of my pickup. Jack said, "Looks like you've been busy tonight." Jack transferred to Olympic National Park the following spring, and in July Alden Nash replaced him. Despite our previous year's efforts getting bears out of the campground, we had just as many black and grizzly bears haunting us in 1965. We continued our trapping efforts and also got the park's only CO_2 rifle back on loan and used it on a regular basis.

That summer I tranquilized more than a dozen free-roaming grizzlies and black bears in the Canyon Campground without a single fatality. We had a number of hair-raising adventures finding the darted animals and getting them tagged and into a trap before the drug wore off. Our timing was so close in some cases that a couple of bears almost walked into the traps on their own power.

As the summer progressed I was getting good hits on bears, but they often would not go down. It was frustrating to have all your strategy and stalking go for naught. One day I was having coffee with the Craigheads at their Canyon operation center and mentioned my problem. They told me that as bears gained layers of fat, it was increasingly difficult to get the Sucostrin into the muscle, especially when you shot them in the rump. They suggested using the less fatty shoulder and/or neck as my target area.

I immediately followed their advice, and my success rate quickly improved. I began talking with them more about the nitty-gritty aspects of tranquilizing and trapping. I learned more about drugging technique while drinking coffee with the Craigheads than I learned from all other sources. The

Canyon seasonal staff participated aggressively in the trapping and drugging efforts. They were a good bunch to work with, always ready to help, and were willing to do what they could to keep visitors and bears safely separated. Before the summer was over, they knew exactly what needed to be done and did it without being asked. We all worked well together as a team in routine incidents and under extreme stress.

We continued our drugging and trapping efforts in 1966. We still had the same mix of bear-proof and non-bear-proof garbage cans in the campground, and while everyone favored the newer bear-proof cans, they were expensive. There did not seem to be any money to upgrade the 200 non-bear-proof garbage cans. The only thing I could do to mitigate the effect of having this copious food attractant in the campground was to continue the aggressive drugging and trapping program. So we stumbled along for another summer.

While we still had numerous bear-caused damages in the campground, we didn't have any serious injuries that season. For some time we had been suggesting that campers sleep in tents rather than on the ground without a tent. In 1966, people sleeping in small pup-tents awoke to find bears sitting on them (two times), jumping on the tent (one time), or pawing at the tent (once). Fortunately the resulting melees produced only minor injuries and some damage to the tents. Two of the incidents were attributed to black bears and two to grizzlies.

One night a party saw a grizzly bear that was walking through a campsite turn abruptly toward a pup tent, jump up-and-down on it, swat the tent twice, and then continue through the campsite, almost without missing a beat. The two surprised occupants of the tent suffered only a strained back and multiple bruises between them. They definitely had a story to tell, and they had a slightly damaged tent to prove it. Once again we adjusted our advice, suggesting that campers sleep in larger tents and that they sleep in the center of the tent, not against the walls. This latter advice was to avoid the tribulation of one sleeping camper who had her buttocks slapped by a passing bear, evidently curious about the bulge in the tent wall.

In 1966 I free darted (darted bears that were at large, not confined in a trap) and removed 13 different grizzlies and almost as many black bears from the Canyon Campground. That turned out to be the most bears I ever tranquilized in a single season. Trapping and removing bears added up to a lot of time, effort, and hard work. And some good bear stories.

One late summer night, just off the campground's A Loop, I got a dose of Sucostrin into a good-sized grizzly. The bear took off running, and we had a difficult time finding him as the minutes ticked away. We were still dragging him to the trap as the drug wore off.

We were in thick woods with lots of downfall, and moving the big bear was very difficult. We wanted this bear, as he was responsible for a number of increasingly serious depredations. We apparently tried too hard for too long. Suddenly the bear was on all four feet, lunging toward Ranger Glen Riley who had been dragging it. Fortunately the bear's hind feet went out from under him and he missed Riley. Glen backed up rapidly but tripped over a log. The bear zeroed in on the sound and again lunged explosively toward Glen.

I shot the bear through the shoulders with my .44 and the bear dropped at Glen's feet. Stepping up to the bear I finished him with two more rounds at the base of the skull. That was as close as I ever came to having to shoot a bear off of an individual. Too close, but we were still in a steep learning curve.

We continued our efforts to keep bears away from human food and out of the campground. One night we had a trap set in a vacant campsite at the apex of the loop. The trap had been set after dark by Canyon patrol, and around 11 p.m. I was called by Comm Center reporting frantic bear activity around the trap site.

I responded, bringing the drug kit. Canyon patrol was on site. There was a black bear cub-of-the-year in the trap. Mama bear was bawling loudly, frantically running around the trap trying to get to her baby, who was bawling loudly for his mom. Surrounding campers were wisely sitting in their cars with their windows rolled up. One of the rangers backed his vehicle up to the trap, and I got out with a 12-gauge shotgun, its magazine loaded with 00 buckshot and one round in the chamber. I aimed at mama bear and stood between her and the trap while one of the patrol rangers hooked up the trap. The frantic mama bear charged and then backed off, charged and then backed off, time after time. My plan was to shoot only if she came close enough to touch the barrel of the shotgun. She always stopped just short.

With lots of luck and buckets of sweat, we slowly pulled the trap, followed by mama bear, out of the campground. Then we tranquilized her with a very light dose and put her in the trap with her baby. She recovered from the drug, and she and her cub lived happily ever after—or at least for the rest of the night. That was the most valiant, protective mother bear I ever encountered, and that includes at least a dozen grizzly moms I ran into in subsequent years in similar circumstances.

Yellowstone's efforts to keep bears away from human foods changed dramatically after the tragedies in Glacier National Park in 1967. On a single night, Saturday, August 12, two young women were killed by two different grizzlies in widely separated areas of the park. Both deaths were in backcountry campsites, and both bears were regular feeders on human garbage. One of the incidents occurred at Granite Park Chalet where guests regularly congregated on the chalet porch to watch grizzly bears feed in the chalet's open-pit dump. An NPS backcountry campsite was nearby.

Shortly after these incidents, I went to Glacier with Dale Nuss, the South District Ranger (and my boss) to help Glacier with several forest fires burning at the time. I was assigned to the fire nearest Granite Park Chalet (I think it was the Glacier Wall fire). When that fire wound down, I took the opportunity of heavy overcast skies and impending rain to "scout" ahead. From a rise above Granite Park Chalet, I studied the scene of the tragedy. Maintained hiking trails intersected the fainter travel routes of grizzly bears. Standing there in the dusk, it felt eerie, almost surreal, to see the juxtaposition of terrain, trails, and travel routes. They explained to me why the incident unfolded the way it did.

I knew we had very similar situations in Yellowstone: wildlife travel routes intersected maintained trails, shared them for a ways, then veered off in independent directions. Bear trails entered the campgrounds at Canyon, Pelican Creek, and Fishing Bridge. There but for the grace of God, I thought. Or maybe it was just luck that something like Glacier had not happened at Canyon, Pelican Creek, or Fishing Bridge. The profound impact of the Glacier scouting trip stayed with me a long time.

Chapter 23

The Closing of the Dumps

BEARS AND THEIR MANAGEMENT ARE CONTROVERSIAL WORLD-wide, and perhaps especially in Yellowstone. In 1968 the NPS closed the park's several garbage dumps "cold turkey," very much in contrast to the gradual closure the Craighead Grizzly Bear Study Team recommended. The Craigheads felt that if the dumps were closed too quickly, the garbage-addicted, hungry bears would rapidly overrun the campgrounds or go outside the park, searching for the same food. The resulting conflicts with people could result in more dead bears and possibly harm to humans. The Craigheads lobbied for slowly phasing out the garbage dumps, believing this would keep the bears safely inside the park and give the bears time to return to natural foods as the supply of garbage diminished.

Then in a short span of time the NPS somehow came up with enough money to convert all non-bear-proof garbage cans in the park to the current state-of-the-art bear-proof can. With this change in place I thought the NPS plan had a chance to work. Otherwise I thought the Craighead idea made more sense, except I favored a three-year phase out. However, no one asked me! The campgrounds did see increased bear activity but survived mainly due to the newly installed, bear-proof garbage cans.

The incinerators that were to replace the dumps were not up to the challenge, however. They were not capable of handling the volume of garbage, and instead of reducing the garbage to ashes, the incinerators burned some of it and just heated the rest. Since the fences around the incinerators were not bear proof, the displaced West Thumb, Trout Creek, and Rabbit Creek grizzlies who found the incinerators basically got hot meals instead of cold snacks.

Unfortunately, there were campgrounds near the incinerators: Bridge Bay Campground was just a few hundred yards from the Bridge Bay incinerator. Grant Village Campground was about one mile from Grant Village Incinerator. As the poet Robert Burns said, "The best laid plans of mice and men gang aft agley."

The temporary solution was to separate wet and dry garbage, with the dry garbage burned at the incinerators and the wet garbage taken to the old dumps which had been re-opened. The Craigheads didn't think this would be enough to hold the bears in the interior of the park. The procedure was only mildly successful and lasted only a year or so, and the final closing of the dumps was 1968 for West Thumb, 1969 for Rabbit Creek, 1970 for Trout Creek, and 1971 for the West Yellowstone dump.

In 1969, Yellowstone started getting serious about keeping campers' food away from bears. Proper food storage was mandatory. Food, garbage, and other attractants had to be stored in hard-sided vehicles or placed in the bear-proof garbage cans, or hung properly (ten feet above the ground and at least four feet from the nearest tree). This was law, not just recommendation, and was strictly enforced. About this same time, NPS maintenance personnel started collecting garbage twice daily (morning and evening) so there was less garbage to arouse a passing bear's curiosity and tempt it to hang around. Garbage cans were lined with heavy-duty trash bags so that little food waste actually touched the cans. This minimized residual odors, and the garbage cans themselves were periodically steam cleaned.

Somewhere in the late-1960s the rapport between the Craigheads and park management began to erode. The Craigheads felt they knew more about Yellowstone's grizzlies and what they needed to survive than the NPS, and they felt their recommendations were ignored. The NPS said there was more to managing Yellowstone than just insuring the survival of the grizzly and that they had the welfare of other species to consider. The Craigheads felt that visible identification of individual bears (tags and radio collars) was essential to their study, but the NPS disagreed and refused to allow further visible markings.

Sometimes the Craigheads would respond to questions from newspapers before they communicated with park management, and the park took exception to finding out about grizzly bear research from the *Billings Gazette*. And the park didn't appreciate front-page criticism of park management practices. The bottom line of the controversy was poor communication in each direction between park management and the Craigheads.

Also, in 1968, the NPS wanted to get rid of the long abandoned Yellowstone Park Company bus barn located south of the Canyon complex. This was part of a park-wide cleanup in anticipation of Yellowstone's upcoming centennial in 1972. As they moved ahead with plans to get rid of this eyesore, the NPS also wanted to remove the nearby wooden building (a former Yellowstone Park Company mess hall), which the Craigheads used as their headquarters. This meant the Craighead operation needed new facilities, and none were available inside the park. They had to move to the gateway town of West Yellowstone, which they felt was a big stumbling block for their continued operation.

Though I was present as all this was happening, I did my best not to get involved in the controversy. I just kept my head down and continued to trap and tranquilize bears as was necessary to get them out of the Lake area campgrounds. I had good rapport with Jay Sumner, a Craighead research assistant. Through all the bickering and recrimination, he was very good about supplying background history and information on the marked bears I handled. It saved me a lot of work and usually meant less handling of the bear. To return the courtesy, I would let him know where we relocated the bear. We talked regularly, even as the Craigheads and park management talked less and less.

In 1971, the Craighead grizzly bear study terminated. They refused to sign a renewal contract to conduct research in Yellowstone because the new contract required them to submit their research findings to the NPS for approval before releasing them to the public. What started in 1959 as a groundbreaking study using radio telemetry to learn the life cycle of the Yellowstone grizzly bear ended with acrimony and counter accusations. Much had been gained through the Craighead team's efforts to study an exceedingly complex and potentially dangerous animal in all kinds of weather and conditions, in very formidable, remote country. Further study of this charismatic creature would have to wait until the creation of the Interagency Grizzly Bear Study Team in 1973.

When Jay Sumner left he gave me a record of all the bears tagged and marked by the Craigheads. It was intended for my use and not to be duplicated or circulated. I used it to simplify identification of bears I trapped and tranquilized. This knowledge led to better decisions.

The dump closures were not just a theoretical issue to me. An experience in late May 1968 gave me a clue of what to expect. Around 6:30 a.m. I turned into the Fishing Bridge Campground, the only campground in the area open that early in the spring. As I entered I saw a large handsome grizzly cruising the area. I radioed our Comm Center to call Alden Nash on the phone and ask him to bring the drug equipment to Fishing Bridge. I was near the exit of C Loop as the bear came out of the trees near a tent. A parked car blocked my view of the campsite's fire ring, but apparently it had a fire because smoke was rising.

I watched fascinated as the bear suddenly focused on something near the fire ring. It crouched down and began stalking carefully, just like a cat stalking an unsuspecting mouse. For a moment I was mesmerized by the huge bear's power, grace, and stealth. Then I suddenly realized the parked car obscured a woman who was bending over and tending the fire.

I gasped and floor boarded the car's accelerator, my heart pounding. The vehicle, not a police package but a run-of-the-mill, worn-out station wagon, whined shrilly and lurched forward, then picked up speed. Reaching the parked car, I slammed on the brakes. As the vehicle skidded in the gravel, I jammed the gear shift into park, undid my seat belt, unzipped the shotgun case, shoved the car door wide open and stepped out, explosively racking a shell into the shotgun's chamber. Then I charged toward the bear.

All through my gravel-skidding arrival, the bear had stayed focused on his potential victim. But when he heard the metallic *rack-rack* of the shotgun, he turned his head and looked at me. The bear gave me an intense, dirty look, focusing right into my eyes, as if saying, "All right, asshole, your turn this time." He held eye contact just long enough to add, "Next time it's my turn." Then he broke eye contact, wheeled around, and sprinted away. Now I don't claim to speak "grizzly bear," but at that stage of my career I felt I could read their body language somewhat. And this was the message that came across to me.

I ran back to my vehicle to start looking for the bear. Enroute, I stopped to see the woman camper. She appeared to be sub-normal but fully functional. Or maybe she just had the wits scared out of her. I never found out. Alden and I looked for the bear the rest of the morning to no avail. When I got back to the campsite, the campers had moved on.

That evening, around 5 p.m., we managed to tranquilize this bear and relocate it. To my knowledge he never showed up again, so this was some kind of minor success story.

We set traps regularly, caught some bears, took most of them to Trout Creek, pointed them toward Canyon, released them, returned to Lake, and waited for them to return. Two weeks later, on June 9, there was another scary and disquieting close call.

This one occurred in the Hamilton Store employee trailer area at Fishing Bridge, which was located near the abandoned incinerator about one-half mile north of the Fishing Bridge Hamilton Store. Around 11 p.m. a large grizzly tried to get into a trailer occupied by seasonal ranger Duane Cunning and his wife.

The bear climbed on the porch, broke a window just over the bed occupied by Duane and his wife, and got partway into the trailer. As the bear scrambled to get in through the window, it grabbed the pillow Mrs. Cunning had just been sleeping on, even as Duane was slapping the bear with another pillow, trying to scare him away. Despite a lot of commotion the bear did not leave the trailer until a neighbor fired a pistol into the air.

Duane, his wife, and the neighbor watched the bear go towards the woods surrounding the trailer area, then circle back toward them at a slow but focused pace. The neighbor went to his trailer, got a .30-06 rifle and offered it to Duane, who shot the bear twice as it continued toward them. The bear fell, stayed down several minutes, then slowly got up and went into the woods. Since they had neither phone or radio, Duane came to Lake Ranger Station and got me.

I responded along with Cecil Pryor, the ranger on patrol. I followed the bear's blood trail; Cecil followed me with a 12-gauge shotgun. We didn't have far to go. The bear was lying down just a short ways into the woods. When he heard us, he got up slowly, turned, and faced us. He started toward us with a somewhat shaky but determined pace, apparently subscribing to the premise that the best defense is a good offense. I put him down for good with my .44. To their credit the Cunnings finished out their season, but to the best of my recollection, they chose not to come back the next season. Some people get their clues early on and act on them, while some of us have to learn the hard way, time and time again. I fit in the latter category most of the time.

I spent increasing time in the campground at night—two, three, or four hours at a time and several nights a week. Unlike previous years, we started carefully documenting the captured bears with tag numbers, sex, weight, color, scars, and other characteristics—anything to help us recognize a bear we had handled before. We were trying to work smarter instead of just working harder.

One day a camper shot a grizzly at Pelican Creek Campground. The bear had come into their campsite as the camper and his family were eating supper at an outside table. They retreated to their car, taking their food with them. The bear left, and in due time the campers went back outside to finish eating. The bear approached them again, this time more boldly. The head of the house, who was a major in the U.S. Army, was ready. He apparently felt one tactical retreat was enough.

The major retrieved his .357 revolver from the car and emptied it into the bear. He reloaded, fired three more rounds into the bear, and then sat down to wait for the ranger. When I arrived the major was polite but unapologetic. He handed me the weapon, butt first with the empty cylinder swung open.

The next day we took the gentleman before the U.S. Magistrate in Mammoth. Judge Brown turned him loose and returned his firearm when the major said he feared for his life and his family's safety.

I am still surprised that shootings like this didn't happen more often in those days before food storage regulations, better garbage pick-up, cleaner campgrounds, and a better-educated public. Looking back at bear management in Yellowstone from today's vantage point, I find it challenging to recreate my mindset and thought process of that long-ago time.

Nor is it easy to recreate the reasoning and attitudes of the other parties. What went wrong in the Craighead-NPS relationship? No doubt ego was involved on both sides. At this late date, does it really matter which side was more correct? For my point of view, I was well treated by the Craigheads and their research staff. They were always gracious and hospitable when I sought information, and they were always willing to suggest better drugging techniques when I asked. The late 1960s and early 1970s was an important transitional period with many ties to the past and many lessons learned for the future. Clearly the grizzly bear is better off today.

Chapter 24

Park Visitors "Jumped" by Bears

LATE ONE AFTERNOON IN JULY 1968 (THE YEAR OF THE FIRST dump closure), the Fishing Bridge Visitor Center called Lake Ranger Station to tell us a visitor had been "jumped" by a bear between Fishing Bridge and the lake. Ranger John Gingles responded immediately, while Rick Smith and I gathered the drug equipment and followed.

A fisherman from Ralston, Nebraska, had taken a short cut to the Yellowstone River through a shallow marsh near Fishing Bridge. He heard splashing behind him, turned and saw a large bear charging directly towards him from only 25 feet away. The man started to run but hampered by his waders, tripped and fell. The bear ran right over him and disappeared. The fisherman was not injured except for a slight wrist strain. He made it to the Fishing Bridge parking area, and someone went to the visitor center to report the incident.

As I crossed Fishing Bridge I saw a man sitting on the open tailgate of a pick-up in the parking lot. The man's right sleeve was rolled up, and a woman was washing that arm. In his left hand the man held what appeared to be a shot glass, and he was drinking from it as fast as the man next to him would fill it up. There was a group of people gathering around him.

Ranger Gingles, with a shotgun, had taken a position between the swamp and the road, while Ranger Smith returned to Lake Ranger Station for a bear trap. In the meantime a couple of other rangers had shown up, and I asked one to finish the interview and to see the man got medical attention. I asked the other to go to the head of the swamp at the lake outlet and not let anyone enter the swamp. I got my .44 from my pack, put it on, and started down the steps to the swamp to retrace the injured party's steps.

Once out of sight of the gathered crowd, I drew my .44, took a good, solid, double-action grip on the gun, and cautiously proceeded along the fisherman's path. Despite paying close attention, there was no warning before I heard a loud splash as a grizzly burst through some willows, charging right at me. I'll be damned, I thought, there really is a bear. I raised the .44, cocked it, moved my sight picture just a little to the right of center-of-mass, focused on the front sight, and waited. The bear never stopped, and I felt as if a runaway freight train was aiming right at me.

When the bear was about five yards away I fired three times. The bullets stopped his running, but momentum kept him sliding right at me through the water, his huge front feet ahead of him. He came to rest about six feet away, and I started breathing again. I watched the bear a few seconds, reloaded (saving my brass shells), stepped to the bear and fired two rounds point-blank at the base of his skull.

We got the bear's body out of the swamp and returned to Lake Ranger Station. The next day we turned over the body to the Craighead team for an autopsy. The bear was a 15-year-old male, weighed 540 pounds, and had been tagged in 1959. The bear had an empty stomach and probably had not eaten in more than 24 hours.

I felt no joy or elation, only remorse for having to kill another grizzly. At that time I felt it was what I had to do; it was a part of the job to resolve a situation and somehow protect people. Nonetheless a lot of people congratulated me as if I had just qualified for the Olympics, while some said nothing and harbored resentment. The fisherman did not blame the bear for its actions, nor express any animosity toward it. He was sorry it had been shot.

Nineteen sixty-nine was much like 1968—a hectic bear year. Again I spent a lot of sleepless hours trying to get bears out of the campgrounds. I asked for overtime for another ranger so he could give me a hand (since the regular patrol rangers were often too busy with other challenges—drunks, accidents, lost kids, etc.—to be able to move bear traps, pick me up, or assist me as needed). I was told there was nothing in the budget for such matters. I didn't ask for overtime for myself because in that era, you were paid overtime only for fires and full-blown tragedies.

After a particularly hard night, I might sleep in when I knew we had adequate coverage and nothing was planned. However, I was told I should instead be in the office at eight a.m. since that was a good time for my supervisor or managers to get updates and information that might affect their day's operations; they thought it was better if I took time off in the middle of the day. Many years later I tried to recreate the atmosphere and conditions of this period for a friend. After listening intently and incredulously, my friend shrugged and said, "Well, at least you got some good bear stories for your efforts."

As the summer rolled on, I noted how much sheer chance affected peoples' lives. Chance placed some people in harm's way while, at the same time, it rapidly extracted others who had tempted fate; 1969 had examples of both. One evening in June, five-year-old Daphne Jax from St. Paul, Minnesota, came out of the restroom at the Fishing Bridge Campground and startled a 400-pound grizzly that had just been chased from an adjacent loop. The bear grabbed Daphne in his mouth and lifted her off the ground. She screamed, and her father and her uncle charged the bear from their nearby campsite. The bear dropped Daphne, moved off 30 feet, and watched as Daphne was retrieved by her father and uncle. As people gathered and the chaos and confusion escalated, the bear faded away.

The little girl was taken to Lake Hospital, where medical staff determined that she had a broken rib and a punctured lung. Park headquarters was notified, and rangers Doug Smith and Terry Penttila soon arrived in separate vehicles and started searching the campground loops for the bear. I arrived a short time later. Interpretive rangers Larry Marcott and Doug Doolittle checked in with me and volunteered their services, and I had one of them go with Smith and the other with Penttila. In this case, two sets of eyes in each patrol car could do a better job.

In short order the bear was located on the south edge of the campground. As I arrived the bear crossed back into the campground from the lakeshore. I got out of my vehicle and approached the bear with my .44 in hand. The bear seemed nonplussed and disconcerted by my somewhat aggressive approach. He hesitated and then stopped, but while the background was safe for shooting, I wanted to move the bear farther away from the campground before I shot. Smith, Penttila, and their associates were on scene, keeping people back.

I was in effect loose-herding the bear out of the campground when I simultaneously heard a rifle shot and saw the bear drop as if the earth had been jerked out from under him. I looked over my shoulder and saw my supervisor, District Ranger Dale Nuss, with his government issued .300 H & H magnum Model 70 Winchester, the barrel smoking. I hadn't known Dale was on site, but he took the opportunity of the safe background and the bear standing broadside to him (while the bear focused on me) to make a good shot. He apologized for shooting without first letting me know he was in the area. The time was 9 p.m. and only thirty-five minutes had elapsed since the time of the injury.

The carcass was taken to the State Wildlife Lab on the Montana State University campus in Bozeman, Montana, for autopsy. Dale was miffed when he found out that his bullet had severed the bear's spinal cord one inch to the right of where he had aimed (the base of the bear's skull).

Fishing Bridge Campground continued to be a crazy, hyperactive place, including considerable nighttime bear activity. About forty days after the Daphne incident, chance (Fate?) was kinder to a young man from Carnegie, Pennsylvania, who was sleeping on the ground without a tent. During the summer of 1969 John Alexander, a friend of ours, was manager of the Lake gas station. Around three a.m. one July night, he was parked in the nurse's dorm parking lot behind Lake Hospital with a nurse friend (discussing English literature I imagine). A car frantically drove up to the hospital's emergency entrance with two people, one of whom had been injured by a bear in Fishing Bridge Campground. While his nurse friend ran to assist, John called me at home.

That year, at that early hour in the morning, our Comm Center wasn't operational. Without John's call I would have been much delayed in responding. As it was, I charged over to the scene of the attack, which was a campsite near the end of the campground and next to the woods. From tracks I confirmed it was a grizzly, got a description (big!) of the bear from witnesses, and raced back to D Loop where there was a pay phone, intending to call for assistance.

As I bailed out of my car at D Loop and ran to the phone, a man holding his bloody head came staggering out of the campground to meet me. He said a big bear had stepped on his head and was slapping him around when I drove up and scared the bear off. I put the man in my still running patrol car and, with .44 in one hand and flashlight in the other, made a hasty search of the area. I did not see the bear but did find where the man had been sleeping on the ground in his sleeping bag. He had been laying with his head right in the middle of the bear's travel route. No wonder the bear was pissed. I took the man to the hospital where I found that his injuries weren't serious. The injuries of the other camper that night were far more serious though not life threatening.

The next night there were 13 people on overtime in Fishing Bridge Campground. This group included the district ranger, the district maintenance supervisor, and other highly paid help, not just GS-4 and GS-5 seasonal rangers. They were set up to kill or tranquilize any grizzly that came into the campground.

At this point in time (39 years later) my memory can't dredge up all the details of that night, but I think one grizzly was killed outright and one was wounded. Don Yestness, a competent seasonal ranger with years of experience, was set up in I-Loop near the site where the most serious injury had occurred. He had Dale's .300 magnum rifle and was monitoring one of the regular travel routes coming from the Pelican Creek area. At one minute before midnight, a grizzly came into the campsite. Yestness shot it in the chest from about

30 yards away. The impact of the bullet drove the bear back four to six inches. Yet the bear wheeled and ran off into the darkness before it dropped dead 50 yards away. It turned out to be a five-year-old tagged male.

In the early morning, almost 24 hours after the injuries, a large bear came out of the woods in another part of the campground. The ranger there, Terry Penttila, shot him with a rifled slug from a 12-gauge shotgun in the center of the left shoulder. It knocked the bear down, but he got up and ran back the way he came before Penttila could get off another shot. I followed the blood trail, backed up by Ranger Cecil Pryor with a shotgun. The blood trail led through the woods to Pelican Creek, turned north, crossed the east entrance road, and went past the RV Park toward Pelican Creek. We didn't find the bear.

About ten days later we got a report of a minor injury from Fishing Bridge RV Park. About one in the morning, a man, sleeping under the stars on a cot wedged between a travel trailer and his van, was bitten on his right big toe by a bear. I interviewed the man both at the hospital and later at the trailer site. He had a puncture wound on the top of his big toe and one on the bottom, both minor. His cot had been recessed back from the loop road by about six feet, and there was hardly enough space between the travel trailer and the van for the cot. Who says bears don't have a sense of humor?

A nearby camper said she had seen a grizzly pass through the area around 1 a.m. on each of the past three mornings. I thought it would be preposterous for it to happen four mornings in a row, but I set up at 10:30 p.m. that night to free dart whatever might show up. A large grizzly strolled by at 30 minutes after midnight, and I hit him with a good dose of Sucostrin. He went down, and on examining him I found a hole in the center of his left shoulder. Rather than take any chances, I administered a lethal dose of the drug.

The next morning we took off the bear's hide and found a broken-up 12-gauge rifled slug. This was the same bear that Pentilla had shot. The slug had hit the bear's shoulder blade at just enough of an angle that it did not penetrate the bone but simply broke up. The bear's shoulder was not broken, nor was the bear limping or impaired in its mobility (that I could see). Who says bears aren't unbelievably tough?

Chapter 25

Hard Lessons Learned Capturing and Relocating Bears

IN 1970 WHEN I WAS THE SUB-DISTRICT RANGER IN CHARGE of the Lake area, several incidents taught us even more about the precautions necessary in capturing and releasing bears. Having a bear securely in a trap as soon as possible was essential for everyone's safety, including the bear. Bear behavior in the trap varied widely from bear to bear. While some were irate and fought the trap, others were very shy and hung their heads. Some cowered, some acted embarrassed, and others blew snot and saliva over anyone who approached. A few relaxed and napped after dining on the bear bait. I always tried to keep folks away from the trap, both for their safety and to afford the bear as much privacy as possible.

Releasing a trapped bear safely was another source of adventure. When dealing with black bears, many people would just drive to a release site, open the gate, bang on the trap with a nightstick or a pick handle, and wait until the bear left. Others backed to the downhill side of a cut-bank, so when the bear stepped out of the trap, he would be going down a steep bank so fast he wouldn't be thinking of the person who released him.

In the days before the battery-operated trap release system

or new drugs, I preferred to release grizzlies from a moving trap. At the release site, I would get up on the trap, brace myself, signal the trusted driver, and raise the trap gate as the vehicle pulled away. Usually the bear jumped out and ran away. While it was usually safer than it sounds, I had a few memorable races to get away from irate, pursuing bears.

In the late spring, a grizzly bear was reported to be sleeping on the front porch of the Lake Lodge, which was not yet open to the public. Apparently this had been happening for several days, so I set a bear trap that night, and the next morning there was a bear in it.

It turned out to be a large, lean, and apparently very old grizzly who was more aggressive and antagonistic to people than any bear I had seen before or since. If a person was in the area, this bear never rested. He charged everyone who came close to the trap and did not quit fighting until the individual left. When I approached the trap to determine if the bear was tagged, he not only charged me and blew snot and saliva all over me, but he bit and pawed frantically at the trap bars, trying to get to me! He was truly one tough, mean SOB. I reported the bear to Dale Nuss, the South District ranger, and he notified the park biologist. The word came back that it was my decision to turn the bear loose or to terminate him. On one hand I was dumbfounded that it was my decision to make. On the other hand, I was glad it was.

I had recently read the Lewis and Clark journals from their expedition in 1804-1806 across what is now the western United States. A short time later I read an article speculating that today's grizzlies are not as aggressive as the grizzlies Lewis and Clark encountered. I also knew a little about the European brown bear, which is related to our grizzly. The European bear is shy and seldom seen. This was speculated to be the result of generations and generations of hunting, which killed off the bolder, more prominent, and more aggressive bears, leaving only shy, timid bears in the gene pool.

As I mulled this over, I didn't know how old my current bear was or if he was still of breeding age. I'm not sure what my rationale was at the time, but I decided to release the bear at Trout Creek Dump. Chuck Anderson, the senior seasonal ranger at Lake Ranger Station, drove us over. When we were in position, I got up on the trap and released the safety latch on the trap door. I nodded for Chuck to start, and he drove slowly forward as I braced myself, drew my .44 as a precaution, and raised the heavy trap door with my left hand. By this time in my career I had released several dozen bears this way.

This bear leaped out of the trap the instant it could, landed on both front feet, pivoted, and immediately started to climb on the trap, intently focused on me. Chuck saw this and promptly accelerated. The bear burst into a run like a fast racehorse out of the starting gate, charging hard to catch up with a rival just ahead of him. He had evidently been trapped before, and he kept his eyes on me on top of the trap.

Chuck went faster and faster. We went a couple hundred yards with the bear going all out, trying to keep up. I could see determination in the bear's eyes as he sucked it up and decided on one last try. With supreme effort, he accelerated and launched himself at me. He almost succeeded. His left paw hit the trailer about two inches from my left boot. But he couldn't maintain his grip on the trailer, and he slipped, fell off, and rolled a couple of times before coming to a stop. (I imagine he was cussing the day of my birth.)

Chuck finally slowed down and stopped. I got off, nursing my bruises, my skinned knuckles, and my sore knees—all the result of tightly hugging the trap as we bounced down the road. I worried about the bear for awhile, wondering if I had done the right thing to let it go. But he never showed up again at Lake (at least during my tenure of another five years).

Nineteen seventy was another active bear year in the campgrounds. Instead of dumping all the captured bears at Trout Creek or taking the bear to the district line, we increasingly used a helicopter to translocate bears to remote backcountry sites. This was made possible by using M-99, a drug that worked on the central nervous system and was able to keep a bear down for hours as opposed to minutes for Sucostrin. A dose of M 50-50 (an M-99 antagonist) would bring the bear out of its slumber in ten to fifteen minutes. The bear would awake fully functioning and totally alert, a sight that was both impressive and breathtaking to watch.

Helicopters, like computers now, were a mixed blessing. They were expensive, not always available, could be usurped for higher priorities, were subject to breakdowns, always seemed due for maintenance, were waiting for the gas truck, and were limited by the pilot's available flying hours. Meanwhile, the bear was waiting, cooped up in a trap. But when everything worked well (and you were back safely on the ground) you felt you had accomplished a lot for the bear by releasing it in prime habitat, in a remote location, and away from the competition and slum-like environment of the dump.

Typically, the helicopter would take the ranger (or drug administrator) to the release site, leave him there, and go back to get the bear. (FAA regulations did not allow helicopters to carry passengers and haul sling loads at the same time.) The bear was transported in a web net hanging from the helicopter. In an emergency, or if the bear prematurely woke up and was thrashing about, the pilot could disengage the sling and the bear, sacrificing the bear but saving the helicopter and the pilot.

After the helicopter pilot had placed the bear on the ground, he would land a hundred yards or so away and shut down. After getting the bear out of the sling and administering the M 50-50 antidote, the ranger would go back to the helicopter and wait with the pilot. They would watch the bear through binoculars, counting the seconds between breaths. When the frequency of breaths became normal and the bear was close to waking, the pilot would start the helicopter and be ready to leave when the bear woke up and ran off.

Sometimes, however, the bear recovered quite suddenly and was off at full steam. That was always a thrill to see. On one occasion, and almost without warning, the bear jumped up and came full tilt toward the helicopter. I had never seen anyone react so quickly as that pilot—both hands and both feet moving simultaneously—pushing pedals, slapping switches, pulling levers, gunning the engine, and lifting off with a whoosh!

The trip back, after a successful translocation to a bear friendly backcountry site, was always an enjoyable part of the operation. I could relax and enjoy the country, study the terrain, and pick out interesting travel routes from the helicopter. In this way I plotted many good cross-country horse rides.

One evening about the second week of August, I was set up in the Fishing Bridge RV Park waiting for a 500-pound grizzly that had been frequenting the area. A bear arrived on schedule, and I got the pre-measured dose of Sucostrin into him. Belatedly, I realized this was not the bear I wanted. Although the bear resembled the other one, this bear weighed much less than the 500 pounds I had prepared the dosage for. By stretching out the bear and pumping on its chest with my foot, I managed to keep it alive while the drug dose wore down.

I had often noted over the years that one big mistake rarely led to tragedy, but rather an accumulation of smaller errors did. This incident definitely started with an error. As we loaded the tranquilized bear into the trap, I saw it was a tagged Craighead bear. The following day I notified the Craigheads and found it was bear #81, a mature female. Concurrently, the NPS biologist's office decided we should relocate the bear by helicopter to Plateau Creek in the southern end of the park. However, because a previous job took longer than anticipated, the helicopter didn't arrive until much later than expected—*another contributing error.*

At 5 p.m. I dosed the bear with one and a half cc of M-99, enough for the bear's estimated weight. The helicopter crew was anxiously waiting to get the bear since they were running short of flying time to do the job and get back to Mammoth. The bear got very drowsy but not near enough to be able to fly her out. NPS workers going past the helispot began to stop and get out of their vehicles to watch. I always tried to work bears in private so I would have fewer people to worry about and keep track of. In the past I had been criticized for this practice by folks who told me if I wanted support and help from employees, I needed to periodically invite them to watch what we were doing with bears. So I decided to let them stay. *Altogether, contributing errors three, four, or five, depending on how you keep count.*

At 5:55 p.m. the bear was still too awake to fly, so I gave her a follow-up dose of three-fourths of a cc of M-99. By then even more people had showed up to watch—concession employees and a few visitors—and I let them stay because the public has a legitimate right to know about government operations. *Big, big contributing error.*

By 6:30 p.m. the bear, while down, was still not unconscious enough to fly. It was breathing very deeply and seemed to be sleeping soundly, but it would bite at a stick placed against its lips. Decidedly not a good sign. Jay Sumner, a Craighead research assistant, had arrived. He asked if the bear was lactating since their records indicated she might have a cub.

I didn't know; I had not checked. I had been so busy pumping the bear's chest to keep her alive that I didn't go through my usual checklist. *One more contributing error.* The question of where to release the bear now seemed to hinge on whether she might have a cub hiding somewhere in the local area.

So we pulled the sleeping bear out of the trap to see if she was lactating. Once the bear was on the ground she immediately got onto her feet and moved rapidly away from the trap. Although she was not charging, she was moving fast enough to cause concern for the spectators, who by then had pretty much encircled the trap. Now they were running away in almost every direction. I drew my .44 and shot the bear multiple times at almost point-blank range. She basically dropped in her tracks. I was aware that people were in the line of fire, but they were well beyond the bear. I kept the muzzle of the .44 pointed down and into the bear. At no time did the muzzle of the .44 cross over anyone (that I was aware of).

I expected the people watching to be irate, indignant, and totally pissed off at me. The only people who approached me, however, thanked me for standing between the bear and them, and some congratulated me on being cool under pressure and for being such a good shot. I was dumbfounded at the response. We released the helicopter crew, and as quickly as possible we loaded the bear in the trap and drove out of there, leaving one ranger to answer questions and clear the area. As soon as I could, I got to a phone and started notifying the chain-of-command. Dale Nuss was first, but he was out of the area so I left a message. I called the chief ranger (Bud Estey) at home and told him what had happened. I was straightforward with my narrative and didn't sugar coat anything. I specifically told the chief that there had been people behind the bear and in the line of fire as I was shooting.

I fully expected to get reamed out, but once again I was surprised. The chief listened carefully, and then in his mild, quiet way, said something to the effect that he was sure I had done what I thought was appropriate and safe, and that was good enough for him. Case closed. I heard no more of the matter.

In this otherwise sorry incident marred by miscalculations there were at least two bright spots: no one was hurt, and the sow was not lactating. In a memo dated August 13, 1970, I covered the incident from my point of view. I recommended we conduct bear management operations as privately as possible. I concluded with possibly the biggest understatement of the day by saying, "… no matter how routine things may appear…there remains a certain amount of inherent danger when handling grizzlies." No shit, Lone Ranger!

Whether it was from compounding errors or simply reaffirming self-imposed safety rules and protocols, I was continually learning. There were many incidents to file away and brood over for years to come. Fishing Bridge Campground provided the locus for many of these lessons. As we used M-99 we found that some bears woke up prematurely despite having been given the proper dose of the drug. Typically, the bear was awakened by a sharp noise or by being abruptly moved. Later that August we learned yet another variation of this syndrome.

The trail from Ten Mile Post to Thorofare and the Bridger-Teton National Forest runs along the east side of Yellowstone Lake. This trail goes through a heavy lodgepole-pine forest. Columbine Creek crosses the trail and enters Yellowstone Lake where the Southeast Arm begins. The Columbine backcountry campsite is at this intersection, and with its extensive meadow and fine views of both the mountains and the lake, it is popular with horse parties and backpackers. Grizzly bears are also fond of it.

Frequent bear sightings early in the summer were followed by reports of a bear digging in the fire ring. When a large grizzly got into a trove of unsecured food early one morning and stayed in the camp, keeping the campers at bay, the campsite was closed. Closing such a strategically located site complicated travel to the southern areas of Yellowstone at the peak of the backcountry travel season. After considering options, it was decided to trap the bear in order to reopen the campsite as soon as possible. This was a big exception to the well-established policy of not trapping bears in the backcountry in order to relocate them to another backcountry area. In a natural area such as Yellowstone, it was considered inappropriate to manage bears in their own territory. Instead, it was usually human use that was regulated.

Maintenance workers hauled a full-sized culvert trap across the lake in their workboat, a converted World War II landing craft. Rolled onto shore, the trap was manhandled across the beach and trail to the spot where the bear had gotten its human food reward. Warning signs were posted, and the area around the trap was posted as "Closed to Public Entry."

We didn't have to wait long. The trap was empty the first two times it was checked the following day, but around 6 p.m. the Lake boat patrol ranger radioed that the trap had an occupant. I assembled the drug kit and other equipment we might need, including ropes, bear net, and bear bite stick, then got the M-99 from the refrigerator and met the boat patrol at Bridge Bay Marina. A couple of off-duty rangers joined me to help. The four of us made the roughly 30-minute trip from Bridge Bay Marina to the Columbine Creek campsite.

The trap held an impressive, handsome, garden-variety Yellowstone grizzly that I estimated to weigh 400 pounds. He was untagged and not particularly happy to see us. He charged, huffed, and blew snot and saliva at us through the mesh of the trap's gate. Using the CO_2 capture rifle, I got the appropriate dose of M-99 into our trapped friend. We backed off and waited for the drug to take effect, and like clockwork the bear went down and was soon sleeping soundly. When the bear passed his snow pole test, we dragged him to the lakeshore. It was getting dark as we called the boat operator, who had been standing by in deeper water.

While the boat came we put the bear into a helicopter transport net and secured it around him. This gave the bear some restraint if he recovered prematurely, and it gave us something to hold onto when handling our captive. With one person standing on the bow of the patrol boat pulling and three of us standing in the cold lake lifting, we managed to get the netted bear onto the bow of the boat without anyone rupturing themselves.

It was full dark as we started the half-hour trip back to the marina. Wearing a life jacket and my .44 to bolster my confidence, I sat on the bow of the boat by the bear in the fresh wind to ensure our four-legged passenger slept the whole trip and did not awaken too soon. The bear was wrapped in the net, and I was babysitting him to make sure he didn't stand up and stare through the boat's windshield at the driver, as had happened six years previously. Competent, experienced boat drivers were hard to find, and like helicopter pilots, they rated special consideration.

We were making good time, cutting comfortably through the lake's evening swells, and I began to enjoy the evening and the ride. We had not gone half way to the marina before our supposedly sound asleep grizzly bear raised his head. Although it was only a brief sniffing of the air it was both unexpected and disquieting. My enjoyment of the evening subsided, and I shifted my position to make my .44 more accessible. The boat operator increased our speed. The bear's second sniff of air lasted longer, and then the bear began looking around and trying to sit up. The patrol boat went faster, and I held onto the boat tightly with my left hand and with my right drew my .44 and held onto it just as tightly. The boat operator called Lake Patrol, who said they were standing by at the marina with a bear trap.

As we went through the narrow entrance to the marina our grizzly friend was making aggressive but drunken-like efforts to sit up. The marina had a "5 MPH, LEAVE NO WAKE" speed limit but the boat operator didn't slow down. I gripped the boat and my .44 harder than ever.

As we turned into the boat-launch area, I saw that the bear trap was backed down to the wooden walkway next to the launch ramp. A ranger stood on the trap behind the raised gate, ready to lower it at a moment's notice. Another ranger stood alertly on the dock with a shotgun at port arms. As the bear struggled drunkenly to free himself from the net, I holstered my .44 and grabbed the bear by the scruff of his neck to try to regulate his head movement. The other two rangers aboard the boat climbed on the bow to help.

A moment before the boat hit the cement of the launch ramp, the operator thrust the engine into reverse, avoiding a crash and providing momentum for us to heave the bear off the bow and onto the wooden walkway next to the trap. One ranger undid the knot securing the net. The bear struggled drunkenly, got out of the net, lunged forward, and tripped into the trap! The ranger on top of the trap dropped the gate. The bear crawled to the back of the trap—and promptly fell sound asleep.

There were no high fives, belly bumping, or chest thumping as when NBA or NFL athletes make a difficult score. I, for one, was emotionally drained and content to let heart rate and breathing return to normal. As we thought about what had happened, we realized the pounding of the boat against the waves had acted somewhat akin to CPR on a stopped heart. It stimulated the nervous system into action. Fine lessons and worthwhile knowledge, but I hoped someday to achieve such knowledge in an easier way.

Chapter 26

A Predatory Grizzly

OUR MOST CHALLENGING GRIZZLY INVESTIGATIONS OCCURRED in 1984 when a young hiker was attacked by a truly predatory grizzly. In my mind, this attack and several others starting six years earlier are related to one another.

In 1978, Gary Grant, who had just barely turned twenty-one, started his first season as a commissioned park ranger. He had spent the previous three seasons at Grant Village as a uniformed park aide working for Janey McDowell, the Grant Village sub-district ranger. Janey thought highly of Gary and encouraged him to take the necessary training to enable him to become a commissioned (law enforcement) ranger.

I was the Snake River district ranger and Janey's supervisor. While I did not share Janey's high opinion of Gary, I went along with her decision to hire him. It was her operation and hers to run without my micromanagement. While Gary looked good in uniform and was fit and trim, I felt he was too young and inexperienced.

June 13 turned out to be the day to challenge Gary's substance, Janey's opinion, and a whole lot more. On this date, a young female concession employee at Signal Mountain Lodge in Grand Teton National Park got up early and went to Heart Lake Trailhead in Yellowstone. She planned to hike to Heart Lake and back the same day. At the trailhead, she slipped around a group of 20 high school and college-age young men from Texas who were about to start a three-day backpacking trip.

I was attending a district ranger's meeting at the Lake Mess Hall, and Gary Grant was on a road patrol working out of Grant Village and covering the whole district. Dick Gifford, a long-time seasonal ranger, was manning the South Entrance Station.

Gary Grant was just leaving the Lewis Lake Campground when a car quickly swerved next to his car and three young men jumped out. They were from the Texas group, and they excitedly told Gary that a bear had attacked the young concession employee a mile and a half from the trailhead. She was still alive when they left but was just barely hanging on. Gary called South Entrance (eight miles south of where he was) and informed Dick Gifford of the situation, asking him to notify Duane McClure, Snake River sub-district ranger (responsible for Heart Lake) and me. He said he was going to the scene. Gifford advised him to wait for a permanent ranger, but Gary did not follow Gifford's advice.

The National Park Service is a bureaucracy modeled after the U.S. Army. Both have a reverence for hierarchy, chain of command, seniority, and experience—justifiably so for the most part. But sometimes young soldiers disregard the advice of older soldiers. Sometimes the young soldiers wind up dead. Often they receive disciplinary action. Once in a while, they wind up being heroes.

Aided by red light and siren, Gary went quickly to Heart Lake Trailhead, four miles north of where he was contacted by the Texans. At 11:25 a.m. he headed down the trail, running, carrying the patrol vehicle's 12-gauge shotgun, an industrial-sized first aid kit, and three wool Army blankets, rolled up individually in plastic bags. He made the mile and a half to the girl in record time. The Texas boys followed Gary and had a hard time keeping up—even though the Texans ran track in their high school.

At Grant Village, Sub-District Ranger Janey McDowell, Senior Seasonal Jerry Jones, and Seasonal Ranger Tim Trainer hustled together more first aid equipment and a wheeled Stokes litter and headed for the trailhead.

McClure had notified me by phone of the incident. As I headed south for Heart Lake Trailhead 30 miles away, I heard McClure check with our Comm Center about getting the park's contract helicopter on stand-by and ready to fly. I asked Comm Center to tell Lake Hospital to get someone ready to fly in to treat a major trauma situation.

I was south of Lake when Gary radioed in his first assessment. The victim was a female, late teens-early twenties, with deep lacerations on the top of the head, a sucking chest wound, a large open wound to the abdomen, and multiple bites and major tissue damage to the buttocks. She had lost a massive amount of blood, her breathing was shallow, and she was semi-conscious. Strain and concern were evident in Gary's voice, but he sounded very professional and in control of a tough situation. I requested the park helicopter be dispatched to the scene after picking up medical staff from the hospital. Gary said a landing site was within a quarter mile of the victim.

About this time, I monitored McDowell, Jones, and Trainer arriving at Heart Lake Trailhead with the Stokes litter. I asked Janey to leave someone at the trailhead to close the trail and keep a log. McClure and Seasonal Ranger Dick Ferguson arrived from the South Entrance shortly after Mc-

Dowell and her party, and they all headed to the attack site. At the trailhead I found Jerry Jones. I left my vehicle running so he could have the advantage of its radio, asked him to keep the area clear in case the helicopter had to land there, to keep the trail closed, and to relay information as needed. Then I ran to the scene.

McDowell, McClure, Trainer, and Ferguson were there along with Gary, who had things well organized. A couple of the Texans provided shade for the injured person and kept flies away while Gary and Janey worked on dressing the victim's numerous wounds. The rest of the Texas group sat quietly, waiting to help as needed. I briefly interrupted Gary to tell him "good job" and then examined the attack site.

Tracks indicated the attack was made by a sow grizzly with cubs of the year. I couldn't determine whether there were two or three cubs. The initial contact site was on the south edge of the trail on a slight bank somewhat above the trail. The Texas group found the young woman in the middle of the trail. The attack took place at the end of a long straight section of trail, unlike a blind corner or limited visibility that mark most confrontation sites.

I knelt by the young lady's head; watched her shallow, uneven breathing for a bit; and then started talking to her. In as soothing a tone as I could muster, I told her everything would be all right, that medical help was coming, that a helicopter would get her to the hospital, and she didn't need to worry. She seemed to acknowledge what I said. I had been told and had observed several times that semi-conscious and/or unconscious people absorb more of their surroundings than most people think.

At 12:30 p.m. we loaded the victim into the Stokes litter and started for the helicopter landing spot. We got there a few minutes before the helicopter arrived, and after cir-cling the small meadow a couple of times, the pilot landed. I helped the two ER doctors (Surgeon Ben Rickers and Anes-thetist Tom Selmack) unload their gear and took them to the victim. After a few frantic moments they were able to get an IV started. With the IV fluids flowing, the woman improved noticeably, but she still had miles to go.

Then came the debate—carry her to the trailhead (45 minutes) and then haul her by ranger vehicle/ambulance to Lake Hospital (another 45 minutes), or transport her in the Stokes litter strapped to the baggage carrier mounted on the skid (landing gear) of the helicopter (15 minutes). The latter would be quicker, but on the flight no one could reach her and provide help if she needed it. They decided to fly her out with Dr. Rickers riding inside the helicopter on the seat just above her. Anesthetist Selmack would hike out and be taken to Lake Hospital by Gary Grant.

When the docs had done everything they could on site, we carried the semi-conscious young woman to the helicopter. We strapped her Stokes litter onto the baggage carrier and made sure she was well covered. The helicopter took off. She was taken to Lake Hospital for further stabilization. Shortly after, she was flown to Salt Lake City where she progressed and continued to recover.

The young woman was Mariana Young, the sister of the wife of a NPS maintenance foreman at Grant Village. When inter-viewed at the hospital in Salt Lake, Mariana said she saw the bear and cubs before they saw her. She stepped off the trail and was watching the bears while slowly retreating when the sow saw her and charged. The sow knocked her down, slapped her around, and was on top of her and biting her when the noise of the approaching Texas group scared the bears away.

Mother grizzlies are known for being aggressive in the protection of their young. They seem more protective of cubs of the year than yearlings. They seem to be even touchier when they have two or three cubs, perhaps from the added stress of trying to keep track of multiple inquisitive, mischievous, fast-moving units. Mariana could not remember whether there were two or three cubs, but she did say that at least one of the cubs joined the mother bear in jumping on her, biting her, and chewing on her. In later years I often recalled these words.

The Heart Lake Trail and area remained closed for some time. Being somewhat early in the season, there were only a few other parties in the backcountry, and each party was met and escorted out by an armed ranger. Today the same area is closed to public use from spring and early summer until July 1. This gives grizzlies and their cubs of the year a little extra time before humans start using the area. Not a bad compromise.

After numerous operations Mariana Young pretty much made a full recovery. A year or two after her encounter she started working for the NPS as an entrance station ranger at South Entrance. She did this for several years and was a valued, conscientious employee. She later worked for the Interpretive Division in the northern part of the park. I have lost track of her and have not heard about her for a number of years.

The same is true of Gary Grant. At this time I can't recall how many seasons he worked as a commissioned ranger or where he ended up. I believe he went to law school in Colorado. I know he earned my undying respect by his actions. If they ever establish a pantheon for park rangers (like the Hall of Fame for professional football players) Gardner L. Grant, Jr., earned admission on June 13, 1978.

Six years later another bear incident involved a slender blond woman. Twenty-five-year-old Brigitta Fredenhagen of Basel, Switzerland, joined her brother and sister-in-law to tour the western United States, including Yellowstone. Andreas and Junko Fredenhagen flew down from Canada. The trio arrived in the park on July 28, 1984, and camped at Grant Village. The following day they toured the park.

Apparently one of Brigitta's goals was to go backpacking in Yellowstone, so the group stopped long enough at Canyon Ranger Station for Ranger Gary Youngblood to issue a backcountry permit to Brigitta for the night of July 30. She planned to start at Pelican Creek Trailhead, go up the valley to Astringent Creek, then up Astringent Creek and down Broad Creek, and out to Canyon the next day. Andreas and Junko did not go since they did not have backpacking equipment with them.

The following morning the group started hiking from the Pelican Trailhead at 11 a.m. Andreas and Junko hiked with Brigitta for five and a half miles to the Astringent Creek junction, where the couple turned around and went back to the trailhead. Before parting, they decided that Brigitta should come back the same way, and Andreas and Junko would meet her at the trailhead about 3:30 p.m. the next day. Brigitta continued on alone.

The following afternoon Andreas and Junko were back at the trailhead on time, but Brigitta was not there. When she failed to show up and none of the returning Pelican day hikers reported seeing her, Andreas and Junko went to Lake Ranger Station and filed a lost person report at 7:30 p.m. with Ranger Mark Marschall, Lake District backcountry supervisor.

The next morning Marschall left Pelican Trailhead on

horseback to check for Brigitta. He also was looking for sign of Chuck Popper, a concession employee who had been overdue several days in the same general area. Marschall went up Astringent Creek and over the divide into the Broad Creek drainage. It was late morning when he approached White Lake.

About 11:24 a.m., Marschall left the main trail to check out a tent he could see pitched under a tree at White Lake's designated campsite (5W1). As he rode toward the tent, his horse spooked and would not approach closer than 20 yards. Marschall secured his horse and went ahead on foot. Everything looked normal, the tent looked intact, and a sleeping bag was stretched out on the ground as if to dry (there had been a good rain overnight). Heeding his horse's behavior, Marschall cautiously went up to the tent. He could see a rip in the tent near the door, but the inside of the tent looked undisturbed.

When he checked the sleeping bag, however, he found a piece of human scalp near the bag and drag marks leading away from the bag. Marschall radioed his findings to Lake Ranger Station, then searched for 20 minutes while waiting for assistance to arrive by a helicopter that was diverted from the Popper search. Lake District Ranger Tim Blank and Dave Spirtes, Lake sub-district ranger, arrived at 12:07 p.m. Forty-five minutes later they found Brigitta's body in the woods 250 feet from the tent. Dead from massive trauma, she had been partially consumed by a bear.

This was apparently a predatory attack. It appeared that the bear took only a couple swipes of his paw to rip a tear in the tent big enough to reach in and grab Brigitta, still in her sleeping bag, and pull her out of the tent without knocking it down.

Several people were dispatched to the scene. I arrived in the second or third helicopter. While I could offer whatever perspective I had from 20 years in Yellowstone, I was basically a bit player on the site for the afternoon.

Usually I only write about situations in which I was involved more directly and completely. However, this incident affected me deeply for several reasons. One was the brutality and circumstance of the death site itself. Routine accidents, rescues, and fatalities (though fairly abundant in my past) just weren't sufficient preparation. This was the first time I had dealt with a grizzly that had deliberately preyed upon a human. Also, this incident (most likely) led to another case I would be more occupied with later. Finally, as more time passed, I began to believe that Brigitta's death may well have had its origin in a bear attack I had been involved with years before.

Looking over the tent site, it was eerie how normal and peaceful everything looked. The campsite was in the middle of an abundant crop of ripe strawberries, which may have been what initially attracted the bear to the area. It was also on a major wildlife travel route and next to an NPS maintained trail. Brigitta had hung her food 12 feet off the ground, suspended between two trees 85 feet east of her campsite. A bear had climbed the tree on the stubs of limbs, much the way Brigitta had. He had pulled down the food and eaten much of it, including the ham left over from Brigitta's supper.

The interior of the tent was orderly and almost totally undisturbed. Inside the tent was a mini tape player in the playing mode but now silent, the batteries having run down. Had the tape player inadvertently been turned on when the bear pulled Brigitta out of the tent? Had she turned it on to bolster her spirits when she heard something prowling around the tent? Or was she simply listening to it before she went to sleep?

Brigitta Fredenhagen's body and belongings were flown out by helicopter to Fishing Bridge that evening. I flew out with one of the later flights and drove home to South, brooding and preoccupied, mind awash with speculation, questions, and theories.

That day Ranger Nick Herring had been dropped off at Fern Lake Patrol Cabin, five miles from the Fredenhagen site. Two people from the Popper search were also supposed to be there that night, but they had been rescheduled elsewhere. The helicopter stood by until the Popper searchers returned, then they quickly packed up and were whisked away to a new assignment. Herring was left alone in the cabin nearest to the Fredenhagen fatality site.

Though he was a competent, experienced ranger (seven seasons at that time), Herring did not relish his situation. Even equipped as he was with his own handgun (a Ruger .357 revolver) and with the government 12-gauge, pump-action shotgun, very few people would have been totally comfortable in this situation.

In routine situations most people would have retired with the cabin as it was. With the image of Brigitta's mangled, partially consumed body in his mind, Herring assessed the cabin's security. While the front door was heavy and solid, it opened inward and had no locking bolt to secure it, only a flimsy lift latch. Before retiring, he closed and bolted the shutters and jammed a nail just above the door latch, preventing it from being raised (in effect providing a flimsy lock bolt). He also shoved the wood box in front of the door.

Before going to bed Herring laid the shotgun on the table and placed his flashlight at his side. Sometime during the night he was awakened by sounds of distant thunder and intermittent rain, which persisted for some time. Lying half awake, dozing, and listening to the thunder, he was startled bolt upright by something forcefully slamming into the door. Shotgun in hand and pointed at the door, he listened as something slapped the latch a couple times, walked across the porch, knocking down a couple of sticks of stacked stove wood, walked off the porch and along the east side of the cabin, stopping to slap and push on the east shutter. Then it continued north out of hearing.

Too awake to go back to sleep, Herring lit a lantern, boiled water, made coffee, and waited until daylight. When it was light enough, he went outside. There were grizzly tracks in the mud along the east side of the cabin and under the shuttered window that had been pushed. Were they tracks of THE grizzly or of a grizzly? It's basically immaterial—the grizzly that left those tracks had made a deliberate and calculated effort to get into a building while it was occupied by a human. Fortunately, the building's occupant had been paying attention and thinking and had a plan. Herring made his own good luck and avoided being another tragic statistic.

Yellowstone remains one of the few places in the continental USA where a human being does not automatically achieve primacy in the ecosystem simply by being a human. And, while I cry for Brigitta's family and say a prayer for her every time I pass her campsite at White Lake, I pray just as hard that Yellowstone will always remain as it is. Yellowstone offers us a perspective not available many other places: we learn humility as human beings. With heightened senses, awareness, and respect we can still enjoy, exult in, and feel awe for all that Yellowstone has to offer.

Herring checked in by radio and then spent the next

few days looking for the Fredenhagen bear. Pairs of rangers combed the woods in the vicinity of White Lake. Two culvert traps were flown into the campsite where one was used to try to trap the bear. The other was used as a secure (but not necessarily comfortable) place for two rangers to monitor the first trap. August 2 was the first night the fatality site was monitored, and other than a long and uncomfortable night, the rangers in the observation trap had little to report.

A third culvert trap was flown to Fern Lake Cabin. Pairs of rangers crisscrossed the area in silence rather than trying to be heard and scare off anything in their path. Kerry Gunther, the Pelican Cone Lookout, tried to keep track of searchers and bears alike. Several piles of bear scat containing human remains were found. A few bears were surprised on their day beds, but none were seen with any evidence indicating they might be the guilty party. Rangers were rotated so no one got stale or had too many nights cramped inside the trap.

On August 4, five days after Brigitta was killed, bear scat containing human remains was found at the Pelican Creek Trailhead. I had a funny feeling on hearing that bit of news, or I guess you could call it a premonition. I was sure we were going to hear from that bear again; I would have bet my own money on it.

I called Pat Ozment, the Grant Village sub-district ranger and told him of my fears. I wanted the rangers to give their nightly bear warnings on foot in certain loops of Grant Village Campground rather than by loudspeaker. Loops G, H, and I faced Big Thumb Creek on their north side, and all three provide easy, surreptitious access to Grant Campground.

Doing the bear safety and food storage warnings on foot took a lot more time but made the ranger available to answer questions. It also increased the likelihood the ranger would not miss seeing any food or ice chests left out. I also wanted Grant patrol to spend a lot of time in the campground and to leave the Grant Village area only for emergencies.

That night the Lynip family of Santa Barbara, California, was camped at Site 319 in I Loop of Grant Village Campground. Bryan Lynip, age 12, and his brother Keith, age 14, were in a tent pitched next to their parents' tent. Their campsite was meticulously clean.

Around 2 a.m., a bear attacked Bryan. His father heard the ripping sounds of the tent as the bear gained access and lifted Bryan out of his tent, still in his sleeping bag. Bryan thought he was having a nightmare and didn't struggle. In a stroke of luck, Bryan fell out of his sleeping bag without the bear noticing. The bear dragged the sleeping bag 109 feet away, then dropped the bag and disappeared. Bryan had received a bite on his right upper arm and a single puncture wound under his right wrist. By 3:04, Bryan was being transported to the Lake Hospital by ambulance, and Lake sent him to West Park Hospital in Cody.

Ozment, Ranger Jon Hildebrandt, and I conferred. We took measurements and interviewed people who were still up and about. Putting together what we found out that morning and later in the day, it appeared that the bear's first contact was with a pop-up tent trailer located two sites south of the Lynips'. The foldout, sleeping portion of the trailer was just the right height for the passing grizzly to scratch his hump on. The bear's vigorous scratching woke the occupants whose subsequent movement may have caused the bear to paw the trailer side and leave bite marks in the siding. Shouts and screams from the occupants caused the bear to drift away and eventually wind up at Bryan Lynip's tent.

Partial bear tracks at the scenes closely matched the Fredenhagen bear tracks. While by no means did I consider myself an expert tracker, I had paid particularly close attention to grizzly tracks for the past 20 years. While the width of the bite of the Fredenhagen bear varied slightly from that of the Lynip bear, I felt the difference could be explained by the fact that the tracks were on two different types of surfaces and were measured by two different people. I believed then, as I do now (2011), that the same bear was responsible for both incidents.

When daylight came I walked the north and east perimeter of the Grant Village Campground. On the north side there were tracks in the sand, evidently grizzly, that matched the general size of the tracks in the Lynip campsite. The bear had made a couple forays into the campground, each time returning to the sandy area next to Big Thumb Creek. Then the tracks led to the eastern perimeter of the campground and headed south. I lost the tracks when they came onto pavement but speculated they were headed to Sewer Creek and/ or the sewage lagoons located on the south side of the Grant Village complex. Maybe they continued south to the Heart Lake trail?

At 10 p.m. that night (August 5), Ozment and I were staked out, watching a culvert trap at Site 319. It was a long, slow, and boring night as nothing showed, and we left at 7 a.m. I monitored the trap the next night. Still nothing. Eventually, when things returned to what passed for normal, we reopened I Loop.

Two weeks later, grizzly bear #88 (numbered from being trapped previously) was trapped in Fishing Bridge RV Park. He seemed to like the Fishing Bridge area at that time of year because he had also been trapped there on July 19, 1982; August 6, 1982; as well as August 12, 1983. Since this was the fourth time in three years that #88 had been trapped in the Fishing Bridge Campground, park management decided to remove him from the population "due to nuisance activity in or near developments and campgrounds." Taken to the state wildlife lab in Bozeman, Bear #88 was euthanized and a necropsy performed. He tested negative for rabies, had no significant lesions, and was considered a normal animal that was seven years old and weighed 375 pounds.

Speculation abounded. Was #88 the Fredenhagen bear? The Lynip bear? A lot of knowledgeable people thought so. Some others didn't. I felt quite certain that the Fredenhagen bear and the Lynip bear were the same, and Bear #88 was a good candidate.

I also think that #88 could be the cub that joined his mother in chewing on Marianna Young in June 1978 on the Heart Lake Trail. Admittedly, the links between the cub that jumped on Mariana Young in 1978 with the bear that stalked and killed Brigitta Fredenhagen in 1984 are more esoteric than tangible, more circumstantial than evidential, and offer many more "possiblys" than "likelys." But I'll make the case here.

I found a striking similarity between Mariana Young and Brigitta Fredenhagen: both were slender blondes (120 pounds) in their 20s who were about five-feet three-inches tall. Mariana was hesitant and retreating; Brigitta was apprehensive and unsure, according to her diary. One of the first things I had observed about grizzlies on my arrival in Yellowstone was how alert and perceptive they were and how they picked up on the slightest nuances.

Through the years I also came to appreciate just how good their memories are. They seem to remember for a lifetime where they got a good meal even once. We know from radio tracking records that on July 28, 1982, Bear #88 was observed a short distance from campsite 5W1 (where Brigitta was killed two years later). Though he was apparently heading back to Fishing Bridge after being translocated to the Gallatin range, it is likely he stopped in the area of 5W1 long enough to feed on the crop of ripe, wild strawberries there. Familiarity with this resource could well be the reason why #88 was in this area at the same time two years later.

We know from the same radio tracking records that on April 28, 1984, Bear #88 was in his den on Silvertip Peak at the head of Crow Creek near the park's east boundary. On May 18 he was east of Trout Creek, near the east end of Hayden Valley some 25 miles away. To me this demonstrated that he could travel long distances when he wanted to, especially considering his route would have been mostly snow-covered or muddy at that time of year.

So, it would be no problem for the bear to leave Grant Village Campground on August 5 and go back north around the lake to Fishing Bridge by August 18 for what became his final trapping, a distance of only 23 miles. In fact, in 13 days, he could have gone the longer route: south to the Heart Lake Trail to check that out, and then around the south end of Yellowstone Lake, up the east shore, and back to Fishing Bridge. That distance is about 62 miles.

Somewhat more challenging to my belief is the question of whether a bear could go from the White Lake campsite to Grant Village Campground in a day, a distance of around 34 miles. My answer is yes (though it would not be something he did routinely). Actually, the time frame could have been more than one day since we don't know when Bear #88 left White Lake, nor do we know when the bear scat containing human remains was deposited at the Pelican Trailhead. We just know the scat was discovered on the afternoon of August 4, and that Bryan Lynip was pulled from his tent around 2:15 a.m. on August 5.

I was surprised we had an incident so soon after the Pelican Trailhead scat was reported, but there are several explanations. There could have been two different bears involved (though I don't think so). Or the bear that left the scat could have deposited it sometime before it was found (it was pretty fresh but of indeterminate age). The Fredenhagen bear could have been one of the bears surprised on its day bed by rangers prowling silently through the woods (on August 2 or 3), and he just decided to go someplace else for a while, especially considering all of the human activity in the area (makes sense to me).

There are a couple more elements concerning the Fredenhagen bear that might support Bear #88's candidacy for that predatory role. One mile south of the fatality site, rangers found bear scat containing human remains. Measurements of nearby grizzly tracks were almost identical to those of Bear #88 as listed in a trapping report of August 12, 1983. While this doesn't prove a connection, neither does it eliminate Bear #88's candidacy for being the Fredenhagen bear.

On the other hand, the Fredenhagen bear climbed a tree to get Brigitta's food. This shifted the focus to a sub-adult bear, not Bear #88, as sub-adults still have claws that are shaped for tree climbing. In retrospect, however, two things come to mind. Brigitta anchored her food line to a tree that many mature grizzlies could climb—it had a number of branch stubs and bumps (the protective growth that had healed about broken limbs) which mature grizzlies could use like steps or rungs on a ladder to ascend the tree. That was apparently how Brigitta climbed it, so my money would be on #88 being able to do that even though he weighed 375 pounds.

Finally, the deliberate stalking of and preying on a human did not seem like the behavior of an inexperienced sub-adult bear. To me, it seemed like the behavior of a bear more used to prowling amongst humans for quite a few years. Shyness is not lost in a day, and boldness is not acquired overnight. It seems to be the cumulative effect of being in close proximity to people. Through the years, time and again, I had watched how bears changed when they were around people, from shy and hesitant during early season to confidant mid-season, to bold and even daring by late season. Without a doubt, in my mind at least, the more a bear is around people—and especially if that bear is drugged, trapped, and handled—the less intimidated it is by humans and human presence. Bear #88 was trapped and handled at least four times, and he was translocated three times.

Of course bears' personalities differ greatly. One rule does not necessarily fit all. Some experts feel strongly that the bear's upbringing and individual nature are the key to how that particular bear will act. I speculate that an encounter on the Heart Lake Trail in 1978 when he was a cub of the year might have prompted Bear #88 to develop a predatory nature. Other contributing factors may have been his long memory and time spent in campgrounds.

Was Bear #88 the Fredenhagen bear? I think so. Bottom line: After Bear #88 was taken out of the population, there were no more grizzly-caused injuries that year, and no more people have been pulled out of tents. One might say, "That's what the FBI refers to as a clue."

Chapter 27

Some Bear Humor

NOT ALL BEAR ACTIVITY IS TRAGIC OR CONTROVERSIAL. SOME of it can be quite humorous. While following a 600-pound grizzly bear in late July 1972, I was carrying a CO_2 capture rifle loaded with a dart dosed for the bear and a follow-up dose in an old cigar container in my shirt pocket. I was wearing my .44 on one hip and carrying a park radio on the other. I had a flashlight tucked in my belt at the small of my back. You might say I was loaded for a bear.

I was in the Fishing Bridge Campground, which was full, around 11 p.m. Ahead of me was a large outfitter-style wall tent. Judging from the voices and the shadows on the tent wall, several people were inside the tent, sitting around a table playing cards. Outside the tent, tied to a pole supporting the tent's awning, was a Chihuahua-sized, yappy dog. When the bear appeared, the little dog began to growl quietly and then tentatively bark as the bear got closer. The bear was minding his own business, not paying attention to the dog or tent, just casually crossing about 10 yards in front of the tent. The dog barked more fiercely with each step the bear took, and finally the bear took exception to the noise and turned toward the dog. The dog got quieter and quieter, barking less fiercely the closer the bear came. Finally the dog sat down and was silent as the large bear came right up to the tiny dog, stopped, and touched his nose to the dog's nose.

As I watched the noses touch, I could imagine the dog, with his eyes shut tightly, not breathing, sitting in a pool of fresh urine and thinking, "Time to kiss my ass good-bye." I was standing 20 yards or so away, heart pumping, and praying that no one would step out of the tent. No one did, and in his own sweet time the bear turned and walked away. I started breathing again and followed the bear. As I went by the tent, the dog was still sitting in the same place, trembling, and I heard someone inside the tent ask, "I wonder what all that ruckus was about?" Another voice answered, "I don't know, but it sounds as if Tuffy scared away whatever it was. Give me two cards."

I managed to get a shot at the bear that Tuffy had "scared off," hitting him in the neck. He jumped, bit at the dart, pranced a step or two and then stopped, sniffing the air all around him. When the drug started taking effect he ran a few steps north on a regular bear travel route and shortly went down.

Three of us loaded the very large grizzly into a trap by running one end of a retired climbing rope through the vent holes in the front of the trap and then out the back. The gate was in the locked open position. We tied this end of the rope with a single overhand knot to one rear leg of the bear and then took a couple half hitches around both of the bear's rear legs.

The opposite end of the rope was tied to a vehicle parked alongside the pick-up that was towing the trailer. The driver of the vehicle with the rope put tension on the rope by driving slowly ahead. The two people outside guided the bear and heaved in unison to get the bear's rear end over the threshold of the trap. It was nice to have an extra person to offer a little control to the bear's head, but we didn't always have that luxury. When a bear was fully in the trap, one person would jump onto the trap and lower the gate. There was a small gate at the front of the trap used to freshen the bait bucket suspended from the trap door release. Working through this gate, the other person would use a variety of hooks to undo the half hitches from the bear's legs. It was hard, stressful, sweaty, and often smelly work that was satisfying when it succeeded. Overall, it was no job for old men.

Visualize the same hour in the same campground at a different date. I was following another very large, seemingly relaxed and nonchalant grizzly. As the bear passed a teepee tent he stood on his hind legs, reached as high as he could, and cuffed the tent, first with his left paw and then his right paw. Pow! Pow! Then the bear moved on. As I passed the tent I heard a woman's voice say, "Honey! Honey! What was that?" A man's voice answered, "Ah, go back to sleep. It wasn't anything. Just your imagination."

Such was life in the bear lane of Fishing Bridge Campground in the late 1960s and early 1970s.

Chapter 28

A Grizzly Bear Charge

To be charged by a grizzly bear can be disquieting or terrifying, but it is always memorable. You may not remember what happened before, and you may not recall what came after, but you remember the encounter clearly. I interacted with a lot of grizzlies over my years in Yellowstone. It helped that I was on horseback most of the time, but even a good horse is no guarantee of safety when dealing with a grizzly. Twice I was charged by a grizzly even though I was mounted.

My most memorable encounter happened in the late 1980s or early 1990s in October. I was the Snake River District ranger, and hunting season was well under way along the south boundary. I rode into Fox Creek Patrol Cabin from Pacific Creek Trailhead on my horse, Scott, and was packing Traveler. Both were experienced mountain horses in great physical condition. Scott was a sorrel and Traveler a grey, just like Robert E. Lee's horse of the same name.

I brought in a load of cabin rations and oats as well as my personal supplies for a week of boundary patrol. At the cabin I met Clair Roberts, a competent and experienced seasonal ranger. Clair had spent the previous week bivouacking on the boundary in an effort to surprise poachers. He had a good week, contacted a few hunters but no poachers, and was ready to hike out over Big Game Ridge for his days off. We spent a pleasant evening updating each other on the past week's happenings.

The following morning was cool, blustery, and mostly cloudy. A serious weather front appeared to be moving in as Clair headed over Big Game Ridge for South Entrance, his home base for the season. I rode east toward the headwaters of the Snake River and other points along the boundary that I liked to check. Early to mid-afternoon I heard Clair call in a weather report from Big Game Ridge.

At this time backcountry rangers were supposed to check in with the park's Comm Center between seven and eight in the morning and again between seven and eight in the evening. This served as a welfare check on the ranger as well as a time to relay messages to him/her. After checking in a little after seven that evening, I left my radio on to listen to the other rangers check in. Most backcountry rangers listened at these times, both for the entertainment factor and to keep up with what was going on around the park. It also served as a crosscheck on the rangers nearest you. I didn't hear Clair check in but assumed he had done so before I had turned on my radio and called in.

The next morning was colder, blowing and trying to snow. I brought in my horses off picket, grained them, and checked in with the Comm Center. They asked if I was also checking in for Clair. I said no, that he should be at Harebell Cabin or at South Entrance. They said that they had not heard from Clair last night or this morning, and that he was usually very prompt about checking in. I could tell the Comm Center operator was concerned, and so was I.

Most backcountry rangers are very comfortable being by themselves, and in fact, many prefer it that way. They fully

realize the pitfalls of being alone in the backcountry. However, most believe that their experience, routine caution, and
extra care were more than a match for the challenge. Whether
the challenge was bears, other wildlife, creek and river crossings, bad weather, bad visitors, or whatever, most backcountry rangers readily subscribed to the "one riot, one ranger"
philosophy. In other words, rangers often have to handle situations on their own.

Nonetheless, rangers are intensely motivated by the thought
that another ranger might need help. Within an hour I had
Scott saddled and Traveler packed with Clair's gear, trash,
and sheet blankets that needed laundering. I closed up the
cabin, left a note for the next cabin user apologizing for the
poor cabin clean-up, splashed across the Snake River west of
Fox Creek Cabin, and urged Scott up the Big Game Ridge
trail. The weather had further deteriorated, and the ridge was
shrouded in clouds. It was colder, snowing, and the wind was
blowing the snowflakes horizontally. I could see Clair's tracks
of yesterday in the frozen mud of the trail and periodically in
the patches of week-old snow. Scott sensed my urgency and
responded well. We were now outside of the park boundary.

I was dressed for the weather—long johns, chaps, down
vest, zipped-up jacket, slicker, insulated gloves, and I had
heavy mittens handy. I was relatively comfortable but hardly
dressed to move quickly or gracefully. We neared the top of
the ridge and were about to enter the last finger of timber
before the final long open area leading up to the pass.

We stopped for a breather, Scott and Traveler were breathing deeply, and I was standing in the stirrups and stretching
when a rifle shot went off immediately in front of us. It was
so close, so loud, that all three of us jumped and started in
unison, focusing sharply on the timber ahead. We listened

and waited. I was just about to urge Scott up the trail when a hunter, his rifle held at port-arms, came hurriedly out of the timber. He was looking back over his shoulder, tripping and stumbling on the trail but catching his balance before he fell. He appeared startled to see us and then became very relieved to have human company. He started talking fast, almost non-stop and somewhat incoherently.

"I was just charged by a grizzly—he was after me—he's guarding something—he wouldn't stop until I shot over his head—I didn't hit him—I'm done hunting—too damn many bears—saw five yesterday—all grizzlies—saw three already today—including the guy that just charged me—he's protecting something—I saw a gut-pile—I don't think that's all—I was crazy to go out by myself this morning—I wouldn't go up there if I were you."

After he calmed down a bit, I was able to ask him a few questions. He was with a group of five that were camped just over the pass from Wolverine Creek on the Fox Creek side. This was their third year hunting up here, and they had seen more bears this year than on the other two years put together. Two of his buddies had their elk, but it was time to go home, to hell with getting another elk, too damn many bears. I asked him if he had seen a ranger yesterday—no. Could he see what the bear might be protecting—there was a gut-pile above the trail, but he thought there must be something more.

For about the third time, he said, "I sure wouldn't go up there if I were you." Then I looked down and saw Clair's footprint in the week-old snow. It was pointed up the trail and into the trees the hunter had just come from. Shit!

Finally the hunter left for his camp, repeating his advice not to go up there. I sat for a few moments contemplating my options. For a fleeting moment I thought of tying Scott and Traveler and going up there on foot. I would be more maneuverable that way, but I decided it would be better to stick with my boys. I decided a bold front with lots of noise would be the best approach. As a precaution, I unsnapped my slicker and raised the zipper on my jacket a few inches to make my .44 somewhat more accessible in case the operation really went to hell.

I transferred Traveler's lead rope to my left side to leave my right hand free, and then we started up the trail. I began to whistle as loud as I could to give the bear as much notice of our approach as possible. We went the 100 or so yards through the trees with Scott stepping lightly and alertly while I continued to whistle. It was still snowing and blowing, and we were enshrouded in cloud. Visibility was poor. When we reached a large open area, the visibility improved a little. Scott suddenly stopped, intently looking to his left, uphill from the trail. Traveler bumped briefly into Scott as both horses focused on the hill. About 15 yards away was an elk gut-pile, the partial skeleton of an elk, and something buried.

About 30 yards farther up the hillside sat a black-colored grizzly, watching us intently. He wasn't a particularly large bear (300 pounds max), but there was no mistaking his confidence that he ruled the world and its contents. Certainly he could kick the ass of anyone or anything that tried to touch his gut-pile and buried treasure. For better or worse I ended the impasse by yelling and waving my right arm at him. The bear charged us like a shot, blowing snot, saliva, fire and brimstone as he came. He didn't hesitate a second, nor did he take his flaming red eyes off of us. At least that's what it looked like to me.

It must have seemed that way to Traveler too. He pivoted away from the bear, slamming into Scott with such force that it knocked Scott to his front knees, then kept on going around, hell-bent on getting away from the black devil bearing down on us. Scott, in an unbelievable effort, surged upright from his knees, saving us from big time chaos, and overtook Traveler a half-second before I would have lost the lead rope. At a wild, full out gallop, Scott took us back through the trees the way we had come up. I never realized Scott was such an athlete or that he could run so fast. Adrenalin can give horses a boost just as it does humans.

When we got back to the opening where we had talked to the hunter, I got Scott turned and running in a circle. We stopped about where we had been when we talked to the hunter. Wow, what a ride! It was Scott's and Traveler's turn to blow snot. They snorted and blew, facing up the trail, poised and ready to continue their flight if need be. When no bear showed up, they relaxed a bit, content that they only had to stand and breathe hard.

I stayed on Scott, let my own breathing get back to normal, and contemplated my next move. I still didn't know where Clair was, or what the bear had buried. On my radio I heard Helitack Foreman Andy Mitchell call the Comm Center and say he was in Helicopter #1 enroute to the Tetons and that he was going to divert to Harebell Cabin to check for Clair. 10-4! Now I had at least a few minutes to rest and consider my options.

The next 15 to 20 minutes took a long time to pass, but then Andy came on to tell Comm Center that Clair was okay! He had spent the night at Harebell and was hiking to South; he had had radio problems. The Comm Center and I were very relieved, as was the rest of the listening audience.

I decided to continue to South with the trash, laundry, and Clair's gear. We dropped way downhill and made a wide loop around the black grizzly. It was a rough detour, and every time we stopped to rest, Scott and Traveler would turn around, making sure that black SOB of a grizzly was not following.

We had a joyful reunion with Clair at South. He apologized for making us worry. No problem. All's well that ends well.

Chapter 29

Country Without Grizzly Bears

Without a doubt grizzlies add depth and dimension to the territory they occupy. Comparing a country without grizzlies to similar country with the great bear is like comparing light beer and skim milk to the real things. Without grizzlies you just do not travel as alertly and as focused as you do when there is the chance to encounter one. To see a grizzly up close and personal can be both exciting and disquieting. It helps to see the bear first and to be psychologically prepared.

Not long ago, I was sitting by myself at our dining room table reflecting on the past while letting my dinner digest. I felt like an over-the-hill bull elk lying on an isolated mountainside in the last rays of the setting sun, chewing his cud, and dreaming of his glory days. I was brooding about my past involvement with Yellowstone's bear management.

After my first season as a permanent ranger in Yellowstone, I became an admirer of grizzlies. I resolved to do everything in my power to see that grizzlies remained a viable, breeding population in the Yellowstone ecosystem—that they survived at least for my lifetime. To that end I worked hundreds of uncompensated hours to keep grizzlies out of the campgrounds, and to keep people and grizzlies safely apart, both at Canyon and Lake. In retrospect, as I contemplate bear management then and now, it is hardly comparable and is almost diametrically opposed. Freedom, flexibility, and individual responsibility (then) as opposed to structure, stipulations, protocols, and shift work (now).

Temperamentally, I was and am better suited to the former. I do, however, see benefits in orientation, training, teamwork, and well thought out protocols. The one riot, one ranger approach cannot survive in today's complex society—especially with the diverse challenges confronting today's ranger. For the most part I was satisfied with my efforts while knowing that some of them should have been better and more effective. I especially was concerned about the times I had to shoot grizzlies. On those occasions were there things I overlooked? Could I have done something better or differently?

I am glad I did what I did to meet my perceived responsibility. At best my responses were to remedy and prevent future problems, not just continue to meet them head on time after time. At worst, the future (today's present) has learned from mistakes made in the past, many of them mine, and will not repeat them.

And I got a few good bear stories for all my monetarily uncompensated time in Canyon and Lake's campgrounds.

Chapter 30

Dusty, my Thousand-pound Partner

THOUGH I HAVE MENTIONED MY ANIMAL FRIENDS THROUGH-out the previous pages, some deserve their own stories in these writings. When I transferred from Grand Canyon to Yellowstone, one of the best things that happened was meeting Dusty. I tend to favor horses over dogs or cats, and while I like most dogs and can tolerate some cats, I feel you form a partnership with a horse when you work together and depend on each other to do a job. When the job is important to you and fun for your horse, your relationship becomes stronger fast.

It is the same relationship a policeman has with his K-9 companion or a searcher with his search dog. All of us are enhanced by our relationships with critters, but having a thousand-pound partner respond promptly to your least request is something to cherish. Dusty was a six-year-old, light bay, Thoroughbred-type gelding, standing 15½ hands. He had kind, intelligent eyes placed well apart in a handsome head topped by active and alert ears that missed very little. His nostrils were wide, flaring, and elastic with the ability to take in and exhale an abundance of air—just as the Plains Indians liked in their buffalo-running ponies. He had a black mane and a black tail. A large white star on his forehead connected with a white stripe that ran the length of his nose, and he had NPS branded on his left hip.

Dusty was well proportioned with good withers and a back that was comfortable to ride without a saddle. He possessed a deep, roomy thorax that had plenty of space for a big heart and impressive lungs. His pasterns were comfortably long and appropriately angled for speed and easy riding. He had long, slender legs and solid, well-shaped hooves. All things considered, Dusty was a good-looking horse. However, it was the way he moved that first attracted my attention, not his looks.

At the suggestion of my supervisor, I had gone to Stephens Creek corrals to meet Red Wetzel, who was in charge of Yellowstone's horse operation. Originally from Pennsylvania, Wetzel had come west to hunt and had worked a few years as a guide, then as a trail crew packer for Yellowstone before taking his current job. Devoted to the 60 to 70 NPS horses and mules he managed, he welcomed everyone genuinely interested in stock use and was polite to those who weren't. He was intolerant of anyone who abused or mistreated his charges. In a mud-caked, past its prime, four-wheel-drive pick-up, Red drove me up a rutted dirt road past the long abandoned coal-mining town of Aldridge to where the NPS horses were on winter range. He stopped at the beginning of a large, open flat where the herd was pawing through a light snow cover for the last summer's cured grass.

When they spotted the pick-up, a mild wave of interest ran through the multi-colored, mixed herd of horses and mules. Some came immediately looking for a handout. Most affected indifference but waited to see if their more eager companions were going to get anything. A few drifted away, convinced that any green pick-up meant work or at least an interruption of the good-life.

We got out and walked among the grazing animals. Red named the horses—Eb, Roger, Billy, Bechler, Jim—as we passed them, telling me which district or individuals they were assigned to. He paused by each unassigned horse and gave me a rundown on what I could expect if I selected this particular one: "He's hard to catch but is a good traveler; he's a good keeper but slow; he shies a lot, but you can catch him anywhere."

I watched a bay horse move away with long, smooth, casual steps. "What horse is that?" I asked. "That's Dusty," Red replied. "He's a recent purchase. He's unassigned but a handful. You can take him if you want." Since Canyon was only assigned two horses, I told Red I wanted horses anyone could ride. I kept looking as Red kept showing, and twice more I noticed a smooth walking horse with a long stride—both times it was Dusty. A month later I stopped at Stephens Creek to select Canyon's two horses. I rode Dusty first, and that was a mistake because no other horse could compare with him. The others rode like rough, out-of-tune tractors compared them with the bay's smooth, Cadillac ride. We went all over the hills around Stephens Creek before I discovered a flaw.

I touched him with my spurs—two jumps later I was sitting on my ass on the ground with dust floating up around me, struggling to hold onto the reins and wondering what the hell happened. I got up with only my pride hurt and dusted off the seat of my pants. I calmed down my horse, calmed myself down, and gingerly remounted. I returned to the corrals, being very careful not to let my spurs touch any part of Dusty's body.

Before the day was out, I had picked out Canyon's horses. While I coveted Dusty, I took two horses everyone could ride. Rosey was a 16-year-old, half-Morgan mare, one of the last sired by Black Baron in Yellowstone's now defunct horse breeding program. She was a chunky, all black, fifteen-hands mare that would not hurt herself or her rider. Jimmy, a couple inches shorter than Rosey, was a sorrel with four white knee-high stockings and a white blaze. Easy to catch and a comfortable ride, Jimmy hated spurs but responded promptly to the tap of a riding crop.

As snow melted and the season progressed, visitor facilities opened, seasonal employees arrived, travel and visitation increased, and bears appeared along the roads and haunted the campgrounds at night. I worked 12- and 14-hour days with frequent night-time call outs. Just when I thought I couldn't take another thing, I got a call from Red Wetzel. "Do you still want Dusty?" he asked. "Of course," I answered, "But I already have two horses here." "I know," was Red's reply, "But if you want Dusty, you can have him and still keep Rosey and Jimmy." "Great!" I said. "I'll take him!"

I didn't realize it until many years later, but this decision started me down the path to becoming a "Yellowstone Ranger" rather than a ranger who would fit into a wide variety of national parks. I never regretted it. The next day Red trailered Dusty out to Canyon. Earlier in the summer he had assigned Dusty to the North District Trail Crew, and in the course of operations, Dusty bucked a trail crewman off. Then another one got dumped, and a third trail crewman, who came from a well-known bronc-riding rodeo family, climbed aboard Dusty to teach him a lesson, and in short order he got bucked off.

After that Dusty was relegated to the trail crew's pack string. When Red found out, he gave the trail crew foreman a piece of his mind and a pack mule in exchange for my Thoroughbred friend. "Dusty's too good a horse just to be in a pack string," Red told me, and as usual he was right. Dusty's arrival at Canyon improved my outlook on life. I rode him a lot in the evenings and on my days off, and he glided like a wisp of wind over the area trails. I left my spurs at home. I didn't need them, as a slight move of my lower leg or the least touch of my heel was all the encouragement my fine bay horse needed.

Many horse users involved with roping, cutting, jumping, or dressage undervalue trail horses. They think just about any horse can make a trail horse. This isn't true in Yellowstone where horse and foot trails mingle with game trails. You share the trail and country with grizzly and black bears, mountain lions, wolves, and coyotes as well as herds of bison and elk. The trails go over steep terrain and are interspersed with vast meadows and grasslands mixed with dense lodgepole pine forests. You and your horse cross miles of fire-burned areas choked with downfall. Trails in Yellowstone have swift and deep water crossings, traverse large thin-crusted thermal areas, and run next to places where the water table is so close to the surface that they are like bottomless pits of Jell-O covered with grass; your horse can sink out of sight if he steps in one. Such trails aren't for sissies or green-broke horses.

On his first trips Dusty wasn't the trail horse he eventually came to be. His fight or flight response was something to behold and even more impressive to experience. I've never seen a horse switch ends so fast. Many of his would-be riders hit the turf or wound up clinging to Dusty's neck after these about-faces. When I became old enough to follow my dad on horseback in Yosemite, he advised me to sit up straight in the saddle, to always ride balanced, and to pay attention to my horse and to the country around me. That advice served me well when I started riding Dusty.

By following dad's advice I survived Dusty's spontaneous about faces. Whenever I saw what prompted his rapid retreat I took time to check it out with him. He improved with every ride, and in time I was able to anticipate some of these responses. I found I could prevent some of these abrupt reactions simply by laying my hand on his neck and talking to him. Dusty learned exceptionally quickly. One day I rode up Observation Peak, past the abandoned lookout, and out along the Washburn Range looking for a poacher's cabin mentioned in an 1890 Army patrol report. Unsuccessful at finding it, I decided to cut cross country down a timbered slope to check the campsites at a pair of nearby lakes. We got into a jackpot of crisscrossed down timber. It was a mess.

Apparently new to Dusty, he resisted crossing down logs, showing his displeasure by rearing and reversing his course of travel. My persistence prevailed, and my bay horse went over the first log like a steeple chaser, clearing it by a couple feet. More backing, rearing, and plunging. With nostrils flaring and saliva flinging as he worked the bit and shook his head in a mini tantrum, Dusty catapulted over the next log and the next. We rested as I debated turning back but decided it was the lesser of two evils to continue. We did, and by the time we got out of the labyrinth of downfall both of us were sweat covered.

The next lesson came less than a week later when I rode out the South Rim Trail to check on a reported carcass. Finding that it was just dried skin and bones and not a bear attractant I headed cross-country through moderate timber to check the campsite at Ribbon Lake. We encountered another jungle of crisscross downfall, not as bad or as extensive as the earlier one. Never liking to backtrack, I decided to see what my mount's response would be, and after one refusal he met the challenge head on. With his steeplechase technique he lunged over each down log with two feet to spare. An improvement to be sure, but I could tell he was not happy at the end of the challenge.

On my next day off I trailered Dusty to Ice Lake and rode back to Canyon. When we neared Cascade Lake I detoured off-trail toward Observation Peak until I located our labyrinth of crisscross downfall that had been our nemesis two weeks earlier. Dusty might well have thought, "Oh shit. Not this again."

I pointed him toward the jungle of downfall, and my boy never hesitated. He went to the first log, stepped over it and continued to the second one with as much aplomb and finesse as if he had done it this way forever. He went through the whole jungle without breaking stride or a sweat and finished not even breathing deeply. For the rest of our time together (14 years), this was the way he handled downfall, assured and sure footed, with never a misstep.

While I was assigned to the Canyon Sub-District the bay horse adapted to grizzly bears and learned not to be intimidated by them. One late September I walked up to the Canyon barn to feed Dusty and five other horses in the fifty-by-fifty-foot corral attached to the barn. I was surprised the boys weren't standing, heads outstretched over the top fence rail, whinnying their greeting to me. Instead, they focused on the center of the corral with their backs to the barn. They were alert and paying attention but didn't appear particularly uncomfortable. A three-year-old, 250-pound grizzly was licking the horse's salt block about seven yards in front of the horses. The bear wheeled around at my approach and ran off. The boys relaxed a bit, and most of them watched the bear run off, while Dusty and one other came to the gate to meet me.

For the rest of our time together Dusty treated grizzlies like any other animal he ran into—pay attention, but no big deal.

The bay horse really came into his own when I was sent to Lake as sub-district ranger in the spring of 1968. After a couple of years he not only had the trails memorized, he seemed to know whether the trip was for patrol or for stocking cabins. My only complaint was that he was such a high-energy horse it took a lot of oats to keep his weight up where it should be.

As well as being a good ride and an enjoyable companion, Dusty was, on his own, a good representative of Yellowstone. I always considered the horse I rode and the animals I packed to be a part of my uniform. Their looks and togetherness in action reflected well on their user and made it easier for me to establish credibility with the outfitters and private horse users. I frequently used Dusty's responsiveness and sensitivity to my advantage, as I did in contacts with Harold Turner. Harold was a third generation outfitter from Jackson Hole.

Steeped in tradition and stubborn by nature, he was reluctant to change to any of the practices adopted by Yellowstone to minimize horse impacts on the land. Harold's standard response was "But we've always done it this way." While apparently good to their clients, the Turner operation was not necessarily equally good to the land. Harold and I often discussed this when we met on the trail, and he was an energetic, persistent debater and always had a litany of grievances against the federal government in general and the NPS in particular. My first thought when I saw him coming down the trail was always how to break off our conversation politely.

One day while on boundary patrol I ran into Harold in the Fox Park area just outside of Yellowstone. He went through his current diatribe of comments and was about to start repeating them when I had an inspiration. I had already mentally outlined my rebuttal points, so when there was an opening I took advantage of it and spoke my points forcefully. Just as I finished, my foot on the side out of Turner's view tapped Dusty's side. Dusty responded with an aggressive jump, and I let him continue down the trail, as I shouted over my shoulder, "Excuse me. My horse is restless. I gotta go. Let's continue this later."

One summer I went to Thorofare to meet with The Trail Riders of the Wilderness, a politically active group of backcountry horse people camped just outside of Yellowstone. I had supper with them one evening, and afterward I talked briefly to the group gathered around the campfire about Yellowstone policy and coming changes.

The following morning I rode into the park with the group president and a couple of the outfitters, escorting them into the backcountry. We spent the morning in the area looking at campsites they might use next year. As we returned to their camp their president rode alongside me and said, "I've been watching your horse all morning and have to tell you that you're way better mounted than any of the other rangers we've met down here in previous years. You're lucky to have such a good horse to ride." That was the first of many compliments I got on my friend through the years. I had to give him credit for representing his park and his brand well.

Three months later Dusty and I were at Trail Creek Cabin at the tip of the Southeast Arm of Yellowstone Lake when I got another clue about the attributes of my partner. It was fall, and we were stocking the south boundary patrol cabins for winter ski trips. The rations had already been taken down by patrol boat and were stockpiled at Trail Creek Cabin, and we worked from there to supply four cabins. This late October morning was overcast and a chilly ten degrees, with almost a foot of snow on the ground. We had planned a day trip to stock the cabin at Cabin Creek, five miles away and across the Yellowstone River. Irwin (the mule) and Rosie were packed, and I was on Dusty leading them, while another ranger followed us.

We had gotten a sweat up in the packing operation and were riding hunched over in our saddles trying to warm up. Ice crystals created by our breathing attached to our caps and eyelashes and onto the horses' nostrils and eye lashes. Dusty moved out, the packs rode well, we warmed up a bit, and life improved, but then we got to the Yellowstone River.

Ice covered the river fifteen to twenty yards out from either side with only the center running free. Much of that was filled with slush flowing rapidly downstream, and it looked cold. While the ford itself was no more than belly deep on Dusty, the ice obscured much of the route, and if he got off course we could wind up swimming in deeper holes on either side of the ford. Not a good idea at that time of year. I looked back to check the packs—they were riding well. I looked at the other ranger and shrugged my shoulders, indicating "What do you think?" He shrugged his shoulders back, indicating, "Whatever you decide is fine with me."

I looked it over again, then touched Dusty gently with the heel of my boot and moved him into the vee-cut in the riverbank leading down to the frozen ford. He went willingly, Irwin followed promptly, and Rosie needed a tug on the lead rope to get started. Dusty stopped at the ice and sniffed it. I had the reins in my left hand and Irwin's lead rope looped around the saddle horn with the running end of the lead rope under my right thigh so I had contact with him but he could pull free if he needed to. I reached down and put my right hand on Dusty's neck and the bay stepped carefully onto the ice. It held, and he took another step and another, and then Irwin followed, but on his fifth step Dusty broke through the ice. I held my breath, my right hand stayed on the bay neck as he calmly pulled his foot out and took another step with no panic, no fuss, just concentrating on his assigned job. The ice held, and I exhaled and started breathing again.

Irwin followed as Dusty continued. As he approached the ice-free center portion of the Yellowstone the bay broke through once again just as Rosie broke through with one leg. Rosie reared back to free her leg, almost breaking the pigging string that tied her to Irwin. She then lunged forward onto the ice behind Irwin, causing Irwin to jump forward and break through the ice right behind Dusty.

In an instant chaos overtook us as horses' hooves churned up the Yellowstone River with chunks of ice and muddy water erupting like geysers. For a moment I thought we had lost it, but when things settled down the horses were standing with their feet on the river bottom, packs were still upright, and the west side of the once-frozen river ford was mostly ice free. Mini-icebergs of slush rolled rapidly downstream as I worked the bay's neck with my right hand and looked back to make sure all was well.

My ranger companion gave a thumbs-up sign. My good horse evidently thought this was a piss-poor place to take a break and stepped out for the east shore. I took a deep breath, got a balanced seat and studied our route as Dusty assuredly headed toward the ice-locked bank ahead. His first two steps onto the ice broke through, but my friend continued as if nothing had happened, and Irwin followed with no problem. Rosie broke the ice for her first three steps but reacted less violently than before and followed Dusty and Irwin onto solid ground.

We all caught our breaths and rested. My right hand trembled with relief as I stroked the bay's neck, and I talked to him quietly, saying "Good! Good! Good! Thank you." I resisted jumping off and hugging my boy around the neck. It would have been difficult as encumbered as I was by my regular clothing plus long underwear, chaps, slicker, mittens, and overshoes. Besides, Dusty was the ultimate professional—he was just doing his job. The rest of the day I marveled at how, once again, we had cheated fate and had been able to accomplish a difficult, seemingly impossible task with a certain amount of style and efficiency just because I had a good partner and the confidence to rely on him. The ranger with me broke the silence, "What a relief. I didn't think you were going to pull that off." "It pays to ride a good horse," was my understated answer.

Two months later, Ranger Gary Brown and I were back at Thorofare to stock the cabin with winter rations and make the final hunting patrol. After getting the rations put away, wood hauled in and stacked neatly, kindling split and stacked, we went out to check the few hunting camps we had been told were still in the area. We visited the outfitter camp on the Yellowstone River several miles south of Hawks Rest. Their hunters had filled out and been packed out the day before. Only guides, the wrangler, and the cook were left, getting ready to break down the camp and leave either the next day or the day after. We had a cup of coffee while we visited about the summer and the season's hunt, and after a short but pleasant respite for us, we left our hosts to return to Thorofare.

They told us that only one camp remained in that area, the outfitter on Two Ocean Pass. Since neither Gary nor I had been to the parting of the waters—where Atlantic Creek flows one way and Pacific Creek flows the opposite direction—we decided to take the opportunity to sightsee and contact a camp not regularly visited by Yellowstone rangers. We knew daylight was short but headed there anyway. It was a pleasant, crisp afternoon with only a flake or two of snow to interrupt our progress. We were dressed for the weather and were comfortable.

Both of us enjoyed seeing the parting of the waters and our stop at the outfitter camp. We stayed at the camp longer than we had intended but enjoyed our conversation, coffee, and a piece of pecan pie that was past its prime but nonetheless delicious. It was dusk as we left camp, full dark by the time we got to the Yellowstone River, and blacker than the ace of spades as we headed north from Hawks Rest. Neither Gary nor I was worried riding in the dark as we were both on solid horses and had faith in them. My only worry was to make sure we got on the trail going around the west side of Bridger Lake. I absolutely did not want to chance the more direct trail I had experienced in August, as the last I had heard it had not been cleared by the end of August.

I found out once again what happens to the best-laid plans of mice and men. It was too late to turn around when we finally came to the conclusion we were on the direct trail, the one with the downfall that probably had not been cleared, but we continued, hoping by some miracle that it had been cleared.

Shit! It wasn't cleared, and from this point it would be five or six additional miles to turn back and take one of the longer trails. It was so dark I could barely see my horse's ears. More out of curiosity than anything else, I rode up to the first log and stopped, then touched Dusty gently with my boot heel. He promptly stepped over the first log, went 20 steps west, reared back and jumped over the next log and did in five minutes what had taken more than 20 minutes in broad daylight the first time around. Gary's horse, anxious not to be left behind, stuck his nose onto Dusty's tail and followed him step for step all the way through the maze. After that it was a routine trip, and in short order we made it back to Thorofare, unsaddled and rubbed down our boys. Needless to say, Dusty got extra oats that night.

I was honored to have my bay horse as a partner for 14 years. He carried me comfortably and safely over fully 90 percent of Yellowstone's trails, and helped me explore many, many drainages on the south end of the park as well as tons of open country. His alertness served me to my advantage many, many times. In all those years, I can't think of meeting a single party that was aware of us before Dusty let me know of them.

I've been blessed with knowing a number of truly outstanding horses and mules in my time. None was smoother riding, more alert, or more intelligent than Dusty. He has been out of my life for over 30 years now but never out of my mind. As Saul Bellow said, "Everybody needs his memories. They keep the wolf of insignificance from the door." Thanks for the memories, my bay friend.

Chapter 31

Irwin the Magnificent

A ROUTINE INCIDENT THAT HAPPENED MAY 15, 1970, WAS DES-tined to influence many of my activities for the next 10 or so years. On that particular date Frank Conrad and Jim Hotch-kiss, who were then responsible for Yellowstone's horse op-eration, purchased two sorrel mules from the Elkhorn Ranch. They paid $300 for each mule.

One of the mules was a good-looking, 16-hands, six-year-old, long-legged molly mule that was broke to ride, pack, or drive. With a bit of a smirk, Hotchkiss and Conrad named her Ellie after Ellie Chamberlain, one of the park's Comm Center operators who was tall, attractive, amply-built, and possessed auburn hair. She also had sense of humor enough to appreciate sharing her name with a National Park Service mule. The second mule was a five-year-old john mule that weighed 1,100 pounds, stood a little over 15 hands, had an alert disposition that didn't miss a thing, and a prominent Roman nose, which to many mule aficionados was not a good sign.

With a bit of malice, Hotchkiss and Conrad named this mule Irwin after Irwin Atwood, the park's property officer. Atwood was a crusty, meticulous bean counter whose cabin inventory form required you to list how many serving spoons a particular patrol cabin had as differentiated from soup spoons and tea spoons. I doubt if Atwood was pleased to have a somewhat homely, Roman-nosed mule with his name listed on the corral operation's property inventory.

At this time I was the Lake sub-district ranger and was introduced to Irwin and Ellie when Hotchkiss delivered Lake's horses and mules toward the end of June. As he unloaded the stock, Jim cautioned that Irwin had a mind of his own and his own agenda. Shortly after their arrival at Lake, Ellie went to Thorofare for the summer. I hardly got to know her. However Irwin stayed at Lake, and I got very well acquainted with him. Irwin proved to be exceptionally strong, athletic, and agile, and had no problem carrying a load 50 to 60 pounds heavier than we would put on any other animal.

When Irwin objected to what his handler wanted him to do and it became a test of wills, Irwin's solution was often to run away. More than one hapless ranger was dragged through the trees, yelling, "Whoa, you SOB. Whoa," when he chose to hang onto Irwin's lead rope during such an episode. The worst trick Irwin ever played on me came late in his first season when he dragged me around Pelican Valley and destroyed beyond repair an almost new, just properly broken-in Class A uniform Stetson. That was the low ebb of our relationship.

To explain the gravitas of this heinous deed, I have to digress momentarily from discussing Irwin to reflect on the significance of the "flat-hat" (Stetson). Some who wore it revered it, while others cussed it. The Stetson certainly made it harder for a tall person to get in or out of a vehicle. Although it was a "uniform" item, the "flat hat" inevitably told quite a bit about its wearer when one contemplated the depth and character of the hat's creases, the shape of its brim, whether the hat was fitted with a "stampede strap," and whether the buckle of the "stampede strap" faced forward or to the rear. Seldom were any two hats similar unless both were fresh out of the box and not yet creased. Those familiar with the ranger "flat hat" used to comment that if at first it doesn't fit, just keep wearing it—sooner or later your head will adjust to the hat's shape.

During this period in Yellowstone uniform regulations were more stringent and much less flexible than they currently are. When out of doors and on duty, a ranger was supposed to wear his Stetson. To be "uncovered" in such circumstances was akin to being seen in public with your fly unzipped. Regardless of crease style, whether the hat was worn tilted forward or tilted back, or tilted to the right or to the left, no ranger liked breaking in a brand-new Stetson. Not only was it hard on the head until head and Stetson were properly mated, wearing a brand new ranger hat made the wearer appear to be a greenhorn. This was an uncomfortable image for any ranger who felt he didn't belong in that category.

This explains why I was thoroughly pissed at Irwin when he destroyed the brim of my almost new but well broken-in Stetson. It was mid-summer and my wife Cindy and I were taking two packhorse loads of supplies and rations to Fern Lake Patrol Cabin. We had just turned onto the Astringent Creek Trail when Cindy, riding in the rear, called to me that Irwin's pack needed attention. I got off Dusty, handed his lead rope to Cindy, and wrapped the lead rope to Rosie, the first packhorse, around the horn of my saddle while I went to adjust Irwin's pack. Irwin was restless and goosey.

Starting out that morning I had tied Irwin to Rosie, a half-Morgan mare and an experienced packhorse, since Irwin was new to the operation, and I had figured this would be the best way to get him used to the "ropes." I untied Irwin to fix his pack since he was fidgety, and I didn't want the attitude to transfer to the horses Cindy was holding.

I jerked on Irwin's lead rope to get his attention and to show him who was boss. He wheeled away and took off forcefully, pulling me with him, and since he outweighed me six to one and had four legs to my two, it was no contest. I lost my footing but hung on because I didn't want to see his pack scattered all over the landscape. He dragged me belly down and headfirst for some distance, across the grass and through the sagebrush. After awhile, he got bored with this and stopped of his own volition and turned, facing me.

I got up gingerly and assessed the damage, and other than rope-burned hands, a grass-stained shirt, bruised elbows, and a bruised ego I seemed to be okay. And, I still had my hat on. Using the patience I should have used initially, I approached my recalcitrant friend to adjust and re-tie his pack. As I tied him back to Rosie, I noticed something in my peripheral vision. On closer scrutiny I saw that the right brim of my Stetson was hanging down. Three-fourths of the brim had broken completely through, and it was hanging by the remaining one-fourth. It was enough to piss off the Pope, and I had to ride with it flapping in my peripheral vision for the rest of the day. It served as a reminder for me to use finesse and not force with my Roman-nosed associate.

The more he was used, the better he became, and Irwin proved to be a fast learner as well as strong and agile. Little escaped his sharp eyes and keen mind. He benefited by the consistency of the few of us in the sub-district who used him. We benefited by his innate good qualities. He had the back and build to carry a load well, was a fast walker, could keep up with any horse without trotting, and rarely bumped his pack into any of the trees close to the trail. I realized I had become attached to the independent, fast moving, hard headed, and Roman-nosed little shit.

On fall cabin stocking forays we often would have to get over substantial trees across the trail where there was no easy way around them. Dusty would cross carefully and quickly. I would hold him back while Rosie, the first packhorse, would grunt and groan getting over the tree one leg at a time. Irwin, third in line and carrying 50 to 60 pounds more than Rosie, would wait until just before there was tension on his lead rope and then, almost effortlessly, hop over the tree. Landing as gracefully as a ballerina, Irwin would stop immediately so he wouldn't jerk the mule behind him. His mind was as impressive as his athletic ability. One observer said Irwin must have had muscles in his shit. I never doubted it.

On boundary patrol during hunting season I would ride Dusty and pack Irwin. They got along well together and made a good team. Once we got to a cabin and unpacked I would set out to visit the outfitter and resident hunting camps outside the park in the national forest. I preferred making these contacts just on my saddle horse and not towing a pack animal—it was one less thing to worry about, and it allowed me to pay closer attention to the folks I was visiting. But what to do with Irwin? I remembered advice from Cary and Marguerite Jackson in Yosemite during my seasonal days—tie a horse you have to leave by himself to a flexible young sapling. With the flexibility of the sapling there's significantly less likelihood the frustrated, lonely critter will be able to rear back and use his full weight to break his lead rope and get free.

I found a suitable sapling close to Howell Creek Patrol Cabin, put a bell on Irwin, and then tied him high and short to the sapling. With more than a little trepidation I headed for the outfitter camp on Dike Creek. I was gone several hours, and when I returned, Irwin was still tied to his tree but it was a mess. So was the area around it. Irwin had pawed around the tree as if he were trying to find a direct route to China. He learned fast, however, and the next time I left him pawing was minimal and rehab was simple. After the third time, he stayed quietly like the gentleman he could be.

Early on in our relationship I tried Irwin on picket. Although it was apparently new to him and he didn't care for the rope around his ankle, he adjusted to the picket rope in just one night. So we had our system in place for the following years—picket Irwin, bell Dusty and let him run free. I always had my horse and mule come the next morning. The three of us spent about eight years together covering both the Lake and the Snake River backcountry.

But not even the mountains last forever. Irwin suffered an unfortunate, untimely and unnecessary death. He had come in from winter pasture with a big bunch of park service horses and mules. At Stephens Creek, the base of Yellowstone's horse operation, the corral operations foreman and the helicopter fire crew were cleaning up the horses and mules, getting them ready for the season's first shoeing. Irwin's tail was full of burrs. Not being one to suffer abrupt handling quietly, Irwin objected forcefully when they tried to remove the burrs, much as he had when teaching me to be gentle brushing mud off his belly. With a lot of animals to work that day, Irwin's handlers didn't have time to waste on an independent mule, so they put Irwin in a squeeze chute to finish the job in a timely manner.

They didn't notice the ice on the bottom of the chute. In his struggles, Irwin slipped on the ice, hyper-extending and breaking his back. Later in the day they put Irwin down. I was devastated, and I blamed myself for not being there. I felt that Irwin would have tolerated my efforts. I cried because Irwin was gone, and I had let him down. Years later, when discussing Irwin with my wife, who knew him well, I said I wish I could apologize to my Roman-nosed friend for not being there for him that day. She was sure he knew. She felt that special animals like Irwin had a spirit that stayed with us and could be an influence on us forever.

She compared it to the souls of departed parents and close friends communicating with us if we are receptive. The more I reflected on this, the more I saw substance in it. I felt I knew of an example of that. The same corral operations foreman, whose decision led to Irwin's demise, was responsible a few years later for bringing horse trainer Buck Branaman to the park to teach a softer, gentler method of horse handling to Yellowstone's staff. The training continues to this day. So Irwin made his point and had the last word. Here's to you, my friend. I still miss you.

Chapter 32

Bit Players and Supporting Roles

SOMETIMES MOVIE BIT PLAYERS AND SUPPORTING ACTORS have more memorable parts than stars. A case in point is Lee Marvin's role as Tully Crow in the John Wayne Western "The Comancheros." While I am a John Wayne fan, I find his performance in this movie indistinguishable from the heroes he played in many other Westerns. Lee Marvin's Tully Crow, on the other hand, sets a gold standard as a mean, no good, squinty-eyed, tobacco-chewing, whisky-swilling, gun-running, son of a bitch. The only thing it lacks is more screen time—he's killed off way too early by the Duke.

This same comparison is often found in the horse world as well. Those taking an outfitted, backcountry horse trip invariably remember the name of the horse they rode. They seldom know or remember the names of the packhorses and mules that made their trip possible. Yet often the packhorses are more significant and talented than the run-of-the-mill, anyone-can-ride-him, just-plod-down-the-trail saddle horse. Some packhorses and mules have laid groundwork for more stories and legends than most saddle horses would dream of—if in fact, horses and mules ever dream.

Max and Ike were notable Yellowstone pack animals who gave rise to more tales then any dozen Yellowstone horses in the 1960s and '70s. Max was a husky sixteen-hands, dirty-grey horse that was easily bored, stumbled frequently, liked to smell wildflowers, and was an incipient racist that considered himself superior to mules. He had a pronounced sheik's mustache on his upper lip, reacted unpredictably, and sometimes after the fact, to threats only he could see. Max could pass wind so loudly that he was often startled by the sound of his own farts. In his day he was known as the Clown Prince of Pack Horses, and everyone who ever used him had his own Max-stories.

Ike was a small, black, wise-old-owl mule that had been there and done that when it came to mule chores. No fence could hold him when he wanted to be on the other side—he could effortlessly go over, under, around, or through any fence in the Lake area. He never ducked work and always managed to show up at the barn when anyone was dishing out oats. Being small, around thirteen and a half hands, Ike had to rely on guile and fleetness of foot to stay healthy. One time I pulled up to the Lake corral where about sixteen ranger and trail crew horses were crowded in. The trail crew was in for the weekend. I was there to feed for the day, filling the three mangers with hay and scattering more on the ground so each animal had his own spot and wouldn't have to compete.

I watched as a dominant horse bared his teeth and gestured toward a horse standing at a prime spot in front of the manger. The chastened horse quickly backed away, snarled at a subordinate to move him out, and took his spot at another manger. The pecking order exercise continued, and one horse with its lips rolled back and teeth bared made a bee-line for Ike's butt as if to say, "At least I can show this little black so-and-so who's boss."

Ike was standing out-of-the-way, next to the corral gate,

and appeared to be sound asleep. Out of the corner of his ever-alert eye Ike glimpsed the approaching horse. Ike neither ran nor kicked, but, without telegraphing his intent, he flexed his muscles and jumped over the five-foot-high corral gate. The other horse closed his teeth only on air as Ike gracefully landed outside the gate and nonchalantly walked over to a lush clump of grass and started grazing.

Ike couldn't hide a slight, enigmatic, but pleased-with-himself smile. He wasn't one to gloat—he was content to eat grass in peace while his unworthy adversary had to compete with others to chew on dry hay. I was so impressed with the little mule's athletic ability that I didn't bother to put him back in the corral but let him continue to free graze in peace. Anyone who could levitate five feet in a standing jump, without a running start, deserved some recognition of his talents. Utilizing his newly discovered capability Ike spent more and more time grazing outside the corral and pasture. He became a fixture in the government residence area and in the meadows along the Fishing Bridge to Lake road.

Grazing next to the road with Yellowstone Lake and the dramatic, snow-capped Absaroka Range in the background, Ike would often create his own wildlife jam. My wife Cindy called him the most photographed moose in Yellowstone after people coming into the Lake Hospital, where she worked, told her of the neat moose picture they got back up the road by the barn.

That particular year was a bad white bark pine nut year. Without that food source to keep them up high, grizzly bears started wandering through the Lake Area in late August looking for an alternate food source. One Monday, Bill Armstrong, Lake maintenance supervisor, told me he had returned late Sunday night from his weekend in Mammoth to find himself locked out of his Lake apartment. While he was gone he let friends use it for the weekend, and they had locked the apartment, which Bill never did. As he walked around back in the dark to get a hide-a-key he bumped into a dark furry object. Both were startled. Bill said the black critter exhaled just as forcibly as he himself had gasped and inhaled. He said it was lucky he had stopped at Mud Volcano to check the restrooms and had relieved his bladder. "It was that damn black mule of yours!" he said.

"Chalk one up for Ike," I thought.

While Ike was athletic and graceful, Max was a klutz and stumbled frequently for a variety of reasons. Max stumbled because he fell asleep and because he was trying to smell the flowers growing along the trail. He was like Ferdinand the Bull but stumbled more—sometimes simply because he wasn't paying attention. I think Max suffered from A. D. D. long before it ever became a part of our vocabulary. Ike was quiet and self-effacing; Max was obstreperous and pushy. Ike was a patient soul who would wait his turn. Max was never shy about trying to be first. And Ike never bumped his pack boxes against trees growing close to the trail. In contrast Max never figured out why he himself could get by a tree without bumping it, but his pack boxes would bump trees and slam back against his ribs.

But Max had redeeming features—he was always glad to see you, and you could catch him anywhere. On a memorable, cold and dismal late October day I rode into Fern Lake Patrol Cabin packing Max with the last of that cabin's winter rations. It was below zero with twelve inches of snow on the ground when I picketed Max, turned my saddle horse loose, and retreated to the cabin to finish cleaning and put the rations away.

The next morning, there was ice in the bucket of water inside the cabin when I started a fire in the cook stove. Going out at first light to bring my horses in for their morning grain, I found Max had pulled his picket pin, and my two horses were heading back to Lake without me, Max dragging his picket rope along with him. It was not a good way to start my day.

I hurried back to the cabin, put more wood on the fire, filled a nose bag with oats, grabbed both halters, and started slogging through a foot of snow after my two runaways who were simply trying to improve their lot in life. While I could see their point of view, I still had work to do before the cabin was ready for winter. And, I certainly didn't relish walking out 15 miles stumbling through a foot of snow and wading two creeks in riding boots and overshoes with temperatures ranging from zero to the low double digits. I went as fast as I was able for a mile and a half and was beginning to sweat despite the cold. I could already feel a rub spot that would soon become a blister if I didn't take care of it.

Then I caught sight of the deserters 300 yards ahead going up Broad Creek toward the divide and home, and they spotted me about the same time. The saddle horse, being the smarter of the two, moved away. Max, good soul that he was, whinnied as if to say, "Hi, Jerry, where the hell have you been? I'm hungry." I caught and haltered Max and gave him a good feed of oats while I worked at unfastening the frozen picket rope. "Max, you homely SOB, you have redeeming features. Thanks for letting me catch you."

I coiled the stiff, semi-frozen picket rope and slid it over his head onto his withers so I wouldn't have to carry it. I found a log to help me struggle onto Max bareback so he could carry me, and we headed back to the cabin. My saddle horse followed, as he evidently didn't feel the "free" part of freedom was worth it by himself. He traded it for companionship and a feed of oats. Max's stock went way up in my estimation when he saved me from the misery of the walk out and the ignominy of having my horses arrive without me. In short order, though, Max was back to his usual self.

In the fall of 1969, Ranger Gary Brown and I worked out of Trail Creek Patrol Cabin to stock the south boundary patrol cabins with winter rations. We spent two weeks or so doing what most any healthy, red-blooded ranger would love to be doing in late October in Yellowstone—riding good horses in great country.

We packed rations and readied the cabins for ski patrols we planned to make that winter. In between cleaning cabins, splitting and stacking wood, we rode the country adjacent to Yellowstone to contact the last few hunters still in the area. Max, Ike, and Rosie were our pack animals. Max was at the peak of his career both physically and as a provider of raw material for stories. We had finished our cabin stocking and patrol chores and were on our way out to Ten Mile Post Trail Head. We were north of Clear Creek, and my saddle horse Dusty was stretched out at his going-home pace. I was leading Rosie, with Max pigtailed (tied) to Rosie's saddle, and Ike pigtailed to Max. Gary brought up the rear surveying the country and watching for packs that might tilt off center.

Max continued to pick on Ike, as he had the whole trip. More than once when I looked back to see how the packs were riding I watched Max eye the slack in his lead rope tied to Rosie's packsaddle. Just before he ran out of slack, Max would turn his head and bare teeth at the little mule causing him to reflexively pull back. When Ike pulled back, Max charged forward to catch up with Rosie before tension on his lead rope jerked his head around. Fourteen hundred pounds of grey horse lunging forward as seven hundred pounds of black mule pulled back was no contest. End result, Ike got jerked around a lot, Gary and I replaced a lot of broken pigtails and Max's full name evolved into "Max You SOB"—when we were polite.

On this last day Max was especially difficult, and in addition to tormenting Ike he refused to follow directly in line behind Rosie but was always offset one horse width to the right or left of her. At first I tried to get him into line like a real packhorse, but he listened only to his own drummer. I either had to shoot him—which would have generated considerable paper work—or tolerate him.

As we were going down the trail tolerating Max's whim, two things happened almost simultaneously—Rosie's lead rope was rudely yanked from my hand, and I heard two loud crashes behind me. It was like BAM—KAPOW! The lead rope left a rope burn in its place. I wheeled Dusty around to see Rosie standing chagrined at having pulled back. Max was behind Rosie, offset a horse width to the right and directly behind a huge tree growing next to the trail. He seemed unsteady on his feet and was shaking his head side to side. Ike was a mule width to Max's left, in direct line with Rosie, and had his head turned away, which was not enough to hide his ear-to-ear smile.

Gary was laughing so much he had a hard time staying in the saddle. When he regained control he tried talking, "You missed it! Max turned his head back to snarl at Ike…then ran forward right into that tree…you should've seen it…I don't know which was louder…Max hitting the tree…or his fart when the wind was knocked out of him! I've never seen anything like it."

We both dismounted, and by the time we walked up to Max, he had stopped shaking his head and was grazing. It pays to have a strong body and a thick skull. We checked packs, led Max around a bit, and he walked as normally as he ever did. When we started back down the trail, I looked back at our entourage, and all was going well. Ike was still smiling to himself, and Gary was still chuckling to himself. I thought to myself, "Chalk one up for Ike."

To his credit, Max behaved himself for the last four miles of that day. I would like to report that Max had experienced an epiphany and was changed forever, but that wouldn't be true. I had many more Max and Ike experiences during my next six years at Lake. Though Max and Ike long ago departed for perpetually green pastures, I remember them often. Both rank high in the pantheon of critters that have enriched my life and the lore of Yellowstone.

Chapter 33

Outlasting Your Warranty

AFTER I RETIRED FROM THE NATIONAL PARK SERVICE ON December 31, 1995, my wife Cindy and I moved to Bozeman, Montana, into a house we had purchased several years before. Required to retire by age restrictions, my only regret is I didn't have another 32 years to work in Yellowstone.

As a retiree, I now live with memories, often looking back at my early goals and aspirations. But defining and contrasting goals and aspirations during your lifetime is somewhat akin to picking flyspecks out of pepper or trying to read and understand the fine print of a government contract. It can be challenging, and it might not be worth the trouble.

I was a permanent park ranger for 36 years, during which I had a few outstanding supervisors, some good supervisors, a few so-so, and one or two really piss-poor supervisors. Through it all, the only guidance I ever really needed was simply wanting to be like Dad and trying to do the kind of job he would have done. Dad was thoughtful and assured in his dealings with all varieties of people and gained cooperation through a combination of quiet presence and the application of practical psychology. However, he was not slow to use demonstrative action when it was appropriate.

My main goal now is to maintain as good of health as possible. Comparing my health as a young man to my health as a senior citizen reminds me of a saying by Bat Masterson (a contemporary of Wyatt Earp's). "Mother Nature is mostly fair; she just gives the rich their ice in the summer and the poor their ice in the winter."

Good health as a youth or as a senior citizen requires that you are upright and taking nourishment. As a young man, I would have steak and eggs, rare and over medium, with whole-wheat toast, hash browns and coffee. I would clean my plate, burp in satisfaction, and then go to work. In my senior version, I have bran flakes and milk, preceded by a fast-acting Lactaid tablet to counter my recently acquired lactose intolerance. After eating my bran flakes, I remain seated, snooze briefly to aid digestion, and then take my bowl to the sink and rinse it.

Before retiring, when I had a difficult memo to write or a letter to answer, I would go for a walk first. The first part of the walk was to clear my mind, and then the second part was the most creative for drafting what I wanted to say. Today, if I get up from the table to get a glass of water to take a pill, I use the stimulus of the walk to remind me to correctly document the taking of the pill.

My warranty ran out in my early fifties when I first needed glasses, not for reading but for distance vision. Then I quit jogging and started walking to make it easier on my joints, and while I was never a real runner, jogging felt good (when I was done with it). And it made me feel more justified in drinking a Rainier Ale to restore my electrolytes.

In 1988, I got dumped off a horse and broke my shoulder and had to have it repaired, which took awhile. Then while on leave visiting my mother, I had to have my appendix out, and my mother oversaw nursing me back to health once again. Shortly after, I developed asthma and that was greatly exacerbated by Yellowstone's fires of '88. Then the doctors discovered I had prostate cancer, which led to the immediate removal of my prostate and the usual complications. Then not too many years ago, they found out I had Parkinson's disease, which slowed me down significantly.

All in all I would rather be healthy. As my grandmother used to say, "It's the shits to get old. But then, dying young isn't so good either."

Chapter 34

Death, Loss, and Change

As I have aged, I have reflected back on my reactions to the deaths of my friends, mentors, and my dad.

Perhaps my earliest experience of death was in 1952. I was nineteen and the fire lookout on Pelican Cone in Yellowstone.

Several people said they would visit me during my two months there, but I was especially surprised that Bernie Long, my best friend and classmate from Notre Dame, did not come. He worked for the Yellowstone Park Company in their warehouse in Gardiner, Montana. My first night back at the end of the season, I had dinner at the Lake Lodge with my friend Dan Yuhr and mentioned my disappointment.

When I mentioned Bernie Long's name, Dan stopped eating, looked away, and then said, "So no one told you?" "Told me what?" I asked. "Bernie was killed in an auto accident a couple weeks after you went up on the cone. I thought they had told you," Dan said quietly, almost whispering

I was stunned. Color must have drained from my face as I felt myself becoming chilled, then flushed, then chilled again. I sat motionless, hardly breathing. I couldn't believe it. Bernie had been so strong, so full of life, dancing out the evening the last time I saw him. "Shit," I said, barely audible. Then, after a few more moments of silence, I asked how it happened. Apparently Bernie and his friends were trying to reach the Melody Supper Club near Livingston, Montana, before it closed.

They had to make a 55-mile trip over a narrow, winding two-lane road in less than one hour. In this case youth, energy and enthusiasm, hampered by booze and a fast car, were no match for the laws of physics and the dynamics of a sharp turn at high speed. They struck the northeast abutment of the bridge and tumbled into the Yellowstone River. They died, as have so many park concession employees before them and after them, when care and caution were outrun by fun and frivolity. Now, whenever I cross the bridge I think of Bernie and figuratively doff my hat to the premature loss of youth and innocence. Joseph Bernard Long, may you rest in peace.

AS THE YEARS DRIFTED ON, SO DID MY MENTORS. FORMER Yosemite Ranger Cary Jackson died peacefully in his sleep. Jackson and his wife Marguerite were old family friends, who nurtured my love of horses and taught me many backcountry skills. I went to look up Bob McGregor, my childhood hero who was in charge of the Yosemite horse operation, to thank him for his patience with me in my youth. I was too late. He had already taken the big journey.

I did see Lou Stockton ten days before he crossed his last river. He was only a shadow of the man who had taught me packing skills in Yosemite. I told him I was still using the spurs he had loaned me years ago, and I thought of him every time I put them on. When my wife Cindy and I got up to leave, Lou had a hard time getting up off the couch. I shook hands with him, and it was hard to let his hand go. I wanted to hug him and tell him how much he meant to me, but I didn't want to embarrass him, and above all, I didn't want him to see me cry.

My biggest personal loss was in May 1983 when I was the Snake River District Ranger in Yellowstone. I was attending a meeting in Mammoth when I received a message to call my wife Cindy. She told me that Dad had passed away. She had made reservations for me to fly out the next day from Jackson, Wyoming, to Asheville, North Carolina, where my folks lived.

I was numb and spent the rest of the afternoon on autopilot. I got my leave approved and then headed south with my mind awash with memories. When I got to Hayden Valley, I slowed down. To the west was the beginning of a truly beautiful sunset. I pulled over, shut off the engine, got out of the car, and savored the traffic-less quiet and the crisp fresh air.

After awhile a sow grizzly with a cub of the year came out of the woods on a high point above me, about 75 yards away. The sow stopped, sniffed the air, and stood up on her hind legs to get a better view. The cub was a cute, bold fellow, which ran to his mom and stood up along side of her, imitating her every move. For some reason I found this comforting, and somehow the cub became an allegory for me—though Dad was gone in one form, he was still present. Just as the cub was a new generation, Dad would continue to be around in a different way. The thought helped clear my head, and I was much calmer as I drove on south.

I flew back to Asheville, tried to comfort Mom, commiserated with my sister and went with them to the funeral Mass for Dad. One fine touch at the otherwise somber service was the presence of three uniformed Blue Ridge Parkway rangers. Though they didn't know Dad personally they came on their own as a gesture of respect for Dad's memory and reputation. I'm sure he appreciated it; I know I did.

Though Dad had been retired many years, he wasn't forgotten. The rangers provided a reminder of the past, and in my mind the grizzly cub provided Dad's connection to the present and the future. I felt Dad would continue to be a guiding force, not just for me but for the many others who knew and respected him. I helped Mom scatter Dad's ashes in their garden in accordance with his wishes, did chores for Mom, and promised to come back in the fall. Then I returned to Yellowstone.

The summer of 1983 in Yellowstone was active and busy as always. I missed Dad and missed knowing I could call him any time, day or night, for advice. I thought often of his continued presence and was comforted when I reflected on how I still carried much of Dad and my other mentors with me.

It dawned on me that I was getting older. I had already begun feeling some of the ravages of time and realized how different I was from the wide-eyed nineteen-year old who arrived in Yellowstone in 1952 to be the Pelican Cone Lookout. I wasn't as discomfited and awed by death as when I heard of Bernie Long's passing. Since then I had hauled bodies out of the backcountry on horseback and recovered bodies from 600 feet down in the Grand Canyon of the Yellowstone. I had pulled bodies out of Yellowstone and Shoshone lakes and searched lakes in the worst possible conditions for bodies that were never found. I had administered CPR and saved people and lost people.

My feelings about spirituality had changed, too, over the years. Later in the summer after Dad died I fully realized how profound the change had been. I was traveling from Snake River Ranger Station to Harebell Patrol Cabin, then over Big

Game Ridge to spend a few days at Fox Creek Patrol Cabin.

As we got to the highpoint of Big Game Ridge I stopped to give the horses a breather and to enjoy the scene. To the northwest was the long ridge sloping down to Mt. Hancock; beyond that was Mt. Sheridan standing guard over Heart Lake and Witch Creek drainage; then farther north was Mt. Holmes. Sweeping to the east was Mt. Washburn, below it the canyon of the Yellowstone River, then over to Broad Creek, Astringent Creek, then to Pelican Cone and the Mirror Plateau, down to Pelican Valley, farther down to Yellowstone Lake, Chicken Ridge and Two Ocean Plateau. Wow!

To the south were the Tetons, the Snake River, and mountains beyond mountains. Straight ahead was the Trident and, partly obscured by Two Ocean Plateau, I could see the depression between the Trident and Hawk's Rest that was the Thorofare River flowing into the Yellowstone River. In the valley beyond Two Ocean Plateau, the Yellowstone River flowed north into Yellowstone Lake, past the Trident, Turret Mountain, and Colter Peak. Unbelievable! Awesome! Majestic!

I stood in the stirrups and stretched, feeling a slight breeze that tempered the warm sun shining on my back. (Bob Flame, ranger?) I sat back in the saddle and said aloud, "Thank you, mountains." "Thank you, God."

I touched my horse Rosita with my heel. As we moved down the ridge I realized how fortunate I was to be there and to be responsible for protecting the area. Again I said, "Thank you, thank you."

I wasn't exactly sure who I was thanking—God, mountains, backcountry, wilderness—or were they one and the same? To me increasingly, the answer was "Yes." While I hadn't been to church for a number of years for a variety of reasons (work and isolation among them), I felt more spiritual than ever. There was more than one way to pay respect and honor a Supreme Being. Showing reverence for His country and helping protect it should be as valid as attending formal services in a traditional church.

Years later, quite a bit older and retired, I habitually read the obituaries in the daily newspaper (to make sure I am not included!). I read the following passage in one of the obituaries: "Life's journey is not to arrive at the grave in a well preserved body. But, rather to skid in sideways, totally worn out, shouting 'holy shit…what a ride!'"

I'll drink to that sentiment. While my body is not yet totally worn out, and I try not to skid anywhere, any way you look at it, I've had a hell of a ride!

A Metaphor

I am an aging Yellowstone grizzly.
I weigh 540 pounds. Two years ago at this
same time I weighed 200 pounds more—
but my teeth have worn out and my
back is sore from being run over by
a bull bison I thought was weak
enough two springs ago that I
could take him.
He fooled me and now I suffer
from C.P.O.S. (chronic pissed off syndrome).
I no longer have the speed and dexterity
that I used to have—I just lumber
along, thankful for wolves that bring
down an elk and then give way to me
when I want to share some of it with them.
I can eat anything and I still remember
every place I ever got a meal.
My mind and senses are still good —
it's just my body that is fading.
Despite a failing body, I still
evoke respect from many—humans
and critters alike…
…Yellowstone has been good to me…

—Jerry Mernin

Epilogue

On December 13, 2011, at the age of 79, Jerry Mernin finished his last ride. The bears he worked so hard to protect did not get him, nor the winter cold of the high Yellowstone ridges, nor a cantankerous mule. He died at home of a massive stroke three days before the 40th anniversary of his marriage to Cindy.

The Mernin Rendezvous

More than 400 people attended the Mernin Rendezvous at the Lake Ranger Station on September 8, 2012, to pay their respects. The event was rich in military-style ceremony. The flag flew at half-staff. A riderless horse and a packhorse were led along the road; the horse bore Jerry's saddle with his boots in the stirrups, pointing backwards.

A color guard of young park rangers, Jerry's protégés, conducted a 21-gun salute before raising and lowering the flag and presenting it to Cindy. While gazing misty eyed over Yellowstone Lake toward the Thorofare, the participants drank a toast of Rainier Ale to their old friend and colleague. Long may his legacy live.

About the Author

Jerry Mernin was destined to be a National Park Service ranger. Born in Sacramento, California, in 1932, Mernin grew up in Yosemite National Park where his father was a ranger. In Yosemite, Mernin developed his life-long love of outdoor skills and wild places.

After graduating from the University of Notre Dame in 1954 and serving two years in the U.S. Army, Mernin enrolled in the Hasting College of Law in San Francisco. During the summers he worked as a seasonal ranger in Yosemite. His parents cautioned Mernin against becoming a ranger just because he was raised in that environment, but after three years of law school, Mernin made that choice. His deep love and respect for his father was a determining factor in the decision.

Mernin's first permanent ranger position was at Bryce Canyon National Park. After a brief time at Grand Canyon National Park, he became a Yellowstone ranger in 1964.

Mernin never left Yellowstone. He was a ranger there for 32 years, serving at Canyon District from 1964-1968, Lake from 1968-1975, and finally at the Snake River District. While at Lake he met Cindy Ferguson, a nurse at the local hospital, and they married in 1971.

Mernin worked in law enforcement, resource management (especially with bear management), and in the backcountry (often on remote boundary patrols). To stay in the park he loved, Mernin declined promotions to other parks. Mernin became a legend in Yellowstone, respected by co-workers and the public because of his skills, knowledge, and competence under pressure.

After his retirement in 1996, Mernin continued to serve Yellowstone as a volunteer, patrolling Yellowstone's backcountry every summer until his health would no longer permit it. In his later years, encouraged by friends and family, Mernin wrote his memoirs, which became *Yellowstone Ranger*. He died on December 13, 2011, five days before his 40th wedding anniversary with Cindy. He was 79.

Index

Park employee and spouse entries indicate the park(s) where Mernin knew them.
Visitor entries include a comma preceding the name of pertinent park.

Akja rescue sled. See Rescue equipment
Albright, Stan (Yosemite) 127, 129–130
Alexander, John (Yellowstone) 273–274
Alta Ski Area 163
Ambler, Marjane 21–26
Anderson, Chuck (Yellowstone) 279
Anderson, Rick (Yosemite) 128
Armstrong, Bill (Yellowstone) 342–343
Astringent Creek (Yellowstone) 295–296, 335, 356
Atwood, Irwin (Yellowstone) 333–334
Badger Pass Ski Area (Yosemite) 23, 54, 75, 121, 127–137
Bailey, Jim (Grand Canyon) 164–166
Barr, Bob (Yosemite) 146–147
Barrett, Bob (Yosemite) 142–147
Bean, Patty (Yellowstone) 238–240
Bear attacks (Yellowstone) 289–306. See also Rescues and retrievals, in Yellowstone
Bear management 247–259
   drug kit use 254–259, 255–256, 269
   dump closures 260–268
   firearms 166, 270
   radio collars/telemetry 262
   trapping and relocation 270, 277–288
Bears, black
   compared to grizzlies 248
Bears, grizzly
   charging 310–316
   compared to black bears 248
   importance of 317–318
   in Mernin apartment 206–210

tree-climbing 305
Bears in campgrounds 247–259, 260–268, 307–309
Big Game Ridge (Yellowstone) 215–216, 311, 356
Big Thumb Creek (Yellowstone) 300, 302
Blank, Tim (Yellowstone) 296
Boulder Pass (Glacier) 46
Bozeman, MT 203, 241, 349
Bridge Bay Marina 286–288
Bridger Lake (Yellowstone) 215, 331
Broad Creek (Yellowstone) 295, 296, 344, 356
Broman, Stan (Yosemite) 156
Brown, Gary (Yellowstone) 330, 345–347
Brown, James W. (Yellowstone) 169, 267
Bryant, John, in Yellowstone 221
Bryce Canyon 155–156
Bryce Canyon permanent ranger 148–149, 155–162, 164
Buck Camp (Yosemite) 63–67
Buffalo Ranch. See Lamar Ranger Station (Yellowstone)
Burleigh, Jim (Yosemite) 64–66
Cabins, Yellowstone backcountry patrol 211–212
   etiquette of use 54–55, 212–217
   Cabin Creek 213, 214, 328
   Fern Lake 238, 241, 298, 300, 335, 343
   Fox Creek 214, 215, 224, 310, 312, 356
   Harebell 223, 224, 311, 315, 355
   Heart Lake 224, 225
   Howell Creek 337
   Park Point 212

Thorofare 214–215

Trail Creek 225, 230, 327, 345

Camp Curry (Yosemite) 107

Campgrounds in Yellowstone
Fishing Bridge 188–189, 264,
269–273, 284–285, 307–309
Grant Village 261, 295–296,
300–302
Pelican Creek 27, 267–268

Carter, Jimmy, and family, in Yellowstone 228–236

Castillo, Ferdinand (Yosemite) 125

Chalcedony Creek (Yellowstone) 242

Chamberlain, Ellie (Yellowstone NP) 333–334

Chapman, Scotty (Yellowstone NP) 36

Clouds Rest (Yosemite NP) 24, 101–105, 123, 151

Cockrell, Ernie, in Yellowstone 221

Cody, WY 203, 301

Coffin, Lynn (Grand Canyon) 164

Columbine Creek (Yellowstone) 285

Conrad, Frank (Yellowstone) 333

Cook, Cappy (Yosemite) 128, 132

Craighead, Frank, in Yellowstone 247

Craighead Grizzly Bear Study Team 247, 251, 262–263, 270
and Yellowstone NP dump closures 260–261

Craighead, John, in Yellowstone 247

Cunning, Duane (Yellowstone) 265

Curry Company 54, 79, 105–106, 107, 148
High Sierra Camp (Yosemite NP) 79

Curry, David and Jennie (Yosemite) 107

Danforth, Mary (Yellowstone) 203

Danforth, Terry (Yellowstone) 186, 203

Doolittle, Doug (Yellowstone) 272

Downing, George (Yellowstone) 168

Ebersold, Wally (Yosemite) 72

Eilers, Marita, in Yellowstone 178–185

Estey, Bud (Grand Canyon, Yellowstone) 164, 284

Ewing, Herb (Yosemite) 81, 94, 98, 113, 122, 140

Ewing, Ruth and Bobby (Yosemite) 140, 141

Ferguson, Dick (Yosemite) 291

Fernandez Pass (Yosemite) 67

Firearms
in Yellowstone 190–191
in Yosemite patrol cars 134, 134–135
Mernin's collection and training 150, 155–162, 165

Firefighting
in Glacier 259
Merced Lake, Yosemite 147–150

Fire-making
one-match fires 54–59

Fishing Bridge RV Park (Yellowstone) 199, 275–276, 281–284, 302–303

Fladmark, Elmer (Yosemite) 132

Flame, Bob (Yosemite) 62, 67, 76

Fonda, John (Grand Teton) 56

Ford, Gerald and party, in Yellowstone 218, 218–227

Fowler, Joe (Yellowstone) 229–231

Fowler, Sandi (Yellowstone) 231

Fox, Dr. (Yellowstone) 201–204

Fredenhagen, Andreas and Junko 295–296

Fredenhagen, Brigitta, in Yellowstone 295–301

Gammill, Walt (Yosemite) 64, 66, 74

Garrison, Lon, in Yellowstone 226

Gifford, Dick (Yosemite) 290

Gingles, John (Yellowstone) 269

Goat Haunt Ranger Station (Glacier) 45

Going to the Sun Road (Glacier) 46
Grand Canyon National Park permanent ranger 164–166
Granite Park Chalet (Glacier) 259
Grant, Gardner L. Jr. (Gary) (Yellowstone) 289–295
Grant Village Campground. See Campgrounds in Yellowstone
Haines, Dallas 61
Half Dome (Yosemite) 102, 104
Hall, Gil (Yellowstone) 200
Harebell patrol cabin. See Cabins, Yellowstone backcountry patrol
Hartung, Bob (Yosemite) 128, 139–141, 148
Hastings College of Law 21, 34, 61–63, 75, 77, 96, 113
Hawks Rest, Forest Service cabin near Yellowstone 215
Hayden Valley (Yellowstone) 304, 354
Heart Lake (Yellowstone) 356
Helicopters
    in bear relocation 280–284
    firefighting 146
    Jimmy Carter family visit 229, 231–233
    rescue 77, 216, 280–281, 291–293, 296, 298–300, 315–316
Hendrickson, Roger (Yosemite) 141
Herring, Nick (Yellowstone) 298
Hippies, as crime suspects 189–192
Hooley, Bart, in Yosemite 88
Horse packing equipment and knots 88
    barrel hitch knot 37
    basket hitch knot 37
    Decker packsaddle 37
    diamond hitch 65
    manties 37, 39, 50
    McClellan saddle 115
Horses and mules
    Alexander Hotshot (AH) 141–143
    Buster 94–95, 98–99

Coyote 66–67
Dusty 57, 230, 234, 319–332
Eb 231–236
Eli 231–236
George 101–105, 122–124
Irwin 333–339
Lady/Babe 66–67, 72, 81, 83–84, 88–91
palamino prejudice 63–64
Red Mule (Red) 81, 84, 89–91, 94
Scott 238, 243–245
Traveler 310
Horse Thief Canyon (Yosemite) 68
Hotchkiss, Jim (Yellowstone) 220, 333
Howe, Wayne (Yosemite) 149
Huffman, Bill (Yellowstone) 220, 222–223
Hughes, Jack (Yellowstone) 247, 254–255
Inspiration Point (Yellowstone) 174, 175
Interagency Grizzly Bear Study Team 263
Jackson, Cary and Marguerite (Yosemite) 74, 353
Jax, Daphne, in Yellowstone 272
Jones, Jerry (Yellowstone) 291–292
Jumar ascenders. See Rescue equipment
Jump, Ted (Yellowstone) 171
Kat, William, in Yosemite 69–70
Knowles, Jack, and family (Yellowstone) 36
Lake Hospital (Yellowstone) 201, 272, 273, 301
    helicopter 291, 293
Lake Hotel (Yellowstone) 225
Lake Ranger Station (Yellowstone) 38, 197, 202–203, 205, 295
Lamar Ranger Station (Yellowstone) 241, 244
Law school. See Hastings College of

Law
Lee, Chuck (Yellowstone) 222, 223
Lennox, Elmer (Yosemite) 87–88, 105
Lennox, Ila (Yosemite) 87–88, 105,
    105–106
Little Yosemite Valley (Yosemite) 82
Lockwood, Clyde (Yosemite) 78, 146
Long, Joseph Bernard (Bernie) (Yel-
    lowstone) 352–353
Lookout Point (Yellowstone)
    and Marita Eilers 179–185
Luther, Homer, in Yellowstone 221
Lynip, Bryan, in Yellowstone 301–302
Lynip family, in Yellowstone 301–302
McClure, Duane (Yellowstone)
    290–292
McDowell, Janey (Yellowstone) 289,
    291–292
McGregor, Bob (Yosemite) 80–81, 93,
    95, 96–97, 353
McKown, Jim (Grand Canyon, Yellow-
    stone) 163, 223, 227
Many Glacier (Glacier) 46, 51
Marcott, Larry (Yellowstone) 272
Marschall, Mark (Yellowstone)
    295–296
Mathias, Barry (Yellowstone) 230
Merced Lake High Sierra Camp (Yo-
    semite) 78
Merced Lake Ranger Station (Yosem-
    ite) 81–95, 83–84
Merced Lake (Yosemite) 82
Mernin, Cindy Ferguson
    as angler 236
    marriage 22, 203, 205–210
    on pack trips 220–227
    support from 22–23, 24, 230–236,
        335–336, 349
Mernin, Emma 21, 31–33
Mernin, Gerald 21, 29–33, 354–355
    as Wawona District Ranger (Yosem-
        ite NP) 74, 160–162
    visiting Jerry at Buck Camp 74

Mernin, Jerry
    bear experiences summary 22
    biography by Marjane Ambler
        21–26
    Canyon sub-district ranger, Yellow-
        stone NP 187–194
    Goat Haunt fireguard, Glacier NP
        45–53
    Lake sub-district ranger, Yellowstone
        NP 277–288
    Pelican Cone fireguard, Yellowstone
        NP 36–44
    Thorofare ski patrol, Yellowstone
        55–59
    University of Notre Dame 21
    U.S. Army service 61
    on Yellowstone and Yosemite 187
    Yosemite seasonal employee 78–95
Mernin, Lynn 32–33, 113–117, 118
Merry, Wayne (Yosemite) 141
Miller, Chet (Yosemite) 140, 142, 145
Milligan, Tom (Yellowstone) 186
Mirror Lake (Yellowstone) 241, 244
Mirror Plateau (Yellowstone) 240–245
Mitchell, Andy (Yellowstone) 315
Moran, Pat (Yellowstone) 172
Morey, Bob (Yellowstone) 55, 179,
    182, 212–214, 250
Morris, Bob (Glacier) 45–46
Mount Holmes (Yellowstone) 356
Mount Sheridan (Yellowstone) 223
Mount Washburn (Yellowstone) 356
Muir, John (authentic), in Yosemite
    cabin site 149
Muir, John (modern version) in Yo-
    semite 69
Nez Perce Indians, in Yellowstone,
    1877 24, 169, 241
North Fork Road (Glacier) 46, 47
Nuss, Dale (Yellowstone) 196, 208,
    259, 273, 278, 284
Observation Peak (Yellowstone) 324,
    325

Old Faithful geyser (Yellowstone) 219, 224

Old Village area (Yosemite) 29, 32

Ottoway Lakes (Yosemite) 106, 108

Ozment, Pat (Yosemite) 300, 301, 302

Pacific Creek (Yellowstone) 310, 331

Pelican Cone Lookout (Yellowstone) 36, 164, 300, 355

Pelican Creek (Yellowstone) 43, 57–59

Penttila, Terry (Yellowstone) 272, 275

Popper, Chuck (Yellowstone) 296, 298

Preston, Betty (Mrs. John) (Yosemite) 109–112

Preston, John (Yosemite) 109, 112–113

Protto, Jim (Yellowstone) 191

Pryor, Cecil (Yellowstone) 266, 275–277

Rescue equipment
   Akja rescue sled 129–131
   Jumar ascenders 170, 171
   Stokes litter 77, 79–95, 172–174, 200, 292–293

Rescues and retrievals, in Yellowstone
   document retrieval, Yellowstone River Canyon 170
   Marita Eilers, fall 178–185
   Brigitta Fredenhagen, bear attack 295–298
   Daphne Jax, bear attack 272–273
   in Lewis River Canyon, fall 199–200
   at Lookout Point, prevention 174–177
   Bryan Lynip, bear attack 301–302
   in Yellowstone River whitewater 172–174
   Mariana Young, bear attack 290–294

Rescues and retrievals, in Yosemite

from Vogelsang High Sierra Camp, Yosemite 143–146
   on Badger Pass ski hill, Yosemite 129–131

Rickers, Ben (Yellowstone) 293

Riley, Glen (Yellowstone) 257

Roberts, Clair (Yellowstone) 310–313, 315–316

Ross, Bud (Yellowstone) 172

Ross, Mike (Yellowstone) 244

Rudolph, Roger (Yellowstone) 229–230

Sanders, Clarence E. (Barney) (Yellowstone) 187–194

Sedergren, Oscar (Yosemite) 63, 75

Selmack, Tom (Yellowstone) 293

Sharsmith, Carl (Yosemite) 105, 115

Sholly, Dan (Yellowstone) 23

Sierra Club 46–53

Spranger, Shar (Yosemite) 146

Stockton, Lou (Yosemite) 65, 68, 73, 78, 84, 85, 353–354

Stockton, Myrtle (Yosemite) 65, 72, 73

Stokes litter. See Rescue equipment

Sturm, Avery (Yosemite) 128, 131, 141

Ten Mile Post Trail (Yellowstone) 285, 345

Thompson, Erwin (Tom) (Yosemite) 105, 106

Thorofare (Yellowstone) 212–213, 216–217, 285, 327

Tioga Pass Entrance Station (Yosemite) 122, 125, 126

Townsley, Elaine (Mrs. John) (Yellowstone) 232, 235

Townsley, John
   (Yellowstone) 218–222, 225–226, 228–229, 234–235
   (Yosemite) 105, 106

The Trail Riders of the Wilderness 327

Trainer, Tim (Yellowstone) 291–292

Tressider, Mary Curry (Yosemite) 107

Trident (Yellowstone) 356

Triple Divide Peak (Yosemite) 68, 75

Trischman, Harry (Yellowstone) 212, 213–214, 215

Trout Creek Dump (Yellowstone) 251, 279, 280

Tucker, Tommy (Yosemite) 134, 136–137, 148

Tuolumne Meadows (Yosemite) 138, 139–140

Two Ocean Plateau (Yellowstone) 225, 356

Uniforms 29, 45, 81–82, 133, 174
    etiquette 107–108, 335
    flat hat style 334
    Park Service Stetson 23, 71, 101, 116, 119, 135, 334–335, 336

University of Notre Dame 21, 45

University of Wisconsin lab bombing (1968) 189

Vogelsang High Sierra Camp (Yosemite) 79, 89, 142–144

Warren, Ray (Yosemite) 72

Waterton Lake, Canada/U.S. 45

Waterton Lakes National Park, Canada 45

Wawona (Yosemite) 45, 54, 64, 73

Westphal, Waine (Yosemite) 30

Wetzel, Red (Yellowstone) 320–321, 322–323

White Lake (Yellowstone) 296, 299–300, 304–305

Widmer, Ed (Yellowstone) 55, 212

Wilcox, Gale (Grand Teton) 56

Witch Creek (Yellowstone) 356

Wolves (Yellowstone) 238–240

Wood, Bob (Yellowstone NP) 214–215

Yellowstone River (Yellowstone) 269, 328–330, 353. See also Rescues and retrievals, in Yellowstone

Yestness, Don (Yellowstone) 274–275

Yosemite Park and Curry Company (Yosemite) 107

Yosemite Valley (Yosemite) 30, 31, 33, 72, 77, 128

Youngblood, Gary (Yellowstone) 295

Young, Mariana (Yellowstone) 289–294

Yuhr, Dan (Yellowstone) 41, 352